LABOR RELATIONS AND PUBLIC POLICY SERIES

REPORT NO. 15

COMPULSORY UNIONISM, THE NLRB, AND THE COURTS

A Legal Analysis of Union Security Agreements

by

THOMAS R. HAGGARD
Professor of Law
School of Law
University of South Carolina

Foreword by HERBERT R. NORTHRUP
Professor of Industry
Director, Industrial Research Unit

INDUSTRIAL RESEARCH UNIT
The Wharton School, Vance Hall/CS
University of Pennsylvania
Philadelphia, Pennsylvania 19104
U.S.A.

Foreword

In 1968, the Industrial Research Unit inaugurated its Labor Relations and Public Policy monographs as a means of examining issues and stimulating discussions in the complex and controversial areas of collective bargaining and the regulation of labor-management disputes. The first four studies and the eighth, ninth, twelfth, and thirteenth in the series dealt with aspects of the National Labor Relations Board and its administration. The fifth report contained papers read at the fiftieth anniversary conference of the Industrial Research Unit at which many aspects of labor relations and public policy were discussed. The sixth monograph—*Welfare and Strikes*—was the first empirical analysis of the impact of government payments to strikers on the American collective bargaining system and on the settlement of disputes under that system. The seventh in the series, *Opening the Skilled Construction Trades to Blacks,* was the initial attempt to determine by detailed field analysis what actually occurs when the federal government insists that the skilled construction trades make a serious effort to increase the number and percentage of Negroes in their work force. The tenth, *The Davis-Bacon Act,* dealt with another aspect of construction in that it involved a critical analysis of the impact and administration of the little known law under which "prevailing wages" are established in the construction industry. The eleventh monograph in the series marked the Industrial Research Unit's first published work in the public employee field since 1966, and the fourteenth, *Old Age, Handicapped and Vietnam-Era Antidiscrimination Legislation,* published earlier in 1977, was the first overall analysis dealing with that subject.

This monograph, No. 15 in the Series, *Compulsory Unionism, the NLRB, and the Courts,* deals with the legal problems of a persistent and vexing question affecting union-management relations on the American scene. Compulsory unionism or "union security" involves various types of agreements requiring union membership as a condition of employment. This issue has continued over the years as a sharp and emotion-packed one, both for union-management relations and for public policy.

Union development was hindered in the United States by a variety of factors which emphasized individual rather than collective activity as the best method of achieving economic progress. Class fluidity bred individual opportunity. The "rags to riches" stories still occur; but in the nineteenth century, when there existed an abundance of free land, open doors to ambitious immigrants, and the development of a continent-wide market, union partisans found neither sympathy nor economic strength for their philosophy. Hindered also by the heterogeneity of races and nationalities, the fierce individualism of employers, and the antagonism of public policy, especially as expressed in the courts, unions also found that they could not depend on class solidarity, so often in evidence in other countries, to maintain union membership, dues, and strength. Instead, they turned to contractual provisions requiring the employer to maintain union membership for them. Today, as in 1877, a primary aim of most unions is "union security," and this has been achieved in the overwhelming majority of union contracts. But although the union objective has been highly successful, the issue of whether compulsory union membership should be permitted remains very much alive.

Whether a union will demand a "closed shop" (under which employees must join a union as a prerequisite to employment) or a "union shop" (under which the employer may hire anyone he chooses, but after a probationary period of thirty to ninety days, all employees must join the union as a condition of employment) will vary with the type of employment and labor market. In general, the closed shop is found among skilled and strategically located trades and in industries in which employment is casual or intermittent. The closed shop differs from the union shop in that it is not only a means of compulsory unionism, but also a method of controlling entrance to the trade or industry.

Early unions in the United States came to believe passionately that the closed or union shop was necessary to their survival. Only if union security was achieved could the union count on effective protection from employer discrimination against union members. Indeed, unions argued, often with considerable evidence, that union security provisions were necessary to induce workers to join a union not so much because of their reluctance to join but because of their fear of consequences in the form of employer retaliation if they joined voluntarily. By equating "open shop" with the complete elimination of unions in the pre-New Deal era, management did much to provide credence to this early union position.

Theoretically, the passage of the National Labor Relations (Wagner) Act in 1935 eliminated much of the need for union security. This Act outlawed employer discrimination against workers because of union membership and required employers to bargain with duly certified unions. Nevertheless, union security demands lost none of their intensity. This was true partly because union leaders and members believed, often with considerable justification, that employers were opposed to unions and could circumvent the law; partly because, emotionally, they could not imagine successful unionism without the closed or union shop; and partly because of a new development—the rise of rival unionism on a scale previously unknown. The existence of a union security provision deters raiding by rival unions and, thus, gives unions "security" from another angle.

Arguments pro and con the closed or union shop are actually matters for individual determination. If one believes that under no condition should a person be compelled to join a union in order to have the right to work, one is opposed to union security. If one believes that persons should be compelled to support an organization which has won certain benefits in which they share, one favors union security provisions. These are irreconcilable value judgments.

In a very real sense, no one has a constitutional or even moral right to work at a particular job or business. What is at stake in union security, or compulsory unionism, is the extent to which an organization endowed with authority by Congress or state legislatures should also be permitted to exert coercive power to require contributions to its maintenance and well-being and the extent to which such an organization should be permitted to determine whether workers, otherwise employable, should be denied or be forced out of work.

In essence, then, the compulsory unionism, or union security, issue is one of power. That the issue is concerned with the union's coercive power over its members seems undeniable. Power over the membership involves, of course, the right of a union to fine, to discipline, or to effectuate the discharge of a member for violation of union rules or conduct, or for the completely indefensible reasons of opposing, antagonizing, or otherwise offending union leadership. Students of labor relations have always recognized that a union must have some authority over its members, particularly when a majority has taken a legitimate position in favor of a legitimate objective. Otherwise, anarchy in industrial relations could result. For example, few disagree with the right of a majority to accept a settlement offered by an employer or to reject the settlement and to choose a strike. But should a union have the power to fine or to discipline a member who crosses a picket line, returns to work during a strike, and thus makes the achievement of the strike goal more difficult for the majority? Questions like this involve complex moral and economic issues which each citizen may answer differently and which the legislatures and the courts likewise find difficult to determine, as this monograph makes clear. The power issue in compulsory unionism also has another, and equally significant, aspect. This involves its impact on union-management relations. There is, for example, little doubt that the passage of so-called right to work laws creates a "climate" hostile in some way to unionism. This is true when any union control law is enacted. It marks a public defeat for the pro-union forces and is both a result in itself and a creator of a political atmosphere unfavorable to unionism to some extent, even though such legislation has the support of those who would "reform," not curtail, legitimate unionism. Because of the emotion engendered by right-to-work legislation, the passage of such laws usually both reflects and results initially in strong feelings on questions relating to unions and union-management relations.

But union security restraints limit union power in more direct ways—by reducing control of the leadership over the membership and by reducing the income to the union. Obviously, the control of the union leadership over the membership is decreased if expulsion from the union does not mean loss of job or if resignation from the union is accompanied by no penalty.

Studies have demonstrated also that where compulsory union agreements are proscribed, 10 to 50 percent of the eligible employees do not join or pay dues to their union bargaining agent.[1] This can be a significant financial loss to the union— the difference between affording key union political action, organizers, or publicity and doing without these essential sources of power attainment.

Given the strong division among proponents and opponents of compulsory unionism and the long controversial history of the

---

[1] *See, e.g.,* Kuhn, *Right to Work Laws—Symbols or Substance,* 14 Industrial and Labor Relations Review, 587-594 (1961) ; and H. NORTHRUP and G. BLOOM, GOVERNMENT AND LABOR, at chapter 8 (1963).

issue, one should not be surprised that public policy concerning it reflects both many compromises and hard fought legal questions. Indeed a whole body of law has developed which is still evolving. Surprisingly, this legal history and development has never before been subject to careful, thorough scrutiny and analysis. Professor Haggard's monograph thus fills a very real need for practitioners, lawyers, and scholars.

The author, Thomas R. Haggard, is Professor of Law and Associate Dean, University of South Carolina Law School. At the time that he commenced this study, he was Professor of Law, Rutgers University-Camden. He received both his undergraduate and law degrees from the University of Texas and is a member of the Texas bar.

The manuscript was edited by the Industrial Research Unit's Chief Editor, Mr. Robert E. Bolick, Jr., and Assistant Editor, Mr. David O. Northrup; Ms. Karen M. Rose checked the citations and prepared the case index; Mrs. Deborah T. Kelsall typed parts of the manuscript; and Mrs. Margaret E. Doyle, the Unit's Office Manager, handled administrative matters associated with the project. Professor Clyde W. Summers, Jefferson B. Fordham Professor of Law, University of Pennsylvania Law School, and a labor law advisor to the Industrial Research Unit, read the manuscript and offered many valuable suggestions. The journal of the Rutgers-Camden Law School has permitted the use of materials from an earlier article by Professor Haggard. Support for the project was provided by the generous, unrestricted grants of the Pew Memorial Trust for work in the Labor Relations and Public Policy Series and by unrestricted funds provided by the sixty-five companies that are members of the Industrial Research Unit's Research Advisory Group.

As in all works published by the Industrial Research Unit, the author is solely responsible for the research and for all opinions expressed, which should not be attributed to the grantors, to the University of Pennsylvania, or to the University of South Carolina.

HERBERT R. NORTHRUP, *Director*
Industrial Research Unit
The Wharton School
University of Pennsylvania

Philadelphia
August 1977

TABLE OF CONTENTS

PART ONE

Introduction

CHAPTER I

The Nature and Scope of the Issue

Controversy surrounding compulsory unionism, or *union security* and the *right to work*, is practically as old as the country itself. The first recorded American labor law case, decided in 1801 by a Philadelphia municipal judge, raised many of the same issues about union security and the right to work as were raised in the 1976 presidential campaigns. In the interim this matter has been a subject of continuing national debate, with the policy of the law sometimes favoring one side, sometimes favoring the other, but most often attempting to achieve a compromise between the two.

THE TERM UNION SECURITY

Union security is not a term with a precise meaning. It pertains to a situation in which a significant percentage of employers. Social and economic boycotts have likewise been used labor union that represents them in collective bargaining. This situation can occur in a number of ways. It can, of course, be achieved whenever a substantial number of employees become and remain members of a union *of their own volition*. Usually, however, union security connotes some kind of external compulsion. At times, unfortunately, it has come in the form of physical violence against nonunion employees and/or their employers. Social and economic boycotts have likewise been used to induce union membership and thus to achieve a state of union security; and finally, the law itself has affirmatively encouraged or even created situations of union security. The provisions of federal law which give majority unions the right to be recognized and bargained with as the exclusive representative of *all* the employees in the unit are a prime example of this.

Although these methods of achieving union security are important in their own right, for the purposes of this study they only form the background and context for an examination of a narrower conception of union security. Specifically, the object of this study is limited to *compulsory union* or *union security agreements*. These are federally sanctioned contracts between a labor union and an employer whereby the employer agrees to require his employees, as a condition of their employment, to affiliate with the union in some way. There are several different kinds of union security agreements. Unfortunately, consistent terminology has not always been used in the description of these various types, a fact contributing substantially to the confusion that exists in both the law and in the popular understanding of exactly what union security is. The most common usage, however, together with a careful study of the legal obligations imposed under the various types of union security agreements, suggests adherence to the following definitions:

Closed Shop Agreement: An individual must be a member [1] of the union in order to be eligible for hire and must retain this membership as a condition of continued employment with the contracting employer.

Union Shop Agreement: An individual who is not a member of the union may be hired but within a specified time after hire must become and remain a member as a condition of continued employment with the contracting employer.

Maintenance-of-Membership Agreement: An employee who is a member of the union at the beginning of the contract or who becomes a member during the term of the contract is obligated to remain a member until the termination of the contract.

Agency Shop Agreement: An individual who is not a member of the union may be hired and retained in employment without the necessity of becoming a member of the union, but he is required to tender the equivalent of initiation fees and periodic dues to the union as a condition of his continued employment with the contracting employer.

Service Fee Agreement: An individual who is not a member of the union may be hired and retained in employment without the necessity of becoming a member of the union, but as a condition of employment he is required to tender to the union his pro rata

---

[1] As used in these definitions, the terms "member" and "membership" connote a formal associational relationship that partakes, in legal contemplation, of the attributes of a contract between the individual employee and the union.

share of the costs incurred by the union in performing its statutory function as the exclusive bargaining representative.

Irrevocable Checkoff Authorization Agreement: An individual who elects to discharge his financial obligation to the union by authorizing the employer to deduct money from his paycheck and forward it to the union is bound to continue this authorization (and the employer is bound to honor it) for a specified term.

Union security agreements are designed to serve a variety of purposes. Control over hiring, if not over entrance into the trade or craft itself, is often accomplished by means of the closed shop, especially where membership in the union is itself restricted or where the employer agrees to hire only persons referred through the union's hiring hall. Another purpose served by the closed shop, as well as the union shop and some forms of maintenance of membership, is that of subjecting employees to the union's power of control. Under such agreements, unions obtain the right to discipline, fine, expel, and even effect the discharge of employees who violate the rules of conduct for union members—rules which range from mandatory attendance at union meetings, to honoring picket lines, and even to restricting one's production. Finally although agency shop and service fee agreements serve *only* this function, all of the forms of union security defined above provide unions with a guarantee of continued financial support from the employees they purport to represent. These various purposes are important in evaluating the kinds of union security that the law allows or should allow.

THE TERM RIGHT TO WORK

As with the term *union security,* the phrase *right to work* is also capable of being construed in a variety of ways. In the broadest sense, it pertains to the liberty of an individual to engage in nonaggressive economic activity free from the coercive restraints either of the state or of other private individuals. So construed, it would appear that the right to work is thus violated on a wholesale basis by a wide range of state and federal laws which do in fact regulate such conduct! The common meaning of the phrase *right to work* is, however, much narrower than this. It most often refers to the liberty of the individual to have a job free from the requirement that he become a member of or be affiliated with a labor organization. In other words, the right to work simply connotes a freedom from the strictures of union security agreements as previously defined.

THE LAWS AFFECTING UNION SECURITY AND
THE RIGHT TO WORK

The legal equilibrium that presently exists between union security and the right to work is statutory in its origin. The Labor-Management Relations Act—or the Taft-Hartley Act—extensively regulates the relationship between most employers, unions, and employees. Under this Act, union security agreements are dealt with in an odd sort of way. The Act prohibits an employer from discriminating against employees on the basis of union membership, and unions are prohibited from inducing or attempting to cause an employer to discriminate on that basis. Certain kinds of union security agreements under certain conditions, however, are exempt from these prohibitions—even though they involve discrimination of the most literal sort. The kinds of union security agreements that are *not* exempt are thus illegal under the provisions *generally* prohibiting discrimination —which is a somewhat complex and indirect way of approaching the problem. The enforcement of these statutory provisions rests initially with the National Labor Relations Board and ultimately with the various federal Courts of Appeals and the Supreme Court.

The Railway Labor Act, which covers employees in the railroad and airlines industries, contains a similar provision, and both statutes contain specific provisions regulating the checkoff. The Taft-Hartley Act, however, differs from the Railway Labor Act in one significant respect. Section 14(b) of the Taft-Hartley Act allows the states to prohibit *all* kinds of union security agreements, even those that would otherwise be legal under the Taft-Hartley Act itself. These state laws are known as *right-to-work laws*. Such laws have no effect, however, on union security agreements negotiated under the authority of the Railway Labor Act.

There is yet another source of law regarding the scope and enforcement of union security agreements. Although the authority for such agreements flows from federal law, the agreements themselves are in the form of private contracts between an employer and the union. If a collective bargaining agreement, of which the union security provision is a part, contains an arbitration clause, as most of them do, then misunderstandings concerning the employees' union membership obligations can be, and often are, resolved through this process.

Insofar as public employees are concerned, the law comes from a variety of sources. Although there is no comprehensive federal-employee labor relations law, a Presidential Executive Order covering employees in that branch of the government and the Postal Reorganization Act covering postal employees guarantee the right of a federal worker to refuse to join or to support a labor union without thereby losing his job. On the other hand, most of the states have public-employee collective bargaining laws covering some or all of the state's employees, and the position of these statutes concerning union security *versus* the right to work varies appreciably from state to state.

Finally, the ultimate source of all law affecting union security and the right to work is the United States Constitution itself. Despite the claim that right-to-work laws infringe upon the unions' constitutional liberty of contract, the Supreme Court has held that such statutes represent a valid exercise of state legislative power; but, the Court has also sustained the power of government to authorize or impose agency shop arrangements on both public and private employees, even in the face of allegations that this constitutes a violation of the employees' liberties of speech, association, and religion. The Court has said that agency shop fees cannot, however, be used to finance political or ideological activities unrelated to collective bargaining.

THE SIGNIFICANCE OF THE ISSUE

Apart from the fact that the union security/right-to-work controversy is a constantly recurring issue in American labor law, the issue is significant for a number of other reasons as well. First, in simple quantitative terms, the issue affects millions of American workers and involves the payment of hundreds of millions of dollars into labor union treasuries.

From a slightly broader perspective, the union security/right-to-work controversy can be viewed as part and parcel of the continuing debate over union power. On the one hand, from the perspective of those who are concerned with the unions' monopoly status and the resultant concentration of power, union security agreements are merely another way in which this power is both enhanced and potentially abused. On the other hand, to those who view strong labor unions as a necessary counterbalance to the economic power of employers, union security is a means to this end, and right-to-work laws are thought of as nothing more than employer-inspired subterfuges for "union busting."

Underlying this union power issue is, however, a deeper and more fundamental philosophical division. What is at issue are the circumstances, if any, under which individual rights and interests can be subordinated to that of the group in order to achieve a so-called common good. The details and implications of the competing philosophical positions are complex, but in the last analysis what is known as the philosophy of "individualism" lends its support to the notion of the right to work, while the justification for union security is founded ultimately on a philosophy that views man primarily as a component of a larger social group whose interests are paramount. It is important to remember that the union security/right-to-work controversy is but a specific manifestation of that broader issue, and that the tension between these philosophies is not apt to ever be resolved absolutely in favor of one side or the other.

In a somewhat more technical sense, the union security and right-to-work issues are significant because they raise fundamental questions about the proper relationship between federal and state legislative power. Section 14(b) is virtually unique in allowing the states to regulate a facet of the employment relationship that would otherwise be subject to the preemptive authority of federal legislation. It is apparent that more is at issue than simply the *substantive* merits and demerits of union security *versus* the right to work; instead, the issue is who should make this determination—the federal government or the state government?

Finally, within the context of public employment, the debate between union security and the right to work touches upon considerations that go to the very heart of the concept of democratic government. If union security enhances union power, and if union power is directed against the government as an employer, and if the government is expected to represent the best interests of *all* the citizens, and if the desires of government employees are inconsistent with the best interests of the citizenry—then the issue is who is the actual *sovereign* within our system of government. A more significant issue would be hard to imagine.

With all of these matters in mind, we can now turn to the controversy in question and to a detailed examination of how current law has attempted to resolve it.

PART TWO

An Analysis of the Law

CHAPTER II

The Legal-Historical Background of Union Security Agreements

To the extent that they can legitimately be considered descendants of the medieval guilds,[1] labor unions have been preoccupied with union security since the very beginning. Guilds were in essence nothing more than a form of what today would be known as a *closed union/closed shop*. Membership in the guild was restricted, and only guild members could do the work. Since under the political philosophy of mercantilism, guilds were both promoted and regulated by the state, one may conclude that initially the law took a favorable attitude toward union security.

In time, however, the pendulum swung in the opposite direction. As mercantilism was replaced by the philosophy of *laissez faire*, the guilds and other privileged economic groups fell from their favored place in the eyes of the law. State-supported union security and "Crown monopolies" gave way to individual enterprise and competition to the point that even *privately* sustained concentrations of economic power were viewed by the law with suspicion, if not with outright hostility. Insofar as workingmen's groups were concerned, in England this attitude manifested itself in the so-called criminal conspiracy doctrine.

THE CRIMINAL CONSPIRACY DOCTRINE

What the English criminal conspiracy doctrine was and whether it had any business being applied within the newly-freed American States were matters of some dispute among the

---

[1] *See* Sultan, *Historical Antecedents to the Right-to-Work Controversy*, 31 S. Cal. L. Rev. 221, 223 (1958).

early judges, lawyers, and politicians—a dispute that modern
legal historians continue to pursue.[2] During the 1800s a doctrine of that name was invoked and applied to the activities
of groups of American workingmen, but the exact nature of the
offense of criminal conspiracy was and continues to be the object
of some confusion and misunderstanding.

The conventional, but largely erroneous view, until *Commonwealth* v.

Hunt, has been that workers who engaged in peaceful
concerted refusals to work for the object of obtaining an increase in their wages were automatically guilty of a common-
law criminal conspiracy. There is language in some of the early
conspiracy decisions to suggest that such a doctrine existed;
but few if any of these cases stand unequivocally for that
proposition.[3] Overt acts of violence, for example, were committed
in most of the cases, and in nearly all instances the immediate
objectives of the striking workers extended beyond the mere
improvement of their own wages.

Typically, these early trade unionists would also demand that
the employer only hire actual or de facto members of their
union—*i.e.*, persons who would either join the union or at
least agree to work only at the union-sanctioned wage rate and
to comply otherwise with the union's internal rules and regula-
tions. Thus, it has been said that "these cases turned upon
the important question known today as the 'open' or 'closed shop,'
that is, the refusal to work with nonunion men." [4] The issue
was not the legality per se of labor unions; it was, rather,
whether these concerted attempts by unionists to obtain a situation of union security within their industry constituted an in-
dictable offense at common law. On this issue the decisions
went both ways. While these cases are not important in themselves, they do provide a good introduction to the underlying
arguments for and against union security arrangements.

---

[2] *See, e.g.*, Forkosch, *The Doctrine of Criminal Conspiracy and its Modern
Application to Labor*, 40 Texas L. Rev. 303 (1962); Sayre, *Criminal Conspiracy*, 35 Harv. L. Rev. 393 (1922).

[3] *See* Witte, *Early Conspiracy Cases*, 35 Yale L. J. 825, 826 (1926); *see
generally*, M. Turner, The Early American Labor Conspiracy Cases—
Their Place in Labor Law (1967).

[4] III. J. Commons, A Documentary History of American Industrial
Society 15 (1958) (hereinafter cited at III. or IV. Commons).

Convictions

Both the *New York Cordwainers* [5] case of 1809 and the *Pittsburg Cordwainers* [6] case of 1815 present relatively pure and uncomplicated examples of what were found to be illegal conspiracies to obtain union security. In neither case were there any overt acts of violence, and in both cases the primary focus was not on the unionists' attempt to raise merely their *own* wages (although the indictments did allege this as an offense) ; the focus, rather, was on their efforts to fix the wages for *everyone* and thus to achieve the closed shop. The instructions of the judge in the *Pittsburg* case suggests some of the reasons why conduct of this kind was thought to be "evil" and thus subject to prohibition:

Confederacies of this kind have a most pernicious effect, as respects the community at large. They restrain trade: they tend to banish many artizans, and to oppress others. It is the interest of the public, and it is the right of every individual, that those who are skilled in any profession, art, or mystery should be unrestrained in the exercise of it. . . .

Did they conspire to compel an employer to hire a certain description of persons? If they did, they are endictable. On this subject the evidence is equally clear. They did not indeed threaten to beat the employer, nor to burn his shop. But the means they used were more efficient; and menaced him with a punishment more dreadful: no less than the total destruction of his trade, and the means of subsistence.

Did the defendants conspire to prevent a man from freely exercising his trade in a particular place? If so, they are endictable. The testimony you have heard enables you readily to answer this question. They did not indeed drive, by personal violence, from the town, any stranger who happened to come into it: but they adopted means which must eventually drive a journeyman from the town, or immerse him in a jail. It would be mere mockery to say that a journeyman shoemaker (without becoming a member of the society) might exercise his trade freely, in Pittsburgh. Was it to be expected that any master workman would employ such stranger, when the consequence must be the ruin of his own business? No! The stranger must become a wretched wanderer, destitute of employment, and of the means of subsistence. Can anything be imagined more prejudicial to the trade and prosperity of the town? It is the interest of the borough to promote the settlement of mechanics and manufacturers amongst them; and to prevent monopolies. . . .

---

[5] III. COMMONS 251.

[6] IV. COMMONS 15.

Did the defendants conspire to compel men to become members of a particular society, or to contribute towards it? If they did either they are endictable. That they did both, you have a mass of testimony. The means used was not in physical force, but exclusion from employment. The man and his family must famish or leave the place. . . . The absurdity and inconvenience of sanctioning such a doctrine, is too apparent to require a comment.[7]

In short, economic injury *in fact*—to the nonunion workman, the employer, and community at large—provided the requisite justification for condemning concerted efforts by unionists to obtain a closed shop.

Acquitals

On the other hand, the defendant unionists under an indictment which charged them with refusing to work "for any boss who should employ any one who was not a member of their society, or who should work for less than their rates" were acquitted of conspiracy charges in the *Hudson Shoemakers* [8] case of 1836. Likewise, in the *Philadelphia Plasterers* [9] case, also of 1836, despite some relatively specific instructions from the judge to the contrary, the jury acquitted two trade unionists who had been indicted for refusing to work in a shop that employed a nonunion member. An account by the *National Laborer* of defense counsel's closing argument is suggestive of the general rationale by which the unionists justified their conduct in these cases. The paper reports:

One illustration we remember was made by Mr. Ingersoll—which was analogous in every point to the case—of a colored woman in his employ. He said she was a faithful, honest, and industrious woman—suited for his family very well, but who unfortunately had a violent temper, and the consequence was, that oftentimes the other servants had come to him and said that they would not stay in the house if he kept her, and many had left because she was retained; and would the Attorney-general, he asked, indict all these people? . . . Many other examples he brought to show how absurdly stupid it was to construct a law to destroy lawful combinations, which must remain unanswered by the enemies of the people.[10]

---

[7] IV. COMMONS 81-85.

[8] IV. COMMONS 277.

[9] IV. COMMONS 335.

[10] IV. COMMONS 341.

Apparently, the jury agreed with this attorney's implied proposition that workers have the right to refuse employment under circumstances that are unsatisfactory to them, even if these circumstances consist of the mere presence of a nonunion employee among them.

Commonwealth v. Hunt

It was not until 1842 that the libertarian view of union security found full and adequate expression in a judicial decision. *Commonwealth v. Hunt* [11] is frequently regarded as "a landmark of American law" [12] and "the Magna Carta of American trade unionism," [13] although the true significance of the case is a matter of dispute among students of labor law history. [14] Nevertheless, the case was decided by the most prestigious common-law court of the time, and Chief Justice Shaw, who wrote the opinion, is universally regarded as one of the outstanding judges of early America. The case is thus worthy of attention.

In the case it was alleged that "the defendants and others formed themselves into a society, and agreed not to work for any person, who should employ any journeyman or other person, not a member of such society, after notice given him to discharge such workman" [15]—to borrow Chief Justice Shaw's streamlined translation of an otherwise verbose indictment. Other counts of the indictment alleged that the defendants conspired to cause the impoverishment of both the bootmaker with whom they refused to work and of his would-be employers.

The defendant unionists took exception to the indictment on the ground that the facts alleged did not, as a matter of law, constitute the crime of conspiracy. It was to this purely legal issue that the court addressed its opinion. Mr. Justice Shaw, though conceding the lack of precision and accuracy, first began by defining a conspiracy as "a combination of two or more persons, by some concerted action, to accomplish some *criminal or unlawful purpose,* or to accomplish some purpose, not in

---

[11] 45 Mass. (4 Met.) 111 (1842).

[12] Nelles, *Commonwealth v. Hunt*, 32 COLUM. L. REV. 1128 (1932).

[13] L. LEVY, THE LAW OF THE COMMONWEALTH AND CHIEF JUSTICE SHAW 183 (1957).

[14] *See generally* TURNER, *supra* n. 3 at 58-72.

[15] 45 Mass. (4 Met.) at 128.

itself criminal or unlawful, by *criminal or unlawful means.*" [16] The court made it clear that "unlawful," as either a means or an end, pertained to any conduct that would be actionable at law, even if only in a private law suit, as for fraud, breach of contract, or tort. The court then proceeded to examine both the purpose and the means of the defendants' action.

The court first noted that the immediate purpose was to induce everyone engaged in the bootmaking profession to become a member of this association; and this, the court said, was not unlawful in and of itself. The court went on to say, however, that it *would* constitute an illegal conspiracy if the association were actually formed "for purposes of oppression and injustice, [or] . . . for purposes injurious to the peace of society or the rights of members." [17] The court did not elaborate upon what these ambiguous phrases meant, but merely noted that the indictment did not contain any affirmants in this regard.

Turning then to the means used to achieve this ostensibly legal purpose, the court observed that "every free man, whether skilled laborer, mechanic, farmer or domestic servant, may work or not work, or work or refuse to work with any company or individual, at his own option, except so far as he is bound by contract." [18] Thus, "in this state of things, we cannot perceive that it is criminal for men to agree together to exercise their own acknowledged rights, in such a manner as best to subserve their own interests." [19] The court, however, distinguished this from a situation where the defendants were striking in breach of a contract, or where they were attempting to induce an employer to breach his contract of employment with another workman. In such cases, individual conduct would be actionable at law, and the court indicated that in concert it would constitute criminal conspiracy.

Finally, with respect to the "impoverishment" counts, the court noted that in a competitive economy many concerted acts have a "tendency" to reduce the income or profits of another, but this is not illegal in and of itself. Eschewing a "motive analysis" some courts were later to adopt, Shaw then said that legality must turn exclusively on the means used. Since the

---

[16] *Id.* at 123 (emphasis added).

[17] *Id.* at 129.

[18] *Id.* at 133.

[19] *Id.* at 130.

legality of the means had already been passed on—*i.e.*, a concerted refusal to work, and there was none other pled—the court concluded that these counts of the indictment also did not state a criminal offense.

In short, *Commonwealth* v. *Hunt* stands for the proposition that a concerted refusal to work for any employer who hires nonunion employees will *not* constitute a criminal conspiracy unless (a) the workers intend to use the closed shop for "oppressive" or "prejudicial" purposes; (b) the refusal to work is itself in breach of contract; (c) the employer is thereby induced to break contracts of employment with nonunion employees; or (d) force or fraud is used in conjunction with the refusal to work.

Although *Commonwealth* v. *Hunt* was an influential decision, it by no means marked the end of the criminal conspiracy doctrine.[20] As an obstacle to the attainment of the closed shop, this doctrine lingered on until the turn of the century, and then it was not so much repudiated as replaced. Injunctions and, later, damage actions became the prevalent methods for resolving labor disputes of this kind. With respect to the substantive legality of attempts to obtain the closed shop through strikes and boycotts, however, the underlying issues remained the same.

PRIVATE REMEDIES—INJUNCTIONS AND DAMAGE SUITS

When the first labor injunction was issued is not exactly known; it was probably in 1883 or 1884.[21] The famous Debs [22] injunction of 1895 provided, however, the impetus for the increased use of this device in lieu of conspiracy prosecutions. Also substituted for the conspiracy doctrine were damage suits by nonunion employees discharged because of union pressure or

---

20 The doctrine was applied within the context of strikes to obtain the closed shop in a number of later cases, although some of them are flavored by allegations of violence. Even so, the dicta, if not the actual holdings of these cases, are basically inconsistent with the tolerant philosophy of *Commonwealth v. Hunt. See, e.g.*, State v. Donaldson, 32 N.J. (3 Vroom) 151 (1867); State v. Stewart, 59 Vt. 273 (1887); Crump v. The Commonwealth, 84 Va. 927 (1888); State v. Dyer, 67 Vt. 690 (1894).

21 *See* Witte, *supra* n. 3 at 832-33.

22 Debs v. United States, 158 U.S. 564 (1895).

a closed shop arrangement. Though the form of these legal remedies was different, the underlying legal and policy considerations were very much the same as those developed in the conspiracy cases.

Broadly speaking, the courts fell into two opposing camps over the issue of the legality of closed shop strikes, although a number of gradations of position existed between the two extremes.[23]

The New York Approach

At one pole, under what has come to be known as the "New York approach," the courts simply adhered to the philosophy of *Commonwealth* v. *Hunt* in holding that a strike to obtain the closed shop was neither enjoinable as a legal wrong nor, if successful, actionable in a suit for damages brought by a discharged employee, although the courts recognized a number of exceptions to this general proposition.

The New York approach took a very *laissez faire* attitude toward governmental regulation of human conduct. It assumed that a man had a natural right to pursue his own self-interest, and that anything short of physical force, fraud, or breach of contract was permissible. If another were injured in this competitive process, then this was simply *damnum absque injuria* (a popularly used Latin phrase indicating a loss, hurt, or harm without "injury" in the legal sense).[24]

National Protective Association of Steam Fitters v. *Cumming* [25] is typical of the New York approach. The court noted that prior decisions "recognize the right of one man to refuse to work for another on any ground that he may regard as sufficient, . . . and the fact that the reason given is that he refused to work with another who is not a member of his organization . . . does not affect his right to stop work nor does it give a cause

---

[23] *See generally* J. COMMONS & J. ANDREWS, PRINCIPLES OF LABOR LEGISLATION 392-93 (4th ed. 1967); I. L. TELLER, LABOR DISPUTES & COLLECTIVE BARGAINING § 97 (1940); Skinner, *Legal and Historical Background of the Right-to-Work Dispute*, 9 LAB. L. J. 411 (1958).

[24] One of the most lucid and complete discussions of this philosophical view within the context of union security can be found in a case decided by the English House of Lords, Allen v. Flood, 1898 App. Cases 1. This case had considerable influence on many of the American decisions. *See, e.g.,* Davis v. United Portable Hoisting Engineers, 51 N.Y.S. 180 (Sup. Ct. App. Div. 1898).

[25] 170 N.Y. 315 (1902).

of action to the workman to whom he objects because the employer sees fit to discharge the man objected to rather than lose 'the service of the objector . . . [T]heir right to stop work is not cut off because the reason seems inadequate or selfish to the employer or to organized society." [26]

A popular exception to this proposition, an exception which the court in *Cumming* noted but apparently did not assent to, was that the legality of a closed shop strike depended on the true purpose of the strike. If the motive behind the drive for a closed shop were simply to obtain more work for union members, or to insure the competency of all the workmen within a plant, or to obtain collective strength for bargaining purposes, then this would legitimize the conduct as self-protection. On the other hand, if the motive were to drive nonunion workers from the market place, or simply to gratify malice and to inflict injury on nonunion members, or even to force them to join the union, then the conduct would be legally wrong.[27]

The problem with this approach is that a strike for a closed shop is always susceptible of being characterized from either perspective. The strike proposes to benefit the union—either by obtaining employment for present members or by obtaining new members for itself; but in achieving this purpose, it necessarily injures others—the other workers, by forcing them either to join the union against their will or to leave the employment, and the employer, by forcing him to hire only a certain class of workers.

How, then, was the court to characterize such a strike? Even though a few of the courts occasionally hinted at what might qualify as evidence of "purpose," [28] no true consensus ever developed over these matters. It would appear that the characterization chosen was more a reflection of the court's general attitude toward this type of activity than it was an objective

---

[26] *Id.* at 321.

[27] *See generally id.* at 326.

[28] *For example,* Mills v. United States Printing Co. of Ohio, 91 N.Y.S. 185 (Sup. Ct. App. Div. 1904). The court suggested that *since* the present employees could retain their jobs if they but joined the union, the union's "purpose was not to drive out nonunion men so that places might be made for union men, but to assure that there should be no employees in this branch who were not members of the union." *Id.* at 190. Buried within this obscure double-talk, thus, is the suggestion that the "purpose" of a closed shop arrangement will be deemed "honorable" where the union is at the same time willing to admit new members.

and independent basis for the decision. The *Cumming* court, for example, whose tolerance toward closed shop arrangements was manifest, said that there was a presumption that a closed shop strike was to benefit the striking group and that the court would "not assume, in the absence of a finding to the contrary, that the object of such a refusal was solely to gratify malice and to inflict injury upon . . . nonmembers."²⁹ On the other hand, courts whose hostility toward the closed shop was equally manifest naturally couched *their* characterizations of "purpose" in highly pejorative terms, as will be seen subsequently.

Another commonly recognized exception to the general legality of a closed shop strike existed if the striking employees did not in fact have the privilege of refusing to continue to work, as for example where they had bound themselves to work for a fixed term. Thus, following *Commonwealth* v. *Hunt*, a number of courts that upheld the legality of a closed shop strike did so on the express premise that the striking employees were not under any continuing contractual obligation to remain at work.³⁰

Concerning another possible exception to the general legality of closed shop strikes, hinted at in *Commonwealth* v. *Hunt*, the courts following the New York approach were more ambivalent. At common law, inducements for breach of contract gave rise to a cause of action by the injured party against the inducer. If a union thus struck to obtain a closed shop and this resulted in the discharge of a nonunion employee who had been hired for a fixed term, would such an employee have a cause of action against the union? Initially, in *Curran* v. *Galen*,³¹ a New York court had allowed an employee to sue the union for causing his discharge pursuant to a closed shop arrangement with the employer. The *Curran* case, however, was predicated on the view that closed shop arrangements were generally contrary to public policy, a view which the New York courts later repudiated,³² and not on the more narrow grounds of inducement of breach of contract; indeed, it would appear that

---

²⁹ 170 N.Y. at 322.

³⁰ *E.g.*, Clemitt v. Watson, 14 Ind. App. 38, 39, 42 N.E. 367, 368 (1895); *see* Carter v. Oster, 134 Mo. App. 146, 148, 112 S.W. 995, 997 (St. Louis Ct. of App. 1908).

³¹ 152 N.Y. 33 (1897).

³² Jacobs v. Cohen, 183 N.Y. 207 (1905).

the employee in that case was not even employed for a fixed term.

Subsequently, however, in *Mills* v. *United States Printing Co. of Ohio,*[33] a New York court did intimate that if an employee had a "right to retention" of his job, presumably contractual, a cause of action would exist if discharge occurred because of a closed shop agreement with a union. In *Cusumano* v. *Schlessinger,*[34] however, another New York court held that the cause of action would lie only against the employer, not against the union that induced the discharge; the court also made it clear that this applied only to a contract for a fixed term, because under an employment at will an employee could be discharged at any time and for any reason.[35]

The New Jersey Exception

Lying somewhere in between the liberal New York approach and the yet-to-be discussed conservative Massachusetts approach is an exception (and it is as much an exception to the one view as it is to the other) articulated most specifically by the New Jersey courts. According to this view, closed shop arrangements were considered contrary to public policy, but only where they covered an entire industry or a substantial geographic area. In short, closed shop agreements were illegal to the extent that they created a "monopoly" in favor of the contracting union.[36]

The Massachusetts Approach

Turning now to the so-called Massachusetts approach, we see an entirely different response. While in *Commonwealth* v. *Hunt* the Massachusetts courts narrowed the criminal conspiracy doctrine and thus provided the inspiration for the disapproving New York attitude toward injunctions and damage suits, the

---

[33] 91 N.Y.S. 185 (Sup. Ct. App. Div. 1904); *see* Davis v. United Portable Hoisting Engineers, 51 N.Y.S. 180, 184 (Sup. Ct. App. Div. 1898) (Ingraham, concurring).

[34] 152 N.Y.S. 1081 (Sup. Ct. App. Div. 1915).

[35] *Accord,* Harmon v. United Mine Workers, 166 Ark. 255, 266 S.W. 84 (1924).

[36] *E.g.,* Wilson v. Newspaper and Mail Deliverers' Union, 197 A. 720 (N.J. Ct. of Ch. 1938); Four Plating Co. v. Mako, 194 A. 53 (N.J. Ct. of Ch. 1937); Polk v. Cleveland Railway, 20 Ohio App. 317, 151 N.E. 808 (1925); 13 Corpus Juris § 439 (1917).

approach of the Massachusetts courts to this latter type of lawsuit remained inexorably favorable. According to the Massachusetts approach, all of the exceptions to the general legality of closed shop strikes and agreements were accumulated into an overwhelming bundle of general illegality.

Plant v. *Woods* [37] is a typical case which involved a suit between two unions, both of which wanted only their members to work for the employer. The defendant union went on strike when the employer refused to discharge some of the plaintiff union's members; an injunction was sought. Although there were some implied threats of violence against the employer (and this undoubtedly had an influence on the decision), the central thrust of the Massachusetts Supreme Court's argument rendered this fact legally irrelevant. The court reasoned that everyone has the right to dispose of his labor free from the unwarranted interference of others; and that if one loses his job through competition, this is *damnum absque injuria*; but that "if it comes from the merely wanton or malicious acts of others, without the justification of competition or the service of interest or lawful purpose, then it stands on different footing." [38] In this case, the defendants intended to damage the plaintiff employees and were successful in doing so. The issue, thus, was whether justification existed. The court said that justification sometimes, as here, turns on motive. [39] If the motive is to build up one's own business or serve one's own self-interest, then the resulting injury is justified. But the motive here was simply to force the employer to hire only the members of one union, and since this was not sufficiently related to the legitimate self-interest of the striking union (*e.g.*, it was unrelated to their wages and working conditions), the resultant injury was without justification. Thus, the strike was enjoined.

Mr. Justice Holmes, while agreeing that the issue should be resolved on the basis of what justification existed for this strike, nevertheless dissented on the grounds that the motive of the union in seeking the closed shop was to enhance its bargaining strength, which would then enable it to obtain higher wages. Thus, the strike could be justified as being in the legitimate self-interest of the striking employees.

---

[37] 176 Mass. 492 (1900).

[38] *Id.* at 498.

[39] *Id.* at 499.

Subsequently, in *Berry* v. *Donovan*[40] an employee who had refused to join the union and who had been discharged pursuant to a closed shop agreement sued the union in tort for the "malicious interference with the plaintiff's contract of employment."[41] The plaintiff prevailed, even though he had merely been employed at will. The Massachusetts court said this did not matter; there had been an injurious interference with his employment relationship that was without justification. The court also noted that "the attempt to force all laborers to combine in unions is against the policy of the law because it aims at *monopoly*."[42]

Finally, in another series of cases the Massachusetts court condemned attempts to obtain a closed shop on the grounds that the striking unions were causing or attempting to induce the breach of contracts with various third parties.[43]

In short, the Massachusetts approach evidenced considerable hostility toward the achievement and enforcement of closed shop arrangements. There were, however, some notable exceptions. In one leading case, *Pickett* v. *Walsh*,[44] the Massachusetts court found that a union's attempt to obtain the equivalent of a closed shop was justified by considerations of self-interest. Here, the court disallowed a tort suit by a workman who had been discharged as a consequence of a union strike over his continued employment. The discharged employee had performed a

---

[40] 188 Mass. 353 (1905).

[41] *Id.* at 354.

[42] *Id.* at 359. The monopoly aspect was also emphasized in Folsom v. Lewis, 208 Mass. 336 (1911).

[43] Moore Drop Forging Co. v. McCarthy, 243 Mass. 554 (1923) (picketing constituted an attempted interference with the contract between an employer and his employees under which the employees had agreed not to join the union) ; Tracey v. Osborne, 226 Mass. 25 (1917) (strike by one union to induce the breach of a closed shop agreement with another union) ; W.A. Snow Iron Works v. Chadwick, 227 Mass. 382 (1917) (strike would have caused the employer to breach his contracts with certain customers) ; Aberthaw Construction Co. v. Cameron, 194 Mass. 208 (1907) (strike construed as a conspiracy to force the owner of building under construction to breach his contract with the plaintiff construction company). In this regard, the United States Supreme Court definitely followed the Massachusetts approach. In Hitchman Coal & Coke Co. v. Mitchell, 245 U.S. 229 (1917), the Court approved an injunction against unionists who were trying to organize employees whose contract of employment contained the stipulation that they not become members of the union.

[44] 192 Mass. 572 (1906).

specific and limited type of work in the construction of brick buildings, and the bricklayers union wanted its members to perform this work exclusively. The court said that in spite of the injury in fact to the discharged employee, the union members were justified in refusing to do one job unless they also got another. In short, when the acquisition of specific jobs for union members is the sole and proximate purpose of a closed shop strike, the strike can be justified in terms of legitimate self-interest.

The Massachusetts courts stopped short of condemning closed shop agreements completely. In *Smith* v. *Bowen* [45] the court noted that "an agreement by an employer with a union to give all his work to members of the union is a legal and valid agreement, and a strike by the members of the union to enforce their rights under such an agreement is a legal strike." [46] Presumably, the court had reference to hirings *subsequent* to the signing of a closed shop agreement; thus, in *Shinsky* v. *O'Neil*,[47] the court refused to enjoin the enforcement of a closed shop agreement against an employee hired in violation of its terms.

The Massachusetts approach, the New York approach, and the various intermediate positions and exceptions show, then, that during the early part of the twentieth century, the law pertaining to union security was in a state of considerable division, confusion, and complexity.

UNION SECURITY AND THE EXECUTIVE BRANCH OF GOVERNMENT

Early in the history of the union security problem, the various issues were dealt with almost exclusively through the judicial branch of government. More recently, legislative involvement

---

[45] 232 Mass. 106 (1919).

[46] *Id.* at 110. A threshold issue which the Massachusetts courts seemed to ignore but which arrested the attention of other common-law courts of the time was whether an "arrangement" between an employer and a labor union over the terms and conditions of employment of individual employees was even a binding contract at all. Prior to 1930, a majority of the courts had held that such arrangements had no binding effect. *E.g.,* Interborough Rapid Transit Co. v. Lavin, 247 N.Y. 65 (1928). *Compare* Whitmer, *Collective Labor Agreements in the Courts,* 48 YALE L.J. 195 (1938), *with* Summers, *Collective Agreements and the Law of Contracts,* 78 YALE L.J. 525 (1969). The legal status of collective agreements generally, however, is beyond the scope of this study.

[47] 232 Mass. 99 (1919).

has predominated, although the judicial influence continues to be exerted through statutory interpretation. Beginning in the 1900s, various actions by the executive branch of the federal government also had a significant impact on the evolution of the law's response to union security.

The shortage of fuel that was caused by the anthracite coal strike of 1902 touched a raw nerve of America's expanding industrial economy.[48] Under public and political pressure to get the coal mines open again as quickly as possible, President Theodore Roosevelt urged the parties to submit to binding arbitration. It was, however, only after Roosevelt threatened to have the mines taken over by the Army that the mine operators acquiesced and asked Roosevelt to appoint an arbitration commission. When the arbitration panel rendered its award, virtually every demand of the union was granted *except* the union's demand for a closed shop. Indeed, the commission mandated total employer neutrality toward the union membership or nonmembership of the employees. The award itself was widely construed as a semigovernmental endorsement of the idea of the open shop, and President Roosevelt contributed to this impression with his "hearty" approval of the nondiscrimination requirement.

Subsequently, in the celebrated case of W. A. Miller against the Government Printing Office, President Roosevelt had occasion to put his opposition to the closed shop into actual practice.[49] Miller, an employee of the Government Printing Office, had been expelled from the International Brotherhood of Bookbinders. Because the members of this union were prohibited by their rules from working with a nonmember, the public printer found it necessary to discharge Miller. The Civil Service Commission, however, ordered his reinstatement; under law, no one could be discharged "except for such cause as will promote the efficiency of the public service," and the Commission held that nonmembership in a labor organization did not constitute "such cause." Over the sharp protests of a delegation of labor unions, President Roosevelt upheld the Commission's decision. This was again construed as a significant victory for the proponents of the open shop.

---

[48] For a discussion of this strike and the presidential response to it, *see* F. DULLES, LABOR IN AMERICA 189-93 (1949); F. STOCKTON, THE CLOSED SHOP IN AMERICAN TRADE UNIONS 45-46 (1911).

[49] *See* STOCKTON, *supra* n. 48 at 46-48.

During World War I, as during World War II, in order to eliminate strike interference with the production of war materials, various dispute settlement boards were established by the President of the United States. The policy of President Wilson's National War Labor Board toward union security was essentially neutral. Existing agreements calling for closed or open shops were to be continued; employers were prohibited from discriminating against union members; and unions gave up their right to strike—for the closed shop or anything else.[50]

At the war's end, when these governmental restrictions were lifted, the open shop and the closed nonunion shop enjoyed a marked resurgence—to the dismay of labor unions. The disagreement between labor and management over such fundamental matters as the nature of collective bargaining, exclusive representation, and union security led President Wilson in 1919 to appoint a National Industrial Conference composed of representatives of management, labor, and the public. The conference, however, was unsuccessful in achieving any consensus over union security or any other pressing issue.[51]

While presidential disfavor of the closed union shop in public employment was reflected in Roosevelt's actions in the Miller case, a favorable presidential attitude toward the closed nonunion shop was to be seen in the Boston policeman's strike of 1919.[52] When the police commissioner of Boston suspended nineteen of his force who had joined a union, the remainder of the policemen went out on strike. President Wilson called the strike a "crime against civilization," and Calvin Coolidge, then governor of Massachusetts, stated that "there is no right to strike against the public safety, by anybody, anywhere, anytime." The suspended policemen were not reinstated, and a closed nonunion shop within the Boston police force was thus accomplished in fact with at least indirect presidential approval.

World War II witnessed the reappearance of presidentially appointed labor disputes boards. Moving slightly away from the neutrality of their World War I counterparts, these disputes boards generally adopted a policy of requiring that existing union members maintain their membership for the duration of

---

[50] *See* P. SULTAN, RIGHT-TO-WORK LAWS: A STUDY IN CONFLICT 27 (1958).

[51] *See* DULLES, *supra* n. 48 at 229; SULTAN, *supra* n. 50 at 27.

[52] *See* DULLES, *supra* n. 48 at 231-32.

the contract.[53] While industry generally objected to such a contractual requirement, the alternative was seizure by the government. Thus, "the total effect was clearly to prepare the way for wider acceptance of . . . stronger forms of union security in the postwar years." [54] This proved to be the case; by 1946 one-half of all the employees covered by a labor agreement, some 7.5 million workers, were subject to closed or union shop requirements.[55]

During the Korean conflict, presidential boards generally tended to recommend a union shop as a part of their suggested contract settlement. President Truman, however, twice backed away from the imposition of a mandatory union shop despite the recommendations of his own boards—first when he seized the steel mills, and second when the government took possession of the railroad industry.[56]

From World War I through the Korean conflict, presidential disputes settlement boards took a variety of postures on the question of union security, but in the last analysis determined employer opposition to any kind of compulsory unionism was relatively successful. Blackman reports forty-nine instances of management refusals to accept the contract ruling of a disputes settlement board. In twenty-six of these, the seizing agencies failed to obtain acceptance, and the properties were returned without ultimate compliance. Significantly, fifteen of these twenty-six involved management's refusal to agree to some form of union security.[57]

EARLY FEDERAL LEGISLATION

Since one of the common-law bases for condemning attempts to obtain the closed shop was that such an arrangement amounted to a monopoly in restraint of trade, it is not surprising that the Sherman Anti-Trust Act of 1890 should likewise be applied, being the first major piece of federal legislation to affect union security. While some have questioned whether Congress origi-

---

[53] *See* J. BLACKMAN, PRESIDENTIAL SEIZURE IN LABOR DISPUTES 184 (1967).

[54] *Id.* at 184; *see* H. NORTHRUP, COMPULSORY ARBITRATION AND GOVERNMENTAL INTERVENTION IN LABOR DISPUTES 20 (1966).

[55] *See* 64 MONTHLY LABOR REVIEW 767 (1947).

[56] *See* BLACKMAN, *supra* n. 53 at 186.

[57] *See* BLACKMAN, *supra* n. 53 at 146-47.

nally intended the Sherman Act to apply to labor unions,[58] the Supreme Court was initially quite willing to subject labor combinations to its strictures. In the famous *Danbury Hatters* case,[59] the Court held that an attempt to obtain the closed shop by means of interstate boycotts was actionable under this law.

In the Clayton Act of 1914, Congress attempted both to narrow the applicability of the antitrust statutes to labor unions and to limit the power of the federal courts to issue injunctions in labor disputes. The Supreme Court, however, in *Duplex Printing Press Co.* v. *Deering*,[60] construed the Clayton Act as neither providing antitrust exemptions for nor prohibiting injunctions against secondary boycotts aimed at obtaining a closed shop arrangement.

Congress then tried again in the Norris-LaGuardia Act of 1932, and in *United States* v. *Hutcheson*,[61] the Supreme Court effectively (but not literally) overruled its prior decisions and found unions to be virtually exempt from the federal antitrust statutes. As a consequence, the Sherman Act could no longer operate as a legislative limitation upon the acquisition or enforcement of closed shop agreements.

Meanwhile, federal legislation more directly affecting union security had been passed in 1898. The Erdman Act related, in general, to the arbitration and settlement of labor disputes of common carriers engaged in interstate commerce. Section 10 of that Act forbad carriers either from requiring their employees to agree as a condition of employment not to become a member of a labor organization or from otherwise discriminating against employees because of their membership in a labor organization. In short, the Act outlawed the so-called yellow dog contract, a pejorative term generally used to describe a closed nonunion shop arrangement.

The Supreme Court, however, held that prohibition to be unconstitutional. In *Adair* v. *United States*,[62] the Court followed the same philosophy which inspired the *Commonwealth* v. *Hunt*

---

[58] *See, e.g.,* Boudin, *The Sherman Act and Labor Disputes: I.* 39 COLUM. L. REV. 1283 (1939); Emery, *Labor Organizations and the Sherman Law,* 20 J. POL. ECON. 599 (1912).

[59] Loewe v. Lawlor, 208 U.S. 274 (1908).

[60] 254 U.S. 443 (1921).

[61] 312 U.S. 219 (1941).

[62] 208 U.S. 161 (1908).

approach to criminal conspiracies and the New York approach to injunctions and damage suits—namely, that the insistence upon certain things as a condition of employment does not amount to a "legal wrong," and that it is, rather, part and parcel of the liberty of contract protected by the Fifth Amendment to the Constitution. Thus, the Supreme Court in *Adair* said:

> [I]t is not within the functions of government—at least in the absence of contract between the parties—to compel any person in the course of his business and against his will to accept or retain the personal services of another, or to compel any person, against his will, to perform personal services for another. The right of a person to sell his labor upon such terms as he deems proper is, in its essence, the same as the right of the purchaser of labor to prescribe the conditions upon which he will accept such labor from the person offering to sell it. So the right of the employee to quit the service of the employer, for whatever reason, is the same as the right of the employer, for whatever reason, to dispense with the services of such employee. It was the legal right of the defendant Adair—however unwise such a course might have been—to discharge Coppage because of his being a member of a labor organization, as it was the legal right of Coppage, if he saw fit to do so—however unwise such a course on his part might have been—to quit the service in which he was engaged, because the defendant employed some persons who were not members of a labor organization.[63]

Subsequently, in *Coppage* v. *Kansas*,[64] the Supreme Court declared unconstitutional a state statute which attempted to outlaw this same kind of closed nonunion shop agreement between an employer and his employees.

Federal pressure against "yellow dog" contracts continued in a different form. In Section 3 of the Norris-LaGuardia Act (mentioned earlier in the context of injunctions and antitrust suits), Congress declared employment contracts stipulating against membership in a labor organization to be contrary to public policy and unenforceable in federal courts. Whatever the actual legal impact of this provision, it undoubtedly influenced public thinking and served as a stepping-stone for further legislative encouragements of union security.

Such encouragement finally came in 1933 in the National Industrial Recovery Act, part of President Roosevelt's New Deal

---

[63] *Id.* at 174-75.

[64] 236 U.S. 1 (1915).

efforts to stimulate a moribund economy. The result of a series
of dubious compromises,[65] the Act allowed industry to write its
own codes of "fair competition," but in response to the demands of labor, it also stipulated that "every code . . . shall
contain the following conditions: . . . (2) that no employee
and no one seeking employment shall be required as a condition
of employment to join any company union or to refrain from
joining, organizing, or assisting a labor organization of his own
choosing. . . ."[66] In short, the Act prohibited an employer from
requiring membership in a "company union" or from requiring
nonunion membership as a condition of employment; but the
Act did *not* prohibit union membership as a condition of employment—*i.e.*, it did not prohibit the closed shop. The NIRA
was subsequently declared unconstitutional on other grounds.[67]

In the following year, however, Congress took a more bal-
anced approach to employment discrimination concerning membership or nonmembership in a labor organization. In the Railway Labor Act of 1926, Congress had established procedures
for the resolution of labor disputes within the railway industry
without providing for comprehensive regulation of the employer-
employee-union relationship or of union security agreements.
The amendments of 1934 did provide such comprehensive regulation; and with respect to union security, Section 2, Fourth stated
that "it shall be unlawful for any carrier . . . to influence or
coerce employees in an effort to induce them to join or remain
or not to join or remain members of any labor organization,
. . . ."[68] In short, *neither* a closed nonunion shop *nor* a closed
union shop was to be permitted. Rather, an employee's membership or nonmembership in a labor organization was irrelevant
to his employment status.

This ostensibly neutral policy toward union security was accepted by the railway unions, both because they had a long
tradition of voluntary unionism and because then they were
more fearful of company unions than they were desirous of
obtaining the closed shop. Compulsory membership in company-

---

[65] *See generally* DULLES, *supra* n. 48 at 264-67.

[66] 48 Stat. 198-99 (1933).

[67] Schechter Poultry Corp. v. United States, 295 U.S. 495 (1935) (the Act
was held to be an unconstitutional delegation of legislative power from Congress to the President).

[68] 48 Stat. 1187 (1934).

dominated unions, together with a compulsory checkoff of dues, was viewed as a serious threat to the very existence of the independent unions. They were thus willing to accept the compromise.[69]

For unions, other than railway unions, Congress adhered to the formula originally spelled out in the National Industrial Recovery Act, and in 1935 it enacted the National Labor Relations Act, a comprehensive piece of legislation covering all industries in interstate commerce. In Section 8(3) of this Act, Congress made it an unfair labor practice for an employer "by discrimination in regard to hire or tenure of employment or any term or condition of employment to encourage or discourage membership in any labor organization." [70] On its face, this provision would appear to outlaw *both* the "yellow dog" contract and the closed shop contract. Congress, however, added a qualifying proviso. It stated:

> Nothing in this Act . . . or in any other statute of the United States, shall preclude an employer from making an agreement with a labor organization (not established, maintained, or assisted by any action defined in this Act as an unfair labor practice) to require as a condition of employment membership therein, if such labor organization is the representative of the employees as provided in section 9(a) in the appropriate collective bargaining unit covered by such agreement when made.[71]

The combined effect of Section 8(3) and this proviso on what a union security agreement could or could not require was as follows: (a) requiring as a condition of employment that an employee *not* be a member of a union was illegal, (b) requiring an employee to join a *company-dominated* union was likewise illegal; (c) but requiring an employee to be a member of a union representing a majority of the employees in an appropriate unit was not illegal. In short, a closed shop agreement was perfectly valid—*at least insofar as federal law was concerned.*

The effect of this statute on state law was not so clear. In addition to the common-law prohibitions against the closed shop which existed in some states, by 1946-47 several states had statutory or constitutional provisions which banned compulsory union membership agreements. The issue, thus, was whether

---

[69] *See* SULTAN, *supra* n. 50 at 29.

[70] 49 Stat. 452 (1935).

[71] *Id.*

these state laws could operate in the face of the Section 8(3) proviso. After evading the issue in one case,[72] the Supreme Court in *Algoma Plywood Co. v. Wisconsin Board*[73] finally upheld the validity of a state law which was more restrictive of union security agreements than was the federal law. The Court noted that Section 8(3) "merely disclaims a national policy hostile to the closed shop or other forms of union security agreement,"[74] and that Congress did not intend to legalize *affirmatively* union security agreements in the face of contrary state law.

Litigation on union security under Section 8(3) and its proviso was relatively limited; much of it focused on such issues as the majority status of the contracting union, whether the union was employer dominated, and the appropriateness of the unit covered by the closed shop agreement. There were, also, a number of cases defining the kinds of union security agreements the proviso protected. As a general matter, the Board and the courts held that a discharge based on the employee's nonmembership in the union would not be considered illegally discriminatory if the collective bargaining agreement provided for a true closed shop, a union shop,[75] or an agency shop;[76] likewise, a "maintenance of union membership" provision was usually deemed protected by the proviso.[77] On the other hand, preferential hiring clauses[78] and other obscure promises of "cooperation" with the union in sustaining its membership were generally deemed insufficient justification for discriminatory discharges, the proviso notwithstanding.[79]

In the years following the passage of the National Labor Relations Act, unions enjoyed a tremendous growth in both

---

[72] AFL v. Watson, 327 U.S. 582 (1946).

[73] 336 U.S. 301 (1948). This interpretation of the National Labor Relations Act came, of course, *after* Congress had already authorized such state laws in Section 14(b) of the Labor-Management Relations Act.

[74] *Id.* at 307; *see also id.* at 307-10.

[75] National Electric Products Corp., 80 N.L.R.B. 995 (1948) (membership required within a certain number of days after hire).

[76] Public Service Co. of Colo., 89 N.L.R.B. 418 (1950) (the payment of dues and fees required in lieu of true membership).

[77] Aluminum Co. of America v. NLRB, 159 F.2d 523 (7th Cir. 1946).

[78] South Atlantic S.S. Co. of Del. v. NLRB, 116 F.2d 480 (5th Cir. 1941), *cert. denied*, 313 U.S. 582 (1941).

[79] Pittsburgh Plate Glass Co., 66 N.L.R.B. 1083 (1946); *see also*, Burroughs-Wellcome & Co., 68 N.L.R.B. 175 (1946).

membership and power—due largely to the Act's allowance of closed shop agreements. As unions gained power, however, they also tended to use it in ways which many people thought were abusive and without justification. Coercion of employees, organizational picketing, secondary boycotts, and the expulsion of union members on arbitrary or malicious grounds (thus causing, under a union security agreement, the individual's discharge from employment) were among the activities most commonly objected to. Consequently, in 1948 the old NLRA was amended, expanded, and reenacted under the name of the Labor-Management Relations Act, or Taft-Hartley as it is more commonly known.

In the new Act, certain types of union conduct were declared to be unfair labor practices. More importantly, however, Congress narrowed the kinds of union security agreements that were to be allowed under the Act, imposed additional limitations with respect to when these agreements could be entered into (only after the employees had authorized such an agreement in a specially conducted election), and specifically authorized the states to outlaw union security agreements altogether if they saw fit.

The union security provisions of the Labor-Management Relations Act were slightly modified in 1951, principally by eliminating the requirement of an "authorization election." In that same year, the Railway Labor Act was amended to bring its union security provisions into conformity with those of the LMRA. This, then, is the law under which union security agreements presently operate; a detailed examination of its terms will occupy the remainder of this section of the study.

CHAPTER III

Union Security Agreements Under the Taft-Hartley Act

Although the original Wagner Act broadly prohibited employment discrimination on the basis of union membership, it also specifically exempted the most obvious and literal form of such discrimination—union security agreements requiring union membership as a condition of employment.[1] Congress retreated from this seemingly anomalous position in the Taft-Hartley Act by outlawing the closed shop, wherein a person is required to be a member of the union in order to be eligible for employment. How much further, however, the Taft-Hartley Congress went in proscribing inherently discriminatory union security agreements has been the subject of considerable confusion.

The conventional wisdom is that the LMRA authorized the union shop. To be sure, that term was frequently bandied about during the legislative debates as a type of union security to be permitted by the amendments; but no one ever proffered a comprehensive definition of the term.[2] Indeed, at one point Senator Taft noted that "the union shop is not defined. No one knows what it is. We did not use the term in the bill." [3] The Supreme Court has also said that the LMRA authorized the

---

[1] Portions of this chapter originally appeared in Haggard, *A Clarification of the Types of Union Security Agreements Affirmatively Permitted by Federal Statutes*, reprinted with permission from the RUTGERS-CAMDEN LAW JOURNAL, Vol. 5, No. 3, pp. 418-452. Copyright 1974 by Rutgers School of Law-Camden.

[2] *See, e.g.*, THE LEGISLATIVE HISTORY OF THE LABOR MANAGEMENT RELATIONS ACT, 1947 (hereinafter cited as LEGIS. HIST. LMRA) at 321, 409, 545, 734, 1009, 1402, 1420 (1974). For the most part, the explanations are bent on distinguishing the *union shop* from the *closed shop* by reference to the time at which an individual's obligation to the union arises; but the legislative history is obscure as to the exact nature of the obligations being contemplated.

[3] LEGIS. HIST. LMRA at 1408.

union shop,[4] but the rulings indicate that the obligations of
the *true* union shop cannot, in fact, be imposed upon employees
under the Act[5]—thus suggesting that the Court too has not
always used the term with punctilious regard for its full meaning. This was implicitly recognized by the Court in one early
decision where, because of its uncertainty about what labels to
attach to the various types of union security agreements, the
Court concluded that it would be "better to avoid the use of any
of them in this opinion."[6]

This lack of a precise and consistently used terminology has
undoubtedly contributed to the confusion that has lingered over
the union security issue for many years now. On the other
hand, the refusal of both Congress and the courts to pin a specific
label on the union security provisions of the Act is fully justified, for the exact form of union security that the Act authorizes
does not fit into any of the customary pigeonholes. Thus the
traditional forms of union security and the labels that are used
to identify them can at best provide a convenient grid against
which to plot the unique characteristics of a "Taft-Hartley Act
union security agreement." In doing this, the obvious place to
begin is with the language of the statute itself.

Section 8(a)(3) of the Act generally prohibits discrimination
which has the effect of encouraging or discouraging union membership. The Section's proviso, however, states:

> [N]othing in this subchapter . . . shall preclude an employer from
> making an agreement with a labor organization . . . to require as
> a condition of employment membership therein on or after the
> thirtieth day following the beginning of such employment. . . .
> *Provided further,* That no employer shall justify any discrimination
> against an employee for nonmembership in a labor organization
> (A) if he has reasonable grounds for believing that such member-
> ship was not available to the employee on the same terms and con-
> ditions generally applicable to other members, or (B) if he has
> reasonable grounds for believing that membership was denied or
> terminated for reasons other than the failure of the employee to
> tender the periodic dues and the initiation fees uniformly required
> as a condition of acquiring or retaining membership. . . .[7]

---

[4] *See, e.g.,* NLRB v. General Motors Corp., 373 U.S. 734 (1963).

[5] *See, e.g.,* NLRB v. General Motors Corp., where the Court held that even
in a "union shop unit" an employee cannot *necessarily* be discharged just
because of his nonmembership status—a conclusion that is inconsistent with
the obligations that obtain under a *true* union shop arrangement.

[6] Lincoln Federal Labor Union v. Northwestern Iron & Metal Co., 335 U.S
525, 528 n. 2 (1949).

[7] 29 U.S.C. § 158(a)(3) (1970).

That is the kind of union security agreement the Taft-Hartley Act allows for. How it compares with the more traditional kinds of union security agreements, as defined in Chapter I, is the subject of this chapter.

AGREEMENTS AFFIRMATIVELY PERMITTED

The Closed Shop

Beyond cavil, Congress intended to prohibit the closed shop. The Section 8(a)(3) proviso clearly does not exempt from illegality union security agreements requiring union membership at any time earlier than the thirtieth day after employment. The Board and the courts have consistently held that an employer and a union cannot agree to make union membership a condition of initially obtaining a job with the employer.[8]

The congressional purpose behind this particular change in the Wagner Act was to eliminate exclusive union control over entrance into a job market, a monopolistic position which Congress felt the unions had frequently abused.[9] By denying union membership for invidious or arbitrary reasons, the unions had been able, under a closed shop agreement, to foreclose even the possibility of an individual obtaining a job with the contracting employer. Where an entire industry was covered by closed shop agreements, the individual was shut out of his occupation or profession altogether. Congress felt that the union's legitimate needs for union security did not go so far as to justify this kind of power and compulsion.

Athough the closed shop is thus illegal per se, "bootleg" or *de facto* closed shop situations have continued to exist, primarily under the aegis of union hiring halls.[10]

The True Union Shop

Despite congressional assertions that the union shop was being authorized under the amended statute, the Section 8(a)(3) proviso clearly does not authorize a *true* union shop, at least not as that term was defined in Chapter I.

---

[8] *See, e.g.*, Operating Engineers Local 542 v. NLRB, 329 F.2d 512 (3d Cir. 1964).

[9] LEGIS. HIST. LMRA at 325.

[10] *See* Chapter IV, *infra.*

The first part of the proviso does allow an agreement making membership in the union within thirty days a condition of continued employment. This would seem to suggest that the union shop is thus authorized. This conclusion, however, is negated by the "provided further" language which states that an employer is not justified in discharging an employee because of nonmembership in the union if such membership was not available to this employee on the same terms and conditions as those enjoyed by other employees, or if the employee had been denied membership for any reason other that the employee's failure to tender periodic dues and fees. Since the traditional union shop agreement regulated neither the internal privileges and obligations of union membership nor the requirements of admission to and retention of membership, it is apparent that in Section 8(a)(3) Congress contemplated something other than the true union shop.

The Statutory *Union Shop*

If, however, the kind of union shop that the statute authorizes is somehow different from the traditional or true union shop, then it becomes necessary to determine exactly what was authorized. The language of the statute itself is somewhat ambiguous, and from this ambiguity have flowed two principal interpretations.

The Union Option *Interpretation.* The *union option* interpretation of the statute partially implements the apparent congressional desire to authorize the union shop, a desire evident in parts of the legislative history. This interpretation views the proviso as having the following structural form. The first part authorizes the negotiation of an agreement which requires as a condition of continued employment full or formal membership in the union, initially requiring an employee to apply for membership in the union that represents him. In this sense, the Act authorizes the union shop.

The two exceptions to this requirement which follow the "provided further" language, were designed to ameliorate the job effects of certain undesirable union practices. Thus, while Congress did not want to regulate the internal affairs of unions, it did provide in the first exception that a union security agreement could not require, as a condition of employment, that an employee become a member of a union if the membership status to which he was being relegated was somehow inferior to the membership status generally afforded other employees. If, however, the union opted to extend the normal prerogatives of formal membership, then presumably the employee would be obliged to accept it.

The second exception—which, insofar as the two competing interpretations are concerned, is the more significant one—was necessary because Congress did not want to regulate the membership policies of unions. Congress felt that it should not force a union to admit into full membership those which the union found obnoxious or inimical to union interests. Thus, Congress intended that even in a union shop situation, a union could exclude certain employees from full membership. The second exception was intended to regulate the rights of the various parties in those situations in which the union had elected to exercise this right of exclusion. On the union's side, to save it from the burden of having to carry the so-called free rider (*i.e.*, the employee who is in the bargaining unit but who is not a member of the union), the proviso requires employees who are excluded from union membership to continue to pay the equivalent of periodic dues and fees. On the employee's side, so long as he continues to pay such dues and fees, he is entitled to remain in his job.

The significance of this interpretation of the Section 8(a)(3) proviso is that it gives the union alone the power or option of determining whether an employee is to be considered a full member and thus subject to the internal rules of the association and to legally enforceable fines for the breach thereof.

The Agency Shop *Interpretation.* The second possible interpretation is less systematic in its approach, insofar as the structure of the statute is concerned. It starts by construing the term "membership" used in the first sentence of the proviso by reference to the substantive content of clause (B) following the "provided further" language. Thus, what the initial sentence authorizes is not a union security agreeement requiring formal membership, but one wherein the employee's obligation is limited solely to the payment of periodic dues and fees, as in the agency shop! The initial sentence of the proviso having been construed in this fashion, clause (B) becomes redundant. Presumably, clause (A) would merely operate to insure that all agency-shop members are treated equally. The significance of this interpretation, apart from the fact that the affected employees are required only to pay the equivalent of dues rather than actually to join the union, is that such employees are not subject to the disciplinary power that unions normally exercise over their membership.

The Existing Case Law

Underlying the debate between the *union option* and the *agency shop* interpretation of the statute is basically this question: What are an employee's obligations to the union under the maximum form of union security agreement allowed by the statute? The Board and the courts have tended to answer this question, in turn, by reference to two subsidiary issues: First, what are the employee's obligations with respect to obtaining union "membership" as that term is used in the statute? Second, what obligations does the union have as a result of the employee's acquisition of this required membership?

Taken as a whole, the case law on these two issues clearly supports the agency shop interpretation. The matter, however, is not entirely free from doubt, and there is one recent case which opposes this interpretation, requiring extensive case analysis.

The Union Starch *Case.* Shortly after the passage of the Taft-Hartley Act, in the *Union Starch* [11] case, the NLRB held that under a valid union security agreement an employee could be required to do nothing more than tender his dues and fees to the union. In this case, several employees had tendered their dues, but the union refused to accept the money. The union indicated that in order to qualify for membership, as was apparently required by the collective bargaining agreement, the employees would have to attend the next regular meeting and be voted upon, take an oath to the union, then pay the initiation fee and the first two months dues. The employees refused to comply with the first two requirements, but continued to tender the necessary money. The union then demanded that the employer discharge these employees; the employer complied, and unfair labor practices charges were brought against both the employer and the union. In finding a violation of the Act, the Board held that the proviso "protects employees who have tendered the requisite of dues and initiation fees and been denied membership for *any other reason,* even though that reason be nondiscriminatory." [12] A valid union security agreement may allow the

---

[11] Union Starch & Refining Co., 87 N.L.R.B. 779 (1949), *enforced,* 186 F.2d 1008 (7th Cir. 1951), *cert. denied,* 342 U.S. 815 (1951).

[12] *Id.* at 783 (emphasis added).

union to force, on pain of discharge, an employee to pay money to the union, but such an agreement cannot be construed as allowing the union to force, on pain of discharge, an employee to do anything in addition to that.

The *Union Starch* doctrine has been consistently adhered to by both the Board and the courts of appeals.[13] Indeed, the *Union Starch* case was cited with approval and the essence of the doctrine adopted by the Supreme Court in *NLRB* v. *General Motors Corp.*[14] Here the Court noted:

> Under the second proviso to § 8(a)(3), the burdens of membership upon which employment may be conditioned are expressly limited to the payment of initiation fees and monthly dues. It is permissible to condition employment upon membership, but membership, insofar as it has significance to employment rights, may in turn be conditioned only upon payment of fees and dues. "Membership" as a condition of employment is whittled down to its financial core.[15]

Despite the directness of this authority, some unions have persisted in their practice of requiring employees under a union security agreement to do more toward joining the union than merely tendering dues and fees. In the 1972 case of *Boilermakers Local 749* v. *NLRB*,[16] the union attempted to require employees to sign a union membership card. In arguing that a union security agreement could validly impose such a requirement, the union alleged that Section 8(a)(3) expressly authorizes the conditioning of employment upon union membership, that a mere willingness to pay dues and fees is not the equivalent of membership, and that the *Union Starch* doctrine is erroneous in that it abolishes the distinction between union shops and agency shops—a distinction which the Congress clearly recognized. The District of Columbia Court of Appeals, however, held that whatever the intrinsic merits of the union's argument, the *Union Starch* doctrine was firmly ensconced under a "long-established

---

[13] *See* Boilermakers Local 749, 192 N.L.R.B. 502 (1971), *enforced*, 466 F.2d 343, 345 (D.C. Cir. 1972), *cert. denied*, 410 U.S. 926 (1973).

[14] 373 U.S. 734 (1963).

[15] *Id.* at 742. The Court also noted that "If an employee in a union shop unit refuses to respect any union-imposed obligations other than the duty to pay dues and fees, and membership in the union is therefore denied or terminated . . . the employee may not be discharged for nonmembership even though he is not a formal member." *Id.* at 743, *citing, inter alia* in n. 10, the *Union Starch* case.

[16] 466 F.2d 343 (D.C. Cir. 1972), *cert. denied*, 410 U.S. 926 (1973).

array of authority"[17] from which the court was not willing to deviate.

Apparently recognizing that a frontal attack on the *Union Starch* doctrine was not apt to succeed, the union in the *Boilermakers* case argued alternatively that the *Union Starch* doctrine was inapplicable where, as in this case, the discharged employee did not desire and had not sought full union membership. This suggests that the union was pursuing a "union option" line of reasoning. The court rejected the argument. It noted that "in terms of an employee's right under Section 8(a)(3) to be protected from discharge for non-union membership, we think it irrelevant whether the employee did or did not desire membership in the union."[18]

The *Union Starch* line of cases stands for the proposition that an employee's obligation with respect to obtaining union membership pursuant to a statutory union security clause is limited to the tender of union dues and fees. Although other requirements may exist as a condition of full or formal membership, these requirements cannot operate as a condition of continued employment. Therefore, insofar as the employee's retention of his job is concerned, his obligations under a statutory union security agreement are no greater than the obligations that attach under what is commonly known as an "agency shop agreement," as previously defined.

Finally, in the recent case of *Abood* v. *Detroit Board of Education,*[19] the Supreme Court specifically identified the "agency shop" (although it was admittedly in dicta) as the maximum form of union security allowed by federal law. The Court noted:

> Under a union-shop agreement, an employee must become a member of the union within a specified period of time after hire, and must as a member pay whatever union dues and fees as are uniformly required. Under both the National Labor Relations Act and the Railway Labor Act, "[i]t is permissible to condition employment upon membership, but membership, insofar as it has significance to employment rights, may in turn be conditioned only upon payment of fees and dues." . . . Hence, although a union shop denies an employee the option of not formally becoming a union member,

---

[17] *Id.* at 345.

[18] *Id.* at 344-45 n. 1.

[19] 45 U.S.L.W. 4473 (1977).

under federal law it is the "practical equivalent" of an agency shop. . . .[20]

The *Union Starch* line of cases, however, stands only for the proposition that nothing more than the mere payment of fees and dues can be made a condition of employment, even if more is normally required to obtain formal membership in the union. The more difficult question, not specifically resolved by the *Union Starch* doctrine, is whether under such a union security agreement the mere payment of dues and fees can, by operation of law, thereby subject the employee to the disciplinary power of the union—specifically, by rendering him civilly liable for the payment of fines for the breach of the obligations of union membership. This, however, is a question that the courts have avoided answering directly. In the *Boilermakers* case, for example, the court noted:

> Our decision here is limited to the issue of discharge from employment. We decide nothing, and we intimate no opinion, as to the extent of a union's power to discipline an employee who, though refusing formal membership, pays union dues and fees.[21]

The decision was silent as to whether, by virtue of a union security agreement, an employee could be said to have extra-monetary obligations to the union which are enforceable through the imposition of union discipline rather than discharge from employment. The court's disinclination to speak to this issue correctly suggests that the issue has not been definitively resolved.

The uncertainty of the present state of the law stems in part from the Supreme Court's rather chaotic opinion in *NLRB* v. *General Motors Corp.*[22] The issue in *General Motors* was whether the employer had a statutory duty to bargain with the union over an agency shop clause. The Court noted that the resolution of that issue ultimately turned on the legality of the agency shop under Section 8(a)(3) since an employer would not commit an unfair labor practice by refusing to bargain over a provision declared illegal under that Section. The Court then examined the legality of the agency shop agreement and found it to fall within the protections of the Section 8(a)(3) proviso. As its point of departure the Court noted that "[t]here is

---

[20] *Id.* at 4475 n. 10 (emphasis added).

[21] *Id.* at 345 n. 3.

[22] 373 U.S. 734 (1963).

much to be said for the Board's view that, if Congress desired . . . to permit . . . the union shop, then it also intended to preserve the status of less vigorous, less compulsory contracts which demanded less adherence to the union." [23] The agency shop is legal because it is less compulsory than the union shop that Congress did intend to legalize. It is clear, however, that the Court was not conforming to the definition given earlier of the term *union shop,* for the Court went on to say that actual membership (which would be required under a real union shop agreement) cannot be a condition of continued employment. What this logically suggests is that the maximum or most compulsory form of union security agreement allowed by the proviso falls somewhere above the mere agency shop but short of the true union shop. Arguably, this could have reference to the kind of hybrid arrangement suggested by the *Boilermakers* footnote, whereby an employee is required to become a formal member, but only to the extent of being subject to union discipline.

Other language in the Court's opinion reinforces this possibility. The Court noted that while the union may not cause a nonmember's discharge for any reason other than non-payment of dues and fees,

> if the union chooses to extend membership even though the employee will meet only the minimum financial burden, and refuses to support or "join" the union in any other affirmative way, *the employee may have to become a "member" under a union shop contract, in the sense that the union may be able to place him on its rolls.* The agency shop arrangement proposed there removes that choice from the union and places the option of membership in the employee while still requiring the same monetary support as does the union shop. *Such a difference between the union and agency shop may be of great importance in some contexts,* but for present purposes it is more formal than real.[24]

A union's power to discipline employees for breaches of the union's internal rules is a context in which the difference between an agency shop and a union shop is of great importance. The Court had not yet passed on the question of whether the Taft-Hartley Act prohibited a union from suing in state court to collect fines from members, a method of enforcement that had come into vogue only in the late 1950s. Nevertheless, the Court was undoubtedly aware of this practice, and it has been

---

[23] *Id.* at 741.

[24] *Id.* at 743-44 (emphasis added).

argued that in *General Motors* the Court was intimating that unions can legally acquire that kind of disciplinary power over unwilling employees through a type of union security agreement which is permitted by the proviso. According to this view, for disciplinary purposes an employee becomes a member of the union and subject to the union's rules and the enforcement thereof simply by virtue of the tender and acceptance of his dues and fees pursuant to a contract term which requires "membership" as a condition of continued employment.

Although this may be a defensible interpretation of the logic and language of the *General Motors* decision itself, prior and subsequent decisions of the Court suggest an entirely different conclusion. For example, in the earlier case of *Radio Officers' Union* v. *NLRB,* the Court said:

> The policy of the Act is to insulate employees' jobs from their organizational rights. Thus §§ 8(a)(3) and 8(b)(2) were designed to allow employees to freely exercise their right to join unions, be good, bad, or indifferent members, or abstain from joining any union without imperiling their livelihood. The only limitation Congress has chosen to impose on this right is specified in the proviso to § 8(a)(3). . . . Lengthy legislative debate preceded the 1947 amendment to the Act which thus limited permissible employer discrimination. *This legislative history clearly indicates that Congress intended to prevent utilization of union security agreements for any purpose other than to compel payment of union dues and fees.*[25]

If by making continued employment plus the tender of dues and fees the legal equivalent of formal union membership, a union security agreement is capable of being used for the purpose of subjecting employees to internal union discipline, then such an agreement is being used "for [a] purpose other than to compel payment of union dues and fees" and should thus be declared violative of Section 8(a)(3).

The *General Motors* opinion must, moreover, be read against the Court's opinion in the companion case of *Retail Clerks Local 1625* v. *Schermerhorn* [26] which involved the issue of whether Section 14(b) authorized the states to prohibit an agency shop or service fee arrangement. The Court's premise was that "[a]t the very least, the agreements requiring 'membership' in a labor

---

[25] 347 U.S. 17 (1954) at 40-41 (emphasis added).

[26] 373 U.S. 746 (1963).

union which are expressly permitted by the proviso are the same 'membership' agreements expressly placed within the reach of state law by § 14(b)." [27] The Court then construed *General Motors* as holding that the agency shop is the "practical equivalent" [28] of the kind of agreement permitted by the proviso. The Court thus concluded that "[w]hatever may be the status of *less stringent* union-security arrangements, the agency shop is within § 14(b)." [29] While the Court's language is not necessarily inconsistent with the prior interpretation of *General Motors,* the "practical equivalent" characterization and the express reference to "less stringent" arrangements lends some support to an inference that the Court might have believed that the agency shop itself was the maximum form of union security permitted by the Section 8(a)(3) proviso. This is strongly reinforced by the language in *General Motors,* which says that the "membership" required by the proviso as a condition of employment "is whittled down to its financial core." This again suggests that membership for the purpose of being subjected to court-enforced union fines is not contemplated by the Act.

Supreme Court Decisions on Union Discipline. The Supreme Court decisions defining the limits of legitimate union discipline under Section 8(b)(1)(A) lend collateral support to this latter interpretation of Section 8(a)(3). In *NLRB* v. *Allis-Chalmers Manufacturing Co.,*[30] the union had imposed a fine on an employee who had crossed the union's picket line. The union security agreement in *Allis-Chalmers* merely required that an employee become and remain "a member of the Union . . . to the extent of paying his monthly dues." The legality of this provision under Section 8(a)(3) was not in issue, but the dissent clearly indicated that if such a contract clause were construed as giving the union disciplinary jurisdiction over unwilling members, then it violated Section 8(a)(3). Relying on *Radio Officers Union,* Mr. Justice Black noted in dissent:

> If the union uses the union security clause to compel employees to pay dues, characterizes such employees as members, and then uses such membership as a basis for imposing court enforced fines upon those employees unwilling to participate in a union strike, then the

---

[27] *Id.* at 751.

[28] *Id.*

[29] *Id.* at 751-52 (emphasis added).

[30] 388 U.S. 175 (1967).

union security clause is being used for a purpose other than "to compel payment of union dues and fees." It is being used to coerce employees to join in union activity in violation of § 8(b) (2).[31]

The majority did not *expressly* disagree with the dissent on that point of law. Rather, the majority simply construed the contract provision as not actually requiring full or formal membership. The Court then adopted as the controlling fact that which was found by the court below: that the disciplined employee had nevertheless become a full member by virtue of his actions in pledging allegiance to the union, taking the oath of membership, and participating in the proceedings which led to the strike. Since in this case the membership status which the employee enjoyed flowed from his own actions rather than from the operation of the union security provision, the imposition of discipline was legal.[32] The Court declined to express any opinion about the legality of union disciplinary action against employees whose membership is *solely* the result of a union security agreement.[33] The decision, therefore, also tells us nothing about the legality of such an agreement, although it would appear that Justice Black's analysis is a sound one.

---

[31] *Id.* at 215 (Black, Jr., dissenting).

[32] The section of the Court's opinion under analysis is somewhat cryptic, and the interpretation presented in the text is contradicted by the Court's assertion that "the relevant inquiry here is not what motivated a member's full membership but whether the Taft-Hartley amendments prohibited disciplinary measures against a full member who crossed his union's picket line." *Id.* at 196. From the perspective of the scope of the union's disciplinary powers over members, it is irrelevant whether the membership is voluntary or a requirement of the collective bargaining agreement. One of two things may be inferred from this. First, the irrelevance of motive makes some sense if agreements requiring full membership are in fact legal under Section 8(a)(3). This inference is negated, however, by the Court's penultimate sentence and accompanying footnote which strongly suggest that something less than full membership—*i.e.*, a membership "limited to the obligation of paying monthly dues"—is the most that is authorized by Section 8(a)(3). *Id.* at 197 and n. 37. Alternatively, one may infer that perhaps the majority thought that Section 8(b)(1) need not be construed *in pari materia* with Section 8(a)(3). Even if a union security clause requiring full membership is illegal under Section 8(a)(3), the union may nevertheless enforce fines against such members without running afoul of Section 8(b)(1). That, however, is patently absurd; nonmembership in the union, to the extent guaranteed by Section 8(a)(3), is clearly a right protected by Section 7, 29 U.S.C. § 157 (1970), and union interference with that right is prohibited by Section 8(b)(1). Moreover, the Court did construe the scope of Section 8(b)(1) by reference to the union security authorizations. *See, e.g., id.* at 185. Thus the interpretation of the Court's rationale as presented in the text is the most plausible one.

[33] *Id.* at 197.

Subsequently, in *Scofield* v. *NLRB* [34] the Court was again confronted with the issue of the legality under Section 8(b)(1) of union discipline. In *Scofield*, fines were imposed upon employees who had exceeded union-established production quotas. The relevant union security agreement gave employees the option of "becoming and remaining a member in good standing of the union, or of declining membership but paying the union a 'service fee.'" [35] The disciplined employees had elected to become members of the union, and the Court held, as it did in *Allis-Chalmers*, that this kind of union control over its own internal affairs was not an unfair labor practice. It is significant to note, however, the manner in which the Court limited the union's power:

> § 8(b)(1) leaves a union free to enforce a properly adopted rule which reflects a legitimate union interest, impairs no policy Congress has imbedded in the labor laws, and is *reasonably enforced against union members who are free to leave the union and escape the rule.*[36]

This could be construed as merely saying that Section 8(b)(1) would be violated by union discipline if the union security agreement prohibited resignation from formal membership. This does not necessarily mean that the union security agreement itself would be illegal under Section 8(a)(3). On the other hand, it is also reasonable to assume that in defining the scope of permissible union discipline under Section 8(b)(1), the Court was acting on the premise that the employees would always have the option of declining to become full members of the union, thus avoiding the union's disciplinary jurisdiction. In other words, it is arguable that the Court assumed that any union security agreement requiring full membership for disciplinary purposes would be as illegal as an agreement requiring full membership for the purposes of avoiding discharge, as under the *Union Starch* doctrine.

Similar Court Cases. Two subsequent Supreme Court cases— *NLRB* v. *Textile Workers, Local 1029* [37] and *Booster Lodge 405, Machinists* v. *NLRB* [38]—involved similar factual situations. Em-

---

[34] 394 U.S. 423 (1969).

[35] *Id.* at 424 n. 1.

[36] *Id.* at 430 (emphasis added).

[37] 409 U.S. 213 (1972).

[38] 412 U.S. 84 (1973).

ployees were fined by the union for engaging in strike-breaking activities. Some of the employees had, however, resigned from the union before engaging in the activity. Such resignations were not prohibited by the express terms of the union constitution, and the previously negotiated union security provisions had expired at the time of the resignations. In both cases the Supreme Court held that once an employee resigns, the legitimate power of the union over him ends, and any attempt by the union to impose or collect disciplinary fines will be deemed violative of Section 8(b)(1). If, and only if, one sifts these two Supreme Court cases with a fine wire mesh, can certain matters of remote relevance to the issue under a discussion be discerned.

In both *Textile Workers* and *Booster Lodge,* the Court was concerned with possible impediments to *effective* resignation from the union—that is, resignation of membership to avoid the imposition of union discipline. In *Textile Workers* the Court focused exclusively on the absence of a contractual relationship between the union and its members restricting resignations:

> We have here no problem of construing a union's constitution or bylaws defining or limiting the circumstances under which a member may resign from the union [*i.e.,* the constitution contained no express restrictions]. We have, therefore, only to apply the law which normally is reflected in our free institutions—the right of the individual to join or to resign from associations, as he sees fit "subject of course to any financial obligations due and owing" the group with which he was associated.[39]

Since in *Textile Workers* there were no express contractual impediments to resignation, the Court went on to say, "We do not now decide to what extent the contractual relationship between union and member may curtail the freedom to resign." [40] One may possibly draw the following inference from this language: Were it possible for this presumptive freedom of resignation to be restricted through certain types of union security agreements, it seems reasonable that the Court would have mentioned it; the failure of the Court to mention it, therefore, suggests that even the most compulsory union security agreement permitted by Section 8(a)(3) cannot be deemed to require

---

[39] 409 U.S. at 216.

[40] *Id.* at 217.

membership for disciplinary purposes.[41] Moreover, the Court's emphasis upon "the law which normally is reflected in our free institutions"—the freedom to join or not join voluntary associations—suggests that Section 8(a)(3) should not be construed to operate in derogation of that more fundamental norm.

In *Booster Lodge* the union security agreement was again of the maintenance-of-membership variety, but unlike the *Textile Workers* agreement, this one appeared to require more than the mere payment of monthly dues.[42] The Court, accordingly, was more concerned with the potential applicability of such an agreement as an impediment to resignation. It noted, "Here, as in *Textile Workers*, the Union's constitution and bylaws are silent on the subject of voluntary resignation from the Union." [43] But then in a footnote the Court also noted, "Since the collective-bargaining agreement expired prior to the times of the resignations, the maintenance-of-membership clause therein was no impediment to resigning." [44] While the specific inclusion of one rationale (expiration) for why the union security clause was not an impediment to resignation does not necessarily mean the exclusion of all other rationales (the affirmative illegality of any agreement having such an effect), it seems, nevertheless, reasonable to assume that the Court might have mentioned this latter possibility were it correct under the law. On the other hand, the Court again emphasized the fundamental law of a free society which recognizes "the right of the individual to join or resign from associations, as he sees fit. . . ." [45]

Finally, in *Florida Power & Light Co.* v. *IBEW*,[46] the Su-

---

[41] This inference is perhaps weakened by the fact that the union security agreement not only had expired, but also did not require full membership. *See* 412 U.S. at 85 n. 1. The union security agreement could not, therefore, under any circumstances have served as an impediment to resignation, and there was no need for the Court to concern itself with such a possibility. On the other hand, in discussing the impediments to resignation that were *not* present, Mr. Justice Blackmun's dissent expressly noted that "[t]he union and the company had no union shop clause in the 1965 collective-bargaining agreement." 409 U.S. at 219 n. 3. This may be taken to suggest that Mr. Justice Blackmun believed that if such a clause had been in the contract, resignation for disciplinary purposes could have been prohibited.

[42] Rather, it seemed to require actual "membership." 412 U.S. at 85 n. 1.

[43] *Id.* at 88.

[44] *Id.* at 88 n. 8.

[45] *Id.* at 88.

[46] 417 U.S. 790 (1974).

preme Court was confronted with the issue of whether the union's attempt to discipline union members who were also supervisory employees constituted illegal restraint or coercion of the employer in his selection of representatives for collective bargaining. In a footnote the Court noted:

> The supervisor-member is, of course, not bound to retain his union membership, *absent a union security clause,* and if, for whatever reason, he chooses to resign from the union, thereby relinquishing his union benefits, he could no longer be disciplined by the union for working during a strike.[47]

Taken as a whole, that quotation clearly suggests that a union security agreement can operate to require formal or actual membership in the union, at least for disciplinary purposes. Supervisory employees are not covered by the act and an agreement requiring *their* formal membership in the union as a condition of employment would not be regulated by Section 8(a)(3). Thus, perhaps the Court did not mean to imply anything at all about a union security agreement affecting only such employees as are covered by the Act. At best, the Court's footnote is inconclusive on the issue.

Where, finally, does all of this laborious analysis leave us? What disciplinary power over employees belongs to a union by virtue of the operation of the kind of union security that is authorized by federal law? There is language in *General Motors* and in *Florida Light & Power* which suggests discipline may be an incident of a valid union security agreement. While that conclusion has never been expressly repudiated by the Supreme Court, strong inferences to the contrary may be drawn from many other decisions of the Court. The view that a valid union security provision cannot operate to vest a union with disciplinary power over employees is more consistent with the Supreme Court decisions than is the contrary view. In short, it would appear that under the most compulsory type of union security agreement allowed by the statute, an employee can satisfy the requirement that he be a member of the union without thereby subjecting himself to the obligations of full union membership or to the disciplinary powers of the union. In this regard the statutory union shop is again the equivalent of what was previously defined as the agency shop in that such obligations likewise do not accrue under that type of union security arrangement.

---

[47] *Id.* at 812 n. 22 (emphasis added).

The agency shop interpretation of the statute represents a synthesis of two lines of cases—one construing the obligation of membership from the perspective of what an employee must do to retain his job, and the other construing it from the perspective of what subsidiary obligations flow therefrom. In *NLRB* v. *Hershey Foods Corp.*,[48] however, the meaning of a union security agreement membership obligation was considered, at least indirectly, from both perspectives.

In *Hershey Foods* the collective bargaining agreement required all employees to become and remain members in good standing of the union. The contract stated that "An employee who shall tender the initiation fee (if not already a member) and the periodic dues . . . shall be deemed to meet this condition." The contract, however, also provided that religious objectors could, upon proper certification from church officials, elect to "pay to the union each month a service charge as a contribution toward the administration of this agreement, in an amount equal to the regular monthly membership dues of the union,"—that is, they could be nonmembers. This certainly suggests that for everyone except religious objectors, the contract contemplated some form of formal membership, notwithstanding the tender-only language.

When the union called a strike at the Hershey plant, an employee by the name of Lloyd Brewer resigned from the union for nonreligious reasons, crossed the picket line, and continued to work. In his letter of resignation to the union, Brewer indicated a willingness to continue paying an amount equal to the established dues, but when Brewer subsequently tendered the equivalent of two months' dues, the union refused to accept the money. It was the union's position that the contract required Brewer to do more than merely tender the equivalent of periodic dues; rather, it also required that Brewer be "willing to be carried on the roster as a union member." An arbitrator subsequently sustained the union's contention, and Brewer was discharged for noncompliance with the terms of the union security provision.

Unfair labor practice charges were brought against the union and the employer. The union argued that what the *Union Starch* line of cases had prohibited was the requirement that an employee, in addition to paying dues, also attend union meetings,

---

[48] 513 F.2d 1083 (9th Cir. 1975), *enforcing* 207 N.L.R.B. 897 (1973).

take the union oath, fill out an application for, or the like. Such additional requirements were not involved in this case, the union noted. Rather, all that was demanded of Brewer was that he rescind his resignation "and affirmatively acquiesce in his being carried on the union roster as a member." The union insisted that the law permits it to make such a demand of an employee as a condition to his continued employment. In support of this latter proposition, the union relied on some of the Supreme Court's language in *General Motors*. In particular, the union relied on the Court's statement that

> if the union chooses to extend membership even though the employee will meet only the minimum financial burden, and refuses to support or "join" the union in any affirmative way, the employee may have to become a "member" under the union shop contract, in the sense that the union may be able to place him on its rolls.[49]

Technically speaking, the *Hershey* case involved only a statutory interpretation of what membership means for the purposes of job preservation—what an employee must do to avoid discharge. The disciplinary incidents of membership were, however, an integral element in the case. The administrative law judge noted that Brewer presumably resigned from the union to avoid the disciplinary powers allowed to unions under the *Allis-Chalmers* decision. Conversely, he indicated that the union wanted Brewer again to become a full member of the union, "presumably because it wished to impose upon him the full obligations of union membership," obligations which if breached would subject the employee to judicially enforceable fines. Although the administrative law judge did not say so expressly, it is evident that he considered the statutory term "membership" to mean the same thing whether it was being construed for the purposes of job preservation or for the purposes of determining the scope of the union's disciplinary jurisdiction. Thus, the administrative law judge noted that under the union's interpretation of what kind of union security provision the law allowed, Brewer

> would be confronted with a dilemma. . . . either he would be required to become a member of Respondent Union and expose himself to the possibility of union disciplinary measures, or if, as he did, he chose to remain a non-member he would forfeit his employment status.[50]

---

[49] 373 U.S. at 743-44.

[50] 207 N.L.R.B. at 903 (ALJ decision).

The administrative law judge eliminated this dilemma by simply construing the term "membership" as used in the statute and in contract clauses negotiated pursuant to the statute to mean nothing more than the payment of fees and dues. Thus, an employee who pays dues to the union pursuant to an authorized (by the statute) union security provision is a member of the union for the purposes of keeping his job, but he is not a member of the union for the purposes of being subjected to union discipline.

In reaching this conclusion, the administrative law judge relied on the *Union Starch, General Motors,* and *Allis-Chalmers* decisions. He did not have much to say about the union's interpretation of the *Union Starch* doctrine, except that it was not supported by *General Motors.* The *General Motors* language upon which the union relied, suggesting that a dues-paying employee might have to become a member of the union if the union so chose, was dealt with by the administrative law judge in a rather novel fashion. He indicated that this language "does not sound in terms of employee obligation toward the union, but more as a statement of permissible union conduct in keeping its own records." [51] In contrast to the union, the administrative law judge read *General Motors* as resting on the premise that in authorizing union security provisions, Congress had intended to do nothing more than eliminate the problem of the so-called free rider, and that the Court recognized this when it said that " 'membership' as a condition of employment is whittled down to its financial core." Thus the administrative law judge concluded

> that it was the broad overall view of the court that whenever an employer and a union sought to make "membership" a condition of employment, the statute did not envisage that full membership with all its obligations could be required, but was holding that "membership" was achieved whenever the employee tendered the required fees, and no more could be asked.[52]

He further supported this conclusion with *Allis-Chalmers* and the Board's decision in *Booster Lodge* which he construed as suggesting that the union's power of discipline over its members exists by virtue of a voluntary contractual relationship rather than by virtue of a union security provision in a col-

---

[51] *Id.* at 902.

[52] *Id.*

lective bargaining agreement. An employee could, thus, never be restrained by a union security provision from resigning from the union and escaping its disciplinary powers.

The administrative law judge's decision in *Hershey Foods* was affirmed by a three member panel of the NLRB with Chairman Miller in dissent. Members Fanning and Jenkins were in accord with the administrative law judge's interpretation of *Union Starch* and *General Motors*. They reinforced his analysis, moreover, by reference to the Supreme Court's decision in that case.

Chairman Miller's dissent was rather brief and to the point. Without hesitation he construed the first proviso of Section 8 (a)(3) as authorizing the negotiation of "union-shop clauses," a term which he did not define but which was clearly intended to refer to a relationship of full or formal membership in the union. He conceded that an employee who is forced to become a union member under a valid union shop clause would be subject to the disciplinary power of the union. Chairman Miller then asserted that the second proviso to Section 8(a)(3) prohibits the enforcement, through discharge, of a union shop clause under two circumstances: (1) if membership was not available to the employee on generally the same terms that it is available to others, or (2) if "membership was terminated or denied for reasons other than the failure of the employee to tender . . . periodic dues and . . . initiation fees. . . ." Chairman Miller then asserted that Brewer was not denied membership for either of these reasons; "[i]ndeed, he plainly assert[ed] that he did not seek or desire to be a member." [53] Since Brewer had not brought himself within either of these two exceptions to enforcement of union shop clauses, Miller concluded that the discharge was not illegal.

Chairman Miller's emphasis upon the fact that Brewer's non-membership in the union was at his own rather than the union's instigation suggests that Chairman Miller was adopting the previously defined union option interpretation of the statute. The majority, on the other hand, was clearly following the agency shop interpretation. From the perspective of both job preservation and subjection to union discipline, the obligations which accrue under a valid union security clause are no greater than the obligations which accrue under a true agency shop.

---

[53] *Id.* at 898.

The Ninth Circuit Court of Appeals was thus faced with as clear a set of alternative interpretations as could be hoped for. The court upheld the interpretation of the majority of the NLRB panel. It rejected the argument that because of the mention of the union shop in the legislative history, Congress truly intended to validate that kind of union security agreement. It reaffirmed the *Union Starch* doctrine and found it irrelevant that an employee's application for and subsequent denial of membership are necessary under the union option interpretation to trigger the applicability of the "dues and fees only" language of the statute. The court held, rather, that "so long as an employee tenders fees uniformly required of union members, he is a 'member' for purposes of sections 8(a)(3) and 8(b)(2)." [54] The court likewise contrasted the liabilities of a statutory union member (the payment of dues and fees only) with those of a full union member by noting that the latter "is subject to union-imposed disciplinary measures enforceable in state courts." [55] In sum, under this court's interpretation of the statute, the kind of union security agreement that the statute allows is for all practical purposes the functional equivalent of the agency shop.

The conclusion that a union security agreement cannot operate so as to compel an employee to acquiesce in the obligations of formal union membership, a compulsion which is allowed by the union option interpretation, was also the basis for a part of the Second Circuit Court of Appeals' recent decision in *Buckley* v. *American Federation of Television and Radio Artists*.[56] In that case political commentators Buckley and Evans had asserted that the union security agreement between AFTRA and CBS was unconstitutional in that it required them not only to pay dues to the union, but also to accept the obligations of "full-fledged" membership. The court held that the required payment of money to the union was not unconstitutional, but declined to pass constitutional judgment on the second part of the plaintiff's claim involving the requirement of formal membership. The court held that this requirement was an "arguable" unfair labor practice and thus within the jurisdiction of the NLRB. The court noted:

---

[54] 513 F.2d at 1083.

[55] *Id.* at 1085.

[56] 496 F.2d 305 (2d Cir. 1974).

In its brief, and at oral argument in the court the union concedes that "the imposition of obligations of membership other than dues-payment will depend on continued full-fledged membership, which . . . cannot be imposed on pain of loss of employment."

The union also acknowledges that Buckley and Evans can avoid any other sanctions which the union might seek to impose on them by resigning from "full-fledged membership while continuing to pay dues." . . . Under Section 7 of the Act, Buckley apparently had the right to refrain from becoming a full-fledged member.[57]

In his concurring opinion, Judge Friendly also noted that "an employee under the union shop provision of the Act need not accept 'full-fledged' membership in the union, and thus can avoid the disciplinary sanctions to which 'full-fledged' members may be subjected." [58]

What the Second Circuit Court of Appeals in the *Buckley* case thought was an "arguable" unfair labor practice, the Board and court in *Hershey Foods* expressly found to be an unfair labor practice; to wit, the attempted imposition, by means of a union security agreement, of the obligations of full union membership on employees otherwise unwilling to be members of the union. In this regard the statutory union shop is actually no different than the so-called agency shop which also does not carry with it the obligations of formal union membership.

Although the bulk of the case law, climaxed by the *Hershey Foods* decision, more nearly supports the agency shop interpretation than the union option interpretation, there is one recent case, dealing with an issue unlike any of those discussed above, that tends to cut in the opposite direction.

In *Local 1104, Communications Workers* v. *NLRB*,[59] the employer and the union had negotiated an agency shop agreement. Subsequently, a number of employees, who during a prior illegal strike had crossed the union's picket line, applied for membership in the union. The union refused to accept them. Membership was similarly denied to an employee who had previously organized on behalf of a rival union. All of these employees then declined to tender the dues required of them under the agency shop agreement, and the union demanded their discharge.

---

[57] *Id.* at 312 n. 5.

[58] *Id.* at 314.

[59] Local 1104, Communications Workers, 211 N.L.R.B. No. 18 (1974), *enforced*, Local 1104, Communications Workers v. NLRB, 520 F.2d 411 (2d Cir. 1975), *cert. denied*, 96 S.Ct. 778 (1976).

This was found to be an unfair labor practice on the union's part.

Local 1104 does not yield easily to analysis. The specific teaching of the case is fairly easy to state: An employee who is denied formal membership in a union because of his exercise of a Section 7 right is thereby relieved of his obligation to tender agency shop fees pursuant to an otherwise valid union security agreement. The case, however, has a much broader significance, for this conclusion is necessarily, albeit tacitly, premised on the union option interpretation of the statute! This can be seen most clearly in the court's response to the union's argument.

The union, relying generally on the agency shop interpretation of the statute and the cases supporting it, had argued that there are two kinds of membership, "full membership" and "financial core membership," and that the statute only contemplates "financial core membership." Thus, when the employees

> applied for full membership and were turned down, they were not denied financial core membership; that denial occurred only when they subsequently refused to pay dues, and was clearly based on that refusal. Therefore, the argument goes, membership—financial core membership—was denied for the failure to pay dues, and it was proper under § 8(b)(2) for the local to seek the employees' discharges.[60]

The court, however, rejected this argument on the grounds that it would in effect read clause (B) out of the act entirely, "for by definition . . . there can be no reason for the denial of financial core membership except the failure to pay dues, since financial core membership means nothing more nor less that the fact that an employee pays his dues." [61] Thus, in order to give clause (B) some independent meaning, the court construed it as pertaining to the reasons a union has for denying full membership rather than merely "financial core" membership. And since the reasons the union had in this case for denying such full membership were something other than the employees' failure to tender fees and dues, the court concluded that the union was not at liberty under Section 8(a)(3) to seek the discharge of these employees under the union security agreement.

---

[60] 520 F.2d at 418.

[61] *Id.* at 418.

Implicit in the court's reasoning is (1) the repudiation of the agency shop interpretation of the statute (upon which the union had relied), and (2) the acceptance of a statutory scheme that is closely akin to the union option interpretation. The court's reasoning makes sense on no other basis; that is, the court apparently assumed that the first part of the Section 8 (a)(3) proviso contemplates the negotiation of some kind of union shop requiring formal membership as a condition of employment. If, however, the union exercises its option of denying the required formal membership for any reason other than the employee's failure to tender periodic dues and fees, then clause (B) provides that the employee cannot be deprived of his job because of such nonmembership. Finally, such an employee also has no further obligations to the union, financial or otherwise.

The construction of the statute, which is similar to the union option interpretation described above, formed the context against which the court resolved the real issue before it; to wit, whether clause (B) has the same effect when the union security agreement in question is of the agency shop rather than union shop variety. In this regard, the court noted:

> An agency shop is generally viewed as a weaker form of union security agreement than a union shop. . . . Under a union shop clause, it is clear that one would look to the reason for denial of full membership in determining whether there was a violation of § 8(b)(2). . . . Yet under the union's theory here the reasons for the denial of full membership would become irrelevant, in effect giving the union a greater degree of coercive power over employees [under an agency shop clause] than it would have in the case of a union shop.[62]

To avoid that anomaly, the court thus concluded that clause (B) of the proviso should operate to relieve an employee of his union security obligations, whether they be of the agency shop or the union shop variety, whenever full union membership had been denied for reasons other than the employee's refusal to tender dues and fees.

Although the theoretical basis of the *Local 1104* decision is clearly inconsistent with that of *Hershey Foods*—the former is predicated on the union option interpretation while the latter adopts the agency shop approach—the court in *Local 1104* at

---

[62] *Id.* at 419.

least tried to achieve a linguistic reconciliation of the two cases. It said that

> the rule resulting from a combination of the two cases would appear to be that, although a union, even under a union shop clause, cannot compel any greater degree of membership than financial core membership, it must nonetheless, even under an agency shop clause, grant full membership to those employees who desire it if it wants to retain its right to receive their dues.[63]

The only way, however, that the statute could be construed to achieve these two results is to assume that "membership" in the first part of the proviso (which defines what an employee's obligation is under a union security agreement) means financial core membership, while "membership" in clause (B) (which imposes limits on the union's right to enforce this obligation) means full or formal membership. Such an interpretation seems highly unlikely, however.[64]

In conclusion, it would appear that a valid union security agreement can neither require an employee to become a formal member of the union as a condition of continued employment nor automatically make him such a member for union discipline purposes. In this regard, the statutory union shop is simply the functional equivalent of the agency shop. On the other hand, under the *Local 1104* decision the statutory union shop differs from a true agency shop in that under the statutory version an employee who is denied formal union membership is also relieved of his obligation to tender dues and fees, a conclusion that is premised to some extent on union option interpretation of the statute.

That, then, is how the Board and courts have construed the statute. The next question is, Which of the two primary interpretations of Section 8(a)(3) most correctly mirrors the intent of Congress?

---

[63] *Id.* at 418 n. 8.

[64] This is not to say, however, that the result of the case is necessarily wrong. In addition to finding the union guilty of an unfair labor practice under the union security provisions of Section 8(b)(2), the NLRB Administrative Law Judge and the court had also found that the union's conduct toward the strike breakers was a violation of Section 8(b)(1)(A), which prohibits a union from restraining or coercing an employee in the exercise of his Section 7 rights. The court's analysis in this regard cannot be faulted.

The Legislative History—Which Interpretation Does It Support?

The legislative history of the union security agreements that were being authorized under the amendments to the Taft-Hartley Act is a virtual potpourri of conflicting statements and inferences. Selected quotations from the debates and from proposed statutory language can be relied upon to support both the union option and the agency shop interpretations.

For example, Congress expressly and repeatedly indicated a desire to authorize what it called the "union shop,"[65] and it may be assumed that at least some congressmen understood that the membership traditionally required under such an arrangement was of the full or formal variety. This is undoubtedly true of those congressmen who were concerned that the union security agreement which the statute authorized would have the effect of forcing unions to accept obnoxious or otherwise undesirable employees into membership,[66] a concern that would be meaningless if membership, as used in the proviso, meant nothing more than the mechanical and impersonal tender of dues and fees. The proponents of the bill responded to this concern not by saying that full membership was not being contemplated, but rather by saying that even under a union shop agreement, to protect its interests the union could decline to extend such membership. Only the union option interpretation, however, effects both the express congressional intent to authorize the union shop and the intent to defer to the union's sensitivities with respect to the admission of obnoxious employees into membership.

The union option interpretation also finds support in most of the more detailed explanations of how the two exceptions to the requirement of union membership were expected to operate. The context of the two exceptions was one in which the union had chosen to exclude or expel an employee who had attempted to obtain the membership supposedly required by the union security agreement. Consider, for example, the explanation of Senator Taft:

> There are two conditions which we have imposed even on the union shop. . . . In the second place, we have proposed a proviso in the case where a man is refused admittance to a union, when an employer employs a nonunion man, and during the first 30 days he

---

[65] *See* n. 2, *supra.*

[66] *See* Legis. Hist. LMRA at 426, 1097, 1141.

goes to the union and says, *"I want to join the union,"* but the union refuses to take him. It is provided that *in such case* the employer shall not be compelled to discharge the man simply because the union will not let him join the union on the same terms and conditions as any other member. . . .

The bill further provides that if the man is admitted to the union, and subsequently is fired from the union for any reason other than nonpayment of dues, then the employer shall not be required to fire that man. . . .[67]

At another point Senator Taft noted:

The union could refuse the man admission to the union, or expel him from the union; *but if he were willing to enter the union and pay the same dues as other members of the union,* he could not be fired from his job because the union refused to take him.[68]

At no time did anyone overtly suggest that the "dues and fees only" exception could be triggered by the employee's own refusal to become or remain a member of the union. To the contrary, the union security provisions of the original House Bill were substantially similar to those as appeared in the final version of the Taft-Hartley Act. The House Bill, however, also made it an unfair labor practice for a union to "deny to any member the right to resign from the organization at any time." What the House Committee Report says about this particular unfair labor practice is, for our purposes, more important for what it says about the kind of union security agreement the bill contemplated. The report states:

The right to resign from any organization is a fundamental right. This section preserves that right for union members. If, when a member resigns, there is in effect as to him an agreement permitted under sec. 8(d)(4) [permitting union security agreements], has [*sic*] *resigning may result in his losing his job,* unless his resignation results from an unfair labor practice by the union under sec. 8(b)(1) or under sec. 8(c).[69]

That the term "membership" in the first part of the proviso means "formal membership" (as per the union option interpretation) rather than "the mere tender of dues and fees" (as per the agency shop interpretation) is also suggested by the language of the first exception to the membership requirement. This exception states that an employer is not justified in dis-

---

[67] *Id.* at 1010 (emphasis added).

[68] *Id.* at 1142 (emphasis added).

[69] *Id.* at 323.

charging an employee for nonmembership in the union if the employer "has reasonable grounds for believing that such membership was not available to the employee on the same terms and conditions generally applicable to other members." The legislative history is rather sparse on the meaning of this particular exception, but the suggestion is that this pertains to the *privileges* of union membership rather than or in addition to the *requirements* of membership (which is adequately dealt with by the second exception).[70] Thus, an employee who was denied the voting rights of a formal member, or who was relegated to a segregated sub-local with no legal rights under the contract, or who was perhaps denied participation in the union pension plan could decline to accept membership in the union but would still be protected in his job. The function of the first exception was to insure that these incidents of union membership were extended on an equal basis. This makes sense only if the membership required under the first part of the proviso carries these privileges, which is true only of full or formal membership.

Finally, at least one of the opponents to the union security provisions of the House Bill recognized that the authorization of the union shop would result in mandatory union membership and the subjection of the employee to union discipline, just as under the closed shop which clearly contemplates membership of a formal nature. In contrast, Congressman Hoffman was in favor of an open shop, which, he said, "meant simply that a man should have the right to join or not to join, to be bound by or not to be bound by, union rules." [71]

On the other hand, the agency shop interpretation finds even stronger and more specific support in the legislative debates. To be sure, the opponents of the Taft–Hartley limitations on union security were aware that for all practical purposes only the equivalent of the agency shop was being authorized. The remarks of Congressman Klein are particularly germane:

> The bill outlaws the closed shop altogether, and permits modified forms of maintenance of membership and union-shop provisions only under specified conditions. . . . [N]o discharges may be made under the agreement except for nonpayment of dues.
> This seems an elaborate, expensive, and dishonest method of dealing with the problem. . . . [I]f we are to allow unions to compel discharge for no reason other than nonpayment of dues, it would

---

[70] *Cf. id.* at 545 and the NLRB decision cited there.

[71] *Id.* at 733.

seem cheaper, more consistent, and more candid to permit the mandatory check-off [*i.e.*, a service fee], . . . Why pretend we are letting the unions have maintenance of membership and union shop? . . . This bill pretends to allow a requirement of membership but really allows only a requirement that dues be paid.[72]

Another member of Congress, who was a proponent of the bill, believed that the union shop was being authorized and that an employee therefore would be required to join the union, but he then elaborated. A man hired into a union shop situation

only has two obligations: No. 1, to pay the initiation fee, which is regulated under this bill, and No. 2 to pay his dues. He is protected from any oppressive tactics on the part of union officials. He undergoes no risk. He undertakes merely the obligation to help support the union which in turn represents him in dealing with his employer.[73]

An employee, thus, may choose to join formally the union and thereby oblige himself to conform to the union's rules at the risk of being disciplined. The quotation suggests that the union security agreement itself does not impose such an obligation, which is consistent only with the agency shop interpretation.

Senator Magnuson objected to the bill on the grounds that the union security agreement being authorized did not automatically vest the unions with the disciplinary power they normally exercised over union members. He asserted that the act "precludes the possibility of the union maintaining discipline by placing *fines* upon its membership for infractions of union rules, such as strike-breakers or lesser infractions." [74] According to the analysis of Senator Murray:

Employees could with impunity completely defy the union even under union security contracts permitted under the bill. He could engage in any type of activity inimical to the interests of the union, such as engaging in wildcat strikes, strike breaking, and racketeering and yet not be subject to its discipline so long as he pays his dues.[75]

Another proponent of the House Bill noted that "a union may bargain with the employer to require that every employee and all new employees shall join the union within 30 days. *That is* . . . all

---

[72] *Id.* at 654.

[73] *Id.* at 736.

[74] *Id.* at 904.

[75] *Id.* at 1578.

workers may be required to pay initiation fees and dues." [76]
This clearly equates joining or being a member of the union in
the statutory sense with the mere payment of dues and fees as
under the agency shop interpretation.

Senator Taft, on the other hand, apparently thought the word
"join" connoted formal membership; he went on to note of the
employee who is subject to the kind of union security agreement
authorized by the act that "if he pays the dues *without joining
the union,* he has the right to be employed." [77]   This certainly
suggests that not joining the union is an option which the
employee has, contrary to the thrust of the union option
interpretation.

Finally, it should be remembered that Senator Taft was one
of the chief proponents of Section 8(b)(1) which makes it an
unfair labor practice for a union to coerce employees in the exercise of their Section 7 rights. In its relevant part, Section 7
provides:

> Employees shall have the right to . . . join . . . labor organizations
> . . . and shall also have the right to refrain from . . . such activities
> except to the extent that such right may be affected by an agree-
> ment requiring membership in a labor organization as a condition
> of employment as authorized in section 8(a)(3).[78]

When Senator Taft was discussing Section 8(b)(1), he was obviously aware of the kind of union security agreement that was
authorized by Section 8(a)(3), noncompliance with which by an
employee was *not* a protected Section 7 right. Senator Taft
explained the kind of union coercion he wanted to outlaw:

> The language [of the old Section 7] is perfectly clear. . . . An
> employer cannot go to an employee and say, "If you join this union
> you will be discharged." . . . Now it is proposed that the union be
> bound in the same way. . . . Why should a union be able to say to
> an employee, "If you do not join this union we will see that you
> cannot work in the plant"? What possible distinction can there be
> between an unfair labor practice of that kind on the part of an
> employer and a similar practice on the part of a union? . . .
> If a man is invited to join a union its members ought to be able
> to persuade him to join, but if they should not be able to persuade

---

[76] *Id.* at 871 (emphasis added).

[77] *Id.* at 1422 (emphasis added).

[78] 29 U.S.C. § 157 (1970).

him they should not be permitted to interfere with him, coerce him, and compel him to join the union. The moment that such a man is threatened with losing his job if he does join, it at once becomes an unfair labor practice. Threats and coercion ought to become unfair labor practices on the part of the union.[79]

It would, of course, be nonsensical to define as an unfair labor practice a "threat" to do something that would be perfectly legal under a statutory union security agreement. Thus, it would appear that Senator Taft did not contemplate that under such an agreement an employee could be required to associate formally with, join, or become a member of a union—as under a true union shop or even the union option variation thereof.

Since the extrapolation from the legislative history of specific quotations leads to conflicting exegeses of the Section 8(a)(3) proviso, it would appear that a different method for determining legislative intent—which is a fiction in any event—must be resorted to. A common approach in such situations is to hypothesize a congressional intent by reference to the broader objectives of Congress in passing the legislation in question. In this regard, the legislative history of the Taft-Hartley Act reveals a congressional consensus on a number of objectives, each of which is relevant to the scope of the Section 8(a)(3) proviso. The interpretation of the proviso that best accommodates *all* of these objectives is the one that we may say Congress intended. The relevant objectives were as follows:

1. Beyond cavil, Congress wanted to eliminate the presence of a union monopoly over access into the labor market. That objective was realized by the outlawry of the closed shop.[80]

2. Since Congress had imposed upon unions the duty to act as the statutory representative of all employees in an appropriate unit, it apparently felt that the alleged beneficiaries of such representation should share in the cost. Thus Congress intended to eliminate the so–called free rider, at least insofar as federal law was concerned.[81]

3. It is apparent from the legislative debates that Congress did not intend by the Taft–Hartley amendments to intrude upon the internal affairs of labor organizations,[82] an intent reflected in the

---

[79] *See* LEGIS. HIST. LMRA at 1025, 1027.

[80] *Id.* at 296, 321, 409, 412, 470, 545, 612.

[81] *Id.* at 1422.

[82] *Id.* at 426, 1097, 1141.

proviso to Section 8(b)(1)(A) which reserved to unions the right to prescribe their own rules "with respect to the acquisition or retention of membership." The second part of the Section 8(a)(3) proviso implicitly guarantees the same result even under a union security agreement.

4. While Congress did not intend to regulate the internal affairs of unions, it was disturbed over the arbitrary power of unions to expel employees from union membership and thus, as under a true union shop agreement, to effect the discharge of such employees.[83] The proviso to Section 8(a)(3) eliminates that possibility by stating that expulsion from union membership will result in discharge from employment only under the specified conditions.

5. This congressional concern with arbitrary expulsions from union membership was but one aspect of a larger objective—generally curtailing the abusive and coercive power that unions had frequently exercised in the employment context.[84] In addition to the Section 8(a)(3) proviso, this larger objective also found manifestation in the amendments that gave employees a right to refrain from engaging in concerted union activities.

While Congress obviously had other objectives in mind when it passed the Taft-Hartley Act, these five are most relevant to the issue under discussion. These five objectives, moreover, are simply the specific manifestations of a broader and slightly more inchoate congressional policy. The primary thrust of each specific objective is to divorce an individual's employment status from all aspects of union activity except his representation by the union as his bargaining agent over wages, hours, and working conditions. Except to the extent that it serves in the narrow capacity of a statutory bargaining representative, a labor union remains a voluntary, contractual association of free individuals.

This broader policy is manifest in the objective of freeing the initiation of an employment relationship from the condition precedent of union membership (first objective). The "elimination of the free rider" rationale (second objective) also reflects this policy. The money which an employee may be required to pay to a union under a Section 8(a)(3) authorized union security agreement must necessarily be limited to money that is used for the

---

[83] *Id.* at 412-13, 545.

[84] *Id.* at 456, 1018, 1028, 1200, 1204-06.

negotiation and administration of the contract.[85] In this regard, the statutory union shop is more a service fee arrangement than it is an agency shop because the law does not authorize a union to extract money to be used by the union in its role as a voluntary association. Allowing a union to exclude or expel anyone it chooses from membership (third objective) but preserving that individual's job (fourth objective), unless the individual fails to carry his allocated share of the financial obligations (second objective), collectively represent a manifestation of the same policy of divorcing the incidents of union membership from the employment relationship to the benefit of both the union and the individual.

Finally, the reconciliation between the (third) objective of noninterference with internal union affairs and the (fifth) objective of protecting employees from the coercive power of the unions to force employees to engage in union activities can be understood only in light of this broader policy of divorcement. In *Allis-Chalmers* [86] the Supreme Court was confronted with a situation in which these two objectives of the law came into conflict. An employee who had crossed his union's picket line to return to work during a strike was fined by the union for this breach of membership obligations. The union was charged with coercing the employee in the exercise of his statutory right to refrain from engaging in concerted union activities. The Supreme Court was required to grapple with this difficult question of reconciling the objective of freeing employees from union coercion with the equally clear and compelling congressional objective of keeping the heavy hand of the law out of purely internal union affairs. The Court responded to this conflict by holding that the union's obligation to refrain from coercing employees to engage in union activities applied primarily, if not exclusively, to employees who were not, and did not want to become, members of the union.[87]

---

[85] Teamsters Local 959, 167 N.L.R.B. 1042 (1967); *cf.* International Ass'n of Machinists v. Street, 367 U.S. 740 (1961), in which the Supreme Court indicated that the union security provisions of the RLA were merely intended "to force employees to share the costs of negotiating and administering collective agreements, and the costs of the adjustment and settlement of disputes." *Id.* at 764 (footnote omitted).

[86] NLRB v. Allis-Chalmers Mfg. Co., 388 U.S. 175 (1967).

[87] *Id.* at 187-89. The Court quoted one Senator as saying that the proposed prohibition against union coercion "is designed to protect employees in their freedom to decide whether or not they desire to join labor organizations, to prevent them from being restrained or coerced." *Id.* at 187-88 (footnote omitted).

Conversely, the Court indicated that what the union does *vis-à-vis* its members cannot be deemed "coercion" because the Act reserves for the union the power over its own internal affairs.[88]

The accommodation of these two objectives makes sense only if union membership is purely voluntary; it is assumed that a union security agreement cannot operate which requires as a condition of continued employment a kind of membership in the union which automatically subjects the employee to the union's disciplinary powers. To hold that only nonmembers of the union have Section 7 rights against the imposition of union fines is meaningful only if employees also have the Section 7 right not to become members of the union for disciplinary-subjection purposes. Otherwise, the nonunion member employee's Section 7 right to refrain from engaging in concerted union activities would be circumvented by the simple expedient of a union security agreement which required such membership. Thus one may infer that Congress did not intend Section 8(a)(3) to authorize union security agreements having such a result.

The Supreme Court in *Allis-Chalmers* was proceeding on this basis by emphasizing the voluntary contractual nature of union membership.[89] Moreover, it is apparent that the Court considered the legislative objectives behind the prohibition of union coercion *in pari materia* with the legislative objectives behind the Section 8(a)(3) proviso. To read Section 8(b)(1) as not being intended by Congress to protect union members from discipline was permissible only because the Court believed that Congress intended union membership to be voluntary and divorced from the conditions of continued employment under the proviso to Section 8(a)(3).[90] The Supreme Court's reconciliation of these two specific congressional objectives suggests the presence of the more fundamental objective advanced above—the divorcement of an individual's employment status from all aspects of union activity except collective bargaining representation.

---

[88] *Id.* at 178-84. The Court noted that "on its face court enforcement of fines imposed on *members* for violation of *membership* obligations is no more conduct to 'restrain or coerce' satisfaction of such obligations than courts . . . awards of damages against a contracting party for nonperformance of a contractual obligation *voluntarily* undertaken." *Id.* at 179 (emphasis added).

[89] *Id.* at 182.

[90] The Court noted that "Congressional emphasis § 8(b)(2) insulated an employee's membership from his job, but left internal union affairs to union self-government, is therefore significant evidence against reading § 8(b)(1)(A) as contemplating regulation of internal discipline." *Id.* at 185.

Thus only the functional equivalent of the agency shop will satisfy all of the identified congressional objectives, including the broader one of divorcing the obligations of union membership from the incidents of the employment relationship. Clearly, the closed shop and the true union shop are disqualified. Likewise, the congressional objectives are not met if the union shop is modified only by the *Union Starch* doctrine, narrowly applied; that is, a union security agreement which prohibits discharge unless the employee's nonmembership status qualifies under the second proviso to Section 8(a)(3), but which does not necessarily preclude the requirement of membership for disciplinary purposes. Such an agreement would not be consistent with the objective of protecting employees who do not desire to join the union or participate in union affairs from the coercive effect of union fines.

The fallacy of the union option interpretation of Section 8(a)(3) is that it focuses exclusively upon the objectives of noninterference with internal union affairs and the elimination of the "free rider." These were important objectives of Congress in wording the Section 8(a)(3) proviso as it did, and clearly some of the explanations of the effect of the proviso had this emphasis.[91] This approach ignores, however, the objective of protecting nonmember employees from union coercion, and more important, it ignores the broader objective of divorcement discussed above. In interpreting Section 8(a)(3) an alternative (the agency shop interpretation) which is consistent with all of the congressional objectives is clearly to be preferred over an interpretation which is only consistent with some (the union option interpretation).

In light of the fact that Congress at least said that it intended to authorize the union shop and then used the term "membership" in the statute, it may seem anomalous to conclude that Congress really only intended to authorize the functional equivalent of the agency shop. That, however, is the only interpretation that makes any sense of the total legislative history, and it is this interpretation that the courts have generally adopted in construing the obligations of an employee under a statutory union security agreement.

De Facto Union Shop Arrangements

Although the existing case law stands clearly for the proposition that an employee may be required to do nothing more than

---

[91] LEGIS. HIST. LMRA at 734, 846, 1068, 1142, 1420.

tender an initiation fee and periodic dues as a condition of continued employment, the requirements of a true union shop are being imposed on many unsuspecting employees. Union security provisions,[92] including the model clause drafted by the NLRB,[93] typically use terms (borrowed from the statute, to be sure) such as "membership," or worse, "membership in good standing," to describe the obligations the employee has to the union. The average worker, unversed in the tortuous complexities of statutory interpretation, would normally construe that to mean membership in the colloquial sense—*i.e.*, formal membership. This toleration, if not encouragement, by the Board of an illegal kind of union security arrangement must surely come to an end. As a court has recently done under the Railway Labor Act,[94] the Board should require employers and unions to notify adequately that under a valid union security agreement all they can be required to do is to tender the correct dues and fees.

The Agency Shop

If, as was argued previously, what the Section 8(a)(3) proviso really authorizes is nothing more than the functional equivalent of the agency shop, then it follows *a fortiori* that an overt agency shop or service fee arrangement is encompassed by the statute.

---

[92] *See, e.g.*, (1976) 2 COLLECTIVE BARGAINING NEGOTIATIONS AND CONTRACTS (BNA) 87:62-63.

[93] In Keystone Coat, Apron & Towel Supply Co., 121 N.L.R.B. 880 (1958), the Board quoted a "model union security clause, deemed by the Board to be the maximum permissible in conformity with the policies of the Act," for contract-bar purposes. *Id.* at 885.
That so-called model clause reads as follows:

> It shall be a condition of employment that all employees of the Employer covered by this agreement who are *members of the Union in good standing* on the effective date of this agreement shall remain members in good standing and those who are not members on the effective date of this agreement shall, on the thirtieth day [or such longer period as the parties may specify] following the effective date of this agreement, *become and remain members in good standing in the Union*. It shall also be a condition of employment that all employees covered by this agreement and hired on or after its effective date shall, on the thirtieth day following the beginning of such employment [or such longer period as the parties may specify] *become and remain members in good standing in the Union*.

Id. (emphasis added, footnote omitted, and brackets in original).

[94] Marden v. International Ass'n of Machinists, 78 CCH Lab. Cas. ¶ 11,412 (S.D. Fla. 1976).

One of the two rationales of the *General Motors*[95] decision proceeds on that basis. The Supreme Court said that "membership" as used in the first part of the proviso (*i.e.*, what a union security agreement can require of an employee as a condition of employment) means nothing more than the payment of dues and fees. Since that and only that is required under an agency shop agreement, such an agreement is authorized by the statute.

Alternatively, the Court held that an agency shop agreement is simply a lesser included form of union security which Congress intended to allow, its intention being only to outlaw agreements "more compulsive" than the "statutory union shop."

In any event, the agency shop is clearly authorized by the statute because the negotiation and enforcement of an agency shop agreement is not an unfair labor practice.

Maintenance-of-Membership

Traditionally, a maintenance-of-membership agreement was simply a less compulsive variation of the union shop. No one had to join the union, but if one did become a member of the union, he was obliged to remain a member for the duration of the contract term. Congress repeatedly expressed a desire to authorize maintenance-of-membership agreements,[96] but this raised the same kind of difficulties as were encountered when Congress approved the so-called union shop. Did Congress really intend that an employee who had become a formal member of the union could, by virtue of a maintenance-of-membership agreement, be required to remain such for the duration of the contract?

The answer to that question must necessarily be "no". It would be anomalous indeed for the membership obligations under a maintenance-of-membership agreement to be in excess of those allowed under a statutory union shop. Rather, whatever obligations of membership that an employee must assume under a statutory union shop are the same obligations of membership that an employee must adhere to once he has voluntarily accepted them under a maintenance-of-membership agreement. Thus, a valid maintenance-of-membership agreement can do no more than require that an employee, having once agreed to pay dues to the union, continue to pay such dues for the duration of the contract. Such an agreement cannot prevent the employee's resignation as a

---

[95] 373 U.S. 734 (1963).

[96] LEGIS. HIST. LMRA at 325, 545, 665.

formal member of the union. Subject to those limitations, maintenance-of-membership agreements are thus authorized by the proviso.[97]

Although many maintenance-of-membership agreements contain an "escape clause" which gives employees a chance to withdraw from the union at the end of the contract term, the law itself does not require this. Under the Board's so-called *Paulding* Doctrine,[98] where

> there is no time lapse between successive collective-bargaining agreements and there are closely similar union-security clauses, of which maintenance of membership is one form, the union-security clauses have continuity and the new contract, at least as to union security, is to be treated as a continuation of the old contract.[99]

Thus, employees who resign their membership effective the last day to the old agreement will nevertheless be required to continue to maintain their membership for the duration of all successive agreements.

Checkoff Authorization Agreements

Although checkoff authorization agreements are commonly thought of as an adjunct form of union security, such agreements apparently do not fall under the protective umbrella of the Section 8(a)(3) proviso. Presumably, this is because the checkoff pertains to the manner in which union dues are paid rather than to the actual obligation to pay them, which is the major concern of the proviso. On the other hand, it is well established that a mandatory checkoff system would not only violate the anti-discrimination provisions of Section 8(a)(3) itself, but also those subsections prohibiting coercion of employees and unlawful employer assistance to labor unions.[100]

Even though a checkoff is being made pursuant to an employee authorization, this does not necessarily guarantee its legality. Under certain circumstances, an employer's deduction of union dues from an employee's paycheck may still violate the unfair labor practice provisions of the Taft-Hartley Act. In addition, the provisions of Section 302 of that Act must be considered.

---

[97] *See* Horwath v. NLRB, 539 F.2d 1093 (7th Cir. 1976).

[98] International Union of Automobile Workers, 142 N.L.R.B. 296 (1963).

[99] Sunbeam Corp., 219 N.L.R.B. 1019 (1975).

[100] *See, e.g.*, NLRB v. Brotherhood of Ry. Clerks, 498 F.2d 1105 (5th Cir. 1974) ; John B. Shriver Co., 103 N.L.R.B. 23 (1953).

Section 302, which was primarily aimed at employer bribery of union officials and union extortion attempts, prohibits an employer from paying anything of value to a labor union and prohibits unions from demanding or even accepting such payments. Willful violations involve criminal penalties enforced by the Department of Justice. The statute, however, provides an exception

> with respect to money deducted from the wages of employees in payment of membership dues in a labor organization: Provided, that the employer has received from each employee, on whose account such deductions are made, a written assignment which shall not be irrevocable for a period of more than one year, or beyond the termination date of the applicable collective agreement, whichever occurs sooner. . . .

Thus a checkoff arrangement will be legal under Section 302 *only* if it satisfies the requirements spelled out in the quoted proviso.

Section 302 and the unfair labor practice provisions have generally been construed as being independent of one another, even though their requirements are substantially the same. Thus a checkoff arrangement that is illegal under Section 302 is not necessarily an unfair labor practice;[101] similarly, the Board will recognize as a bar to a new election a collective bargaining agreement even though it contains a checkoff provision illegal under Section 302.[102] Conversely, however, because Section 302 is a criminal provision, the term "membership dues" as used there has been construed more broadly than has the same term under the proviso to Section 8(a)(3).[103] Thus, although a checkoff deduction which includes assessments and fines will not be illegal under Section 302, the payment of such monies cannot be made a condition of employment under Section 8(a)(3).

In order to be valid, an employee's checkoff authorization must be signed voluntarily, and if coercion is used this will be an unfair labor practice. Thus, an employer cannot threaten an employee with loss of his job unless he signs an authorization.[104] Similarly, an unfair labor practice was found where an employee, in order to comply with a union security agreement, was forced to choose

---

[101] 29 U.S.C. § 302(c) (1970).

[102] NLRB v. Penn Cork & Closures, 376 F.2d 52 (2d Cir. 1967), *cert. denied*, 389 U.S. 843 (1967); Crown Products Co., 99 N.L.R.B. 602 (1952).

[103] NLRB v. Food Fair Stores, 307 F.2d 3 (3d Cir. 1962).

[104] Dura Corp. 153 N.L.R.B. 592 (1965); Federal Stores Div. of Speigel, 91 N.L.R.B. 647 (1950).

between signing a checkoff authorization or paying the required dues in person at the union's office in a distant town.[105]

Section 302 expressly provides that a checkoff authorization shall not be irrevocable for longer than one year. An authorization, however, can be automatically renewed every year without the necessity of a new authorization being signed, provided the employees are given a reasonable period at the end of the year within which to revoke their authorization.[106] Under certain circumstances, a checkoff authorization may be terminated sooner than that. For example, the NLRB has held that a checkoff authorization is automatically terminated at the severance of the employment relationship; if the employee is later rehired, a new authorization must be obtained.[107] Under this rule, it is necessary for the Board to determine whether the interruption in the continuity of service represents an actual severance and rehire, or whether it represents something akin to a "layoff," in which case the checkoff authorization remains effective.[108] In determining this, however, the Board does not consider the employee's subjective motivation; it is simply a matter of whether the conduct itself amounts to, in legal contemplation, a severance of the employment relationship.[109]

Although union security agreements and checkoff authorizations are generally thought to be independent contracts, the Board has held that once the employees have revoked the union's authority to negotiate such an agreement, the employees must also be free to revoke their own checkoff authorizations.[110] That is, the Board has assumed that *but for* the union security agreement, the employees would not have authorized the checkoff in the first place; and once the union security agreement is repealed, the employees should again have a free choice in the matter. On the other hand, the Board has also held that checkoff authorizations (as well as

---

[105] American Screw Co., 122 N.L.R.B. 485 (1958).

[106] Monroe Lodge 770, IAM v. Litton Business Systems, 334 F. Supp. 310 (W.D. Va. 1971), *affirmed*, 80 L.R.R.M. 2379 (4th Cir. 1972), *cert. denied*, 409 U.S. 879 (1972) ; *see also* Justice Dept. Op., 22 L.R.R.M. 46 (1948).

[107] NLRB v. Brotherhood of Ry. Clerks, 498 F.2d 1105 (5th Cir. 1974).

[108] *Compare* NLRB v. Industrial Towel & Uniform Serv., 473 F.2d 1258 (6th Cir. 1973).

[109] NLRB v. Brotherhood of Ry. Clerks, 498 F.2d 1105 (5th Cir. 1974).

[110] Penn Cork & Closures, 156 N.L.R.B. 411 (1965), *enforced*, 376 F.2d 52 (2d Cir. 1967), *cert. denied*, 389 U.S. 843 (1967).

union security agreements, and other parts of the contract), remain effective even if the union loses its representative status during the term of the contract.[111]

OTHER STATUTORY RESTRICTIONS

Time Restrictions for Joining the Union

The Taft-Hartley Act authorizes union security agreements requiring membership in the union "on or after the thirtieth day following the beginning of such employment or the effective date of such agreement, whichever is the later. . . ." It is thus an unfair labor practice to require an employee to join the union (tender the requisite dues and fees) within a lesser period of time.[112] Contracts making the membership obligation a retroactive one are likewise illegal.[113] If, as is often the case, the "effective date" of the contract is earlier than the date on which the contract is actually signed, then the latter date rather than the former marks the running of the thirty-day grace period.[114] Finally, an employee may not be required to "join" the union within the thirty-day period nor to sign a membership application [115] nor to express even an intent to join within this period.[116]

Although at one point the Board and the courts looked on favorably on vague and ambiguously worded union security agreements,[117] the present emphasis, insofar as the thirty-day grace period is involved, seems to be more upon the manner in which the contract is enforced rather than upon how it is written. Thus, it is not even absolutely necessary that the union security agreement be an express thirty-day grace period, provided the

---

[111] Fender Musical Instruments, 175 N.L.R.B. 873 (1969).

[112] *See, e.g.,* Toy Workers Local 18 v. NLRB, 369 F.2d 226 (7th Cir. 1966); NLRB v. Industrial Rayon Corp., 297 F.2d 62 (6th Cir. 1961).

[113] Colonie Fibre Co. v. NLRB, 163 F.2d 65 (2d Cir. 1947).

[114] Associated Machines, Inc., 114 N.L.R.B. 390 (1955), *enforced per curiam,* 239 F.2d 858 (6th Cir. 1956).

[115] NLRB v. Hribar Trucking, Inc., 406 F.2d 854 (7th Cir. 1969).

[116] Argo Steel Construction Co., 122 N.L.R.B. 1077 (1959).

[117] *See, e.g.,* NLRB v. E. F. Shuck Construction Co., 243 F.2d 519 (9th Cir. 1957); Red Star Exp. Lines v. NLRB, 196 F.2d 78 (2d Cir. 1952); NLRB v. Gottfried Baking Co., 210 F.2d 772 (2d Cir. 1954); Local 1566, Longshoremen, 122 N.L.R.B. 967 (1959). *But see* NLRB v. News Syndicate Co., 365 U.S. 695 (1961).

parties honor this limitation in fact.[118] Likewise, the Board has held that a contract which requires union membership "within 30 days" is sufficiently close to the statutory language to be considered legal.[119] As a counter-balance to the vagueness of many union security agreements, the Board requires unions seeking to enforce such an agreement to notify adequately delinquent employees that refusal to pay the required fees will result in a discharge.[120] This duty is particularly difficult in oral union security agreements, which the Board will recognize, but subject only to the following conditions:

> Parties, who would defend action taken on the basis of such oral agreements, must therefore satisfy a stringent burden of proof in establishing the existence and precise terms and conditions of the agreement and in further establishing that affected employees have been fully and unmistakably notified thereof.[121]

Although most contracts adopt the statutory thirty-day grace period, the parties are free to provide for a longer period if they desire. Where they do so, however, or where the *practice* of the parties has been to allow for a period longer than that spelled out in the contract, then the thirty-day statutory period cannot be relied upon as a justification for a discharge at the expiration of thirty days.[122] The employee must instead be given the time that is contemplated by either the contract or the past practice of the parties.

There has been one curious exception to this statutory thirty-day grace period ruling by the Board. In the *Krause Milling Co.*[123] case the Board held that

> the 30-day grace period must be accorded *only* to those employees who are not members of the union on the effective date of the union security clause of the contract, and to new employees [whether members of the union or not][124] hired after said date.[125]

---

[118] American Seating Co., 98 N.L.R.B. 800 (1952).

[119] NLRB v. Television & Radio Broadcasting Studio Employees Local 804, 315 F.2d 398 (3d Cir. 1963).

[120] NLRB v. Local 182, Teamsters, 401 F.2d 509 (2d Cir. 1968); Chemical Workers Local 50, 169 N.L.R.B. 1009 (1968).

[121] Pacific Iron & Metal Co., 175 N.L.R.B. 604 (1969).

[122] Busch Kredit Jewelry Co., 108 N.L.R.B. 1214 (1954).

[123] 97 N.L.R.B. 536 (1951).

[124] Electrical Workers Local 1842, 124 N.L.R.B. 794, *enforced on other grounds*, 283 F.2d 112 (6th Cir. 1960).

[125] 97 N.L.R.B. at 539 (emphasis added).

The Board supported this deviation from the express statutory language by reference to both legislative history and policy considerations. The Board noted that the original House version of what later became Section 8(a)(3) spoke in terms of a permissible discharge of an employee who "fails to *become* a member" within thirty days, and the Board construed this as evidencing an intent to exclude employees who were already members of the union at the time the agreement was signed. The purpose of the thirty-day grace period, the Board said, was simply to eliminate the closed shop, whereby existing employees who are not members of the union and new employees are required to join the union immediately as a condition of employment. The "elimination of the closed shop" rationale would not, the Board concluded, apply to employees who are already members of the union at the time the contract is signed. From a policy perspective, the Board asserted that it would be impractical and illogical to allow an employee to withdraw from the union for a thirty-day period, only to be required to rejoin the union at the end of that period. Finally, the Board noted that the general policy against free riders lent at least some support to its narrow reading of the thirty-day grace period exception. Despite the Board's ruling, however, this decision ignores the central fact that Congress did not intend to make union membership a condition of employment during the first thirty days of an agreement. From this perspective, it is totally irrelevant whether the employee in question is already a member of the union or not; during that period, such membership cannot be made a condition of employment.

Another exception to the normal thirty-day grace period is contained in Section 8(f), which was added by the Landrum-Griffin amendments of 1959. This section provides, *inter alia,* that in the building and construction trades, a union security agreement may require membership in the union "after the seventh day following the beginning of . . . employment or the effective day of the agreement, whichever is later. . . ." The shorter grace period here has been justified by reference to the fact that building and construction workers move frequently from job to job, many of them lasting less than thirty days. To be meaningful, the union security agreement must be able to require membership within a relatively short period of time, but the full seven days must be allowed.[126]

---

[126] Harder's Construction Co., 146 N.L.R.B. 698 (1964). A comprehensive discussion of who is covered by Section 8(f) can be found in Forest City/

When an employee fails to pay his initial dues and fees within the required period or when he becomes delinquent in payment of periodic dues but makes a "belated tender," the employee may be discharged, depending upon the sequence of events. If the tender comes after the union's request for the enforcement of the union security agreement against this employee, then the employer can refuse the tender and discharge the employee. The record must show, however, that this was the sole reason for the union's request and for the subsequent discharge by the employer.[127]

Apart from the fact that motivation is the controlling consideration in a case involving discharge for nonunion membership, practical considerations are also said to support this rule. In *International Ass'n of Machinists* v. *NLRB*,[128] the Second Circuit explained:

> If labor organizations are to be allowed effective enforcement of union security provisions, they must be free to invoke the sanction of loss of employment against those union members who are delinquent in tendering their periodic dues. This sanction might become meaningless if an employee could avoid its impact by an eleventh hour tender of back dues just prior to actual discharge.[129]

On the other hand, the Board has also held that when an employee makes a "belated tender" prior to the union's request for discharge, then it will be an unfair labor practice for an employer to acquiesce in that request.[130] This is because a belated tender in these circumstances will not "frustrate or undermine in a significant degree the orderly administration of a union security agreement," [131] at least not in the manner described above.

"Periodic Dues and Fees"

Under Section 8(a)(3), an employee's obligation is merely to tender to the union an amount of money equivalent to "the periodic dues and the initiation fees uniformly required as a condition of acquiring or retaining membership . . ." in that union. This implicitly limits what the union can demand of an employee

---

Dillon-Tecon, 209 N.L.R.B. 867 (1974), *enf'd in part*, 522 F.2d 1107 (9th Cir. 1975).

[127] General Motors Corp. Packard Electric Div., 134 N.L.R.B. 1107 (1961).

[128] 247 F.2d 414 (2d Cir. 1957).

[129] *Id.* at 420.

[130] IAM Lodge 508, 190 N.L.R.B. 61 (1971).

[131] *Id.* at 68.

by way of monetary payments. In addition, Section 8(b)(5) makes it an unfair labor practice for a labor union to charge an initiation fee "in an amount which the Board finds excessive or discriminatory under all the circumstances." A number of issues have arisen over the meaning of these two provisions.

It is well established that a union, acting through the employer, cannot require an employee to pay dues for periods antecedent to negotiation of the union security agreement [132] or of that employee's date of hire. [133] Thus, an employee who is in arrears when he is hired can be required to pay *only* the current dues. Some unions, however, have attempted to circumvent this rule through the use of "reinstatement fees." Generally speaking, reinstatement fees are considered to be a form of initiation fee and are certainly not illegal per se. [134] Moreover, the reinstatement fee can be larger than the usual initiation fee, provided there is some legitimate justification for it. [135] But, as the court put it in *NLRB* v. *Fishermen Local 33* :

> A union may not charge a reinstatement fee larger than its initiation fee where the difference in the amounts represents either the amount of back dues not properly owing [as a condition of employment] or a penalty for not paying such dues. [136]

It is not always easy to determine, however, whether a reinstatement fee will be found to represent a "camouflaged attempt to collect back dues," or something more legitimate. [137] Similarly, whether an initiation fee or a reinstatement fee represents a penalty against an employee for failing to join or to remain a member of the union at a time when the employee had no employment obligation to do so is a difficult issue, but one that is most often

---

[132] NLRB v. Eclipse Lumber Co., 199 F.2d 684 (9th Cir. 1952) ; Oil, Chemical & Atomic Workers, 152 N.L.R.B. 436 (1965).

[133] NLRB v. Spector Freight System, Inc., 273 F.2d 272 (8th Cir. 1960) ; United Brotherhood of Carpenters, 224 N.L.R.B. No. 186 (1976).

[134] Metal Workers' Alliance, Inc., 172 N.L.R.B. 815 (1968).

[135] Machinists Lodge 1600, 120 N.L.R.B. 1223 (1958).

[136] 448 F.2d 225 (9th Cir. 1971).

[137] *See* Operating Engineers Local 139, 172 N.L.R.B. 173 (1968), *enforced on other grounds*, 425 F.2d 17 (7th Cir. 1970) where the Board and the court did not even agree on the appropriate test to be used. For a clear violation, *see* Boilermakers Local 338, 166 N.L.R.B. 874 (1967), *enforced*, 409 F.2d 922 (10th Cir. 1969).

determined by reference to the supposed motive of the union in imposing the fee.[138]

Fines, as such, are not encompassed by the term "periodic dues," and an employee's refusal to pay a union fine cannot be a grounds for discharge under union security agreement.[139] For example, fines for nonattendance at union meetings [140] and fines for the late payment of union dues [141] cannot be enforced through the employment relationship. But in both these instances, the unions have found a way to circumvent this rule.

In the *Great Atlantic & Pacific Tea Co.*[142] case, the union imposed and attempted to collect through threat of discharge a $1.00 fine for the late payment of dues. The Board found this to be illegal. Subsequently, the union increased its dues and offered a $1.00 discount for prompt payment, but the Board found this to be nothing more than an illegal attempt to accomplish the same result in a different way. A court of appeals, however, found to the contrary. In *NLRB* v. *Bakery & Confectionery Workers*,[143] the court held that offering such a discount did not amount to a "fine" for late payment but was a legitimate inducement for prompt payment.

The court also rejected as irrelevant the fact that the discount was proportionately larger than that normally offered in a commercial context. Apparently, the Board has not acquiesced on that latter point, for in *Teamsters Local 959* [144] the Board specifically noted in a similar context that the General Counsel had not proved "that the discount granted for prompt payment of dues does not bear a reasonable relationship to the additional cost of collecting delinquent accounts." [145] This certainly suggests that where such a reasonable relationship could be disproved, then the

---

[138] *Compare* Ferro Stamping & Mfg. Co., 93 N.L.R.B. 1459 (1951) *with* Food Machinery & Chemical Corp., 99 N.L.R.B. 1430 (1952) *and* Metal Workers' Alliance, Inc., 172 N.L.R.B. 815 (1968).

[139] *See, e.g.,* Roofers Local 4, 140 N.L.R.B. 384 (1962) ; Pen & Pencil Workers Local 19593, 91 N.L.R.B. 883 (1950).

[140] Federal Telephone & Radio Corp., 98 N.L.R.B. 1324 (1952).

[141] Great Atlantic & Pacific Tea Co., 110 N.L.R.B. 918 (1954).

[142] *Id.*

[143] 245 F.2d 211 (3d Cir. 1957).

[144] 167 N.L.R.B. 1042 (1967).

[145] *Id.* at 1044.

Board would find the alleged discount to be an illegal fine or assessment.

With respect to "discounts" or "rebates" for attending union meetings, the Board itself has taken contrary positions. In *Electric Auto-Lite Company* [146] the union dues were set at $2.00 per month. But as a practical matter the employees only paid $1.50, and the extra 50 cents did not become due until after the employee failed to attend the union meeting for that month. The Board found this extra payment to represent a fine that could not be enforced as a part of the union security agreement. Subsequently, in *Leece-Neville Co.*,[147] the Board extended this holding to encompass a situation where the union gave a monthly cash rebate to employees who attended the union meetings. The Board recognized that attendance at union meetings was a legitimate union objective; but just as this could not be made a direct condition of employment under the *Union Starch* [148] doctrine, so also, the Board found, was it impermissible for the union to link nonattendance with the total amount of dues an employee was required to pay as a condition of employment. As the Supreme Court had emphasized in *Radio Officers,*[149] Congress intended that the institutional aspects of union membership—including attendance or nonattendance at union meetings—should be *totally* divorced from the employment relationship. An employee's obligation was limited to his duty to bear a proportionate share of the expenses of his representation by the union in its capacity as the statutory bargaining agent of all the employees, and in *Leece-Neville* the Board simply refused to let this policy be circumvented through the transparent ploy adopted by the union.

The *Auto-Lite* and *Leece-Neville* decisions were both enforced by courts of appeals.[150] In spite of this, however, in 1967 the

---

[146] 92 N.L.R.B. 1073 (1950).

[147] 140 N.L.R.B. 56 (1962); *see also* United Packinghouse Workers Local 673, 142 N.L.R.B. 768 (1963).

[148] The Union Starch doctrine holds that the maximum employee obligation under a union security agreement is to tender dues and fees; membership oaths, attendance at union meetings, and the like cannot, however, be imposed as conditions of employment.

[149] Radio Officers' Union v. NLRB, 347 U.S. 17 (1954).

[150] NLRB v. Leece-Neville Co., 330 F.2d 242 (6th Cir. 1964), *cert. denied,* 379 U.S. 819 (1964); NLRB v. Electric Auto-Lite Co., 196 F.2d 500 (6th Cir. 1952), cited with approval in NLRB v. Kaiser Steel Corp., 506 F.2d 1057 (9th Cir. 1974).

Board reversed its position. In *Local 171, Pulp & Paper Workers,*[151] the Board held that such a rebate system did not violate the Act. The basis of the Board's decision is not altogether clear. It emphasized the fact that an active and involved union membership is socially desirable, but there is no evidence of a congressional intent to make this a direct or indirect condition of employment. The Board further noted that giving a partial refund of dues for attendance at union meetings was essentially no different than serving refreshments, awarding door prizes, or providing entertainment, all of which were mere "inducements" toward responsible union membership. This simply begs the question, for it is doubtful that monies obtained through a union security agreement can legitimately be used for such noncollective bargaining purposes. Thus far, the *Pulp & Paper* doctrine has not received any judicial approval.

Union assessments are another monetary obligation not included in the statutory term "periodic dues."[152] Thus, an employee cannot be required, as a condition of employment, to make a donation to a special strike support fund.[153] The difference between an assessment and periodic dues is not always easy to determine. In *NLRB v. Food Fair Stores, Inc.,*[154] the court attempted to define the difference as follows:

> It is clear that the term "periodic dues" in the usual and ordinary sense means the regular payments imposed for the benefits to be derived from membership to be made at fixed intervals for the maintenance of the organization. An assessment, on the other hand, is a charge levied on each member in the nature of a tax or some other burden for a special purpose, not having the character of being susceptible of anticipation as a regularly recurring obligation as in the case of "periodic dues."[155]

Clearly, as this quotation suggests, in order to qualify as dues, a monetary extraction must have the elements of "regularity and periodicity," and where the "time and amount of the assessment are variable and not a matter of certain prediction," the Board

---

[151] 165 N.L.R.B. 971 (1967).

[152] *See, e.g.,* Muehlstein & Co., 118 N.L.R.B. 268 (1957); Tom's Monarch Laundry & Cleaning Co., 161 N.L.R.B. 740 (1966).

[153] NLRB v. Die & Tool Makers Lodge 113, 231 F.2d 298 (7th Cir. 1956), *cert. denied,* 352 U.S. 833 (1956).

[154] 307 F.2d 3 (3d Cir. 1962).

[155] *Id.* at 11.

has disallowed its payment as a condition of employment.[156] On the other hand, a payment that is uniformly and periodically imposed may nevertheless be found to be an assessment if this is what the union intended it to be.[157]

Another possible way of identifying assessments has been by reference to how the money is used. In *Teamsters, Local 959*,[158] the union charged special working dues in order to finance a credit union and building program. The Board found that these dues were not the kind of payment that could be made a condition of employment under a union security agreement because the union was using the money "to accomplish ends not encompassed in its duties as a collective bargaining agent of the employees." [159] The Board noted that the free rider rationale goes no further than permitting, as a condition of employment, the compulsory payment of money to defray the expenses of collective bargaining and contract administration. From this perspective, the statutory term "periodic dues" should not be construed as encompassing any money that is used by the union in its capacity as a "voluntary association." Any such money should be viewed as an "assessment" beyond the power of the union to extract upon threat of discharge.

The *Local 959* decision was sound law and should have been adhered to by the Board. In 1971, however, in *Detroit Mailers Union*,[160] the Board repudiated this interpretation of the term "periodic dues":

> Neither on its face nor in the congressional purpose behind this provision can any warrant be found for making any distinction here between dues which may be allocated for collective bargaining purposes and those earmarked for institutional expenses of the union. . . . Dues may be required from an employee under a union-security contract so long as they are periodic and uniformly required and are not devoted to a purpose which would make their mandatory extraction otherwise inimical to public policy.[161]

---

[156] International Harvester Co., 95 N.L.R.B. 730 (1951).

[157] *See* Teamsters Local 959, 167 N.L.R.B. 1042 (1967); Anaconda Copper Mining Co., 110 N.L.R.B. 1925 (1954).

[158] 167 N.L.R.B. 1042 (1967).

[159] *Id.* at 1044.

[160] 192 N.L.R.B. 951 (1971).

[161] *Id.* at 952. *Compare* Ellis v. Brotherhood of Railway Clerks, 91 L.R.R.M. 2339 (S.D. Cal. 1976).

Another problem that has arisen with respect to union dues and fees pertains to their uniformity, or the lack thereof. In order to qualify as a condition of employment under Section 8(a)(3), the payment that is demanded of an employee must be "uniformly required." This does not mean, however, that a union cannot change its fees from time to time; indeed, at any given point in time, the fee need not even be the same for all employees. As the Board put it in *Metal Workers' Alliance, Inc.*: [162]

> The uniformity requirement does not prohibit unions from charging different fees to different classifications of employees entering or reentering the Union, provided that there is a reasonable and not unlawful basis for the classification.[163]

In that case, higher fees for former employees than for new employees were justified by reference to the fact that these former employees received greater benefits under the union contract. On the other hand, if the disparity in the amount of fees charged various employees is "motivated by a purpose to penalize them for not having obtained or retained membership and paid dues during an earlier period when they were not legally obligated to do so," [164] then a violation will be found. Moreover, one court of appeals has suggested that the difference that is charged must somehow be related to the union's performance of its statutory collective bargaining duties. In *NLRB* v. *Kaiser Steel Corp.*,[165] the union's reinstatement fee schedule had the effect of imposing a charge on employees who exercised their contractual rights to "bump" employees with less seniority who worked in different job classifications. The court held that a fee computed on this basis "went beyond the fees and dues required to support Union representation," [166] and thus violated the uniformity requirement of Section 8(a)(3). On the other hand, the Board has upheld fee discriminations in favor of veterans, even though a classification on that basis normally has no nexus with the union's performance of its collective bargaining duties.[167]

---

[162] 172 N.L.R.B. 815 (1968).

[163] *Id.* at 816.

[164] *Id.*

[165] 506 F.2d 1057 (9th Cir. 1974).

[166] *Id.* at 1060.

[167] Food Machinery & Chemical Corp., 99 N.L.R.B. 1430 (1952).

The uniformity requirement of Section 8(a)(3) is duplicated to a considerable extent by the prohibition against discrimination in Section 8(b)(5); that is, an impermissible disparity also constitutes illegal discrimination. Under Section 8(a)(5), however, a fee that is uniform may nevertheless be considered *discriminatory*, in the broader sense of that word, if it is imposed for the purpose of discouraging nonunion members from applying for employment. This is often done, for example, through the institution of an unusually high initiation fee, which as a practical matter brings about the kind of closed shop situation Congress expressly intended to prohibit.[168]

An initiation fee, however, may be illegal, whether it was imposed for discriminatory reasons or not, if it is in fact excessive. For example, in *Boilermakers Local 749*,[169] there were no allegations of illegal discrimination, and yet the union's fees were held to be higher than what Section 8(b)(5) allows. In determining whether a fee is excessive or not, the Board normally considers whether it is disproportionate to the employees' pay, compares it with fees charged by other unions in the industry, and also considers the union's asserted justification for the fee.[170]

Statutory Exemptions for Religious Objectors

Health Care Institution Employees. In 1974 Congress amended the Taft-Hartley Act to extend its coverage to employees of health care institutions. With respect to such employees, the new amendments also provide:

> Any employee of a health care institution who is a member of and adheres to established and traditional tenets or teachings of a bona fide religion, body, or sect which has historically held conscientious objections to joining or financially supporting labor organizations shall not be required to join or financially support any labor organization as a condition of employment; except that such employee may be required, in lieu of periodic dues and initiation fees, to pay sums equal to such dues and initiation fees, to a nonreligious charitable fund exempt from taxation under section 501(c)(3) of

---

[168] *See, e.g.*, NLRB v. Television & Radio Broadcasting Studio Employees Local 804, 315 F.2d 398 (3d Cir. 1963); Longshoremen Local 1419, 186 N.L.R.B. 674 (1970); Television & Radio Broadcasting Studio Employees Local 841, 225 N.L.R.B. No. 144 (1976).

[169] 192 N.L.R.B. 502 (1971).

[170] *See* cases cited n.168 and n.169.

Title 26, chosen by such employees from a list of at least three such funds, designated in a contract between such institution and a labor organization, or if the contract fails to designate such funds, then to any such fund chosen by the employee.[171]

The original Senate version of the "health care institution employees" bill contained no specific exemption for religious objectors. Senator Dominick, however, proposed an amendment that would have added to *Section 8(a)(3)* an across-the-board exemption for all employees who object to union security on religious grounds.[172] Although this amendment was not limited to health care employees, Senator Dominick was apparently motivated by the fact that Seventh-Day Adventists, one of several religious groups that oppose union membership by their adherents, also operate a number of hospitals and would thus be directly affected by the extension of the Taft-Hartley Act to their institutions.[173]

The amendment was opposed on several grounds. Senator Williams, for example, asserted that it was "unnecessary and redundant" because "union policy and practice already fully recognize the religious convictions of individuals"—whereupon he cited several collective bargaining agreements providing exemptions for religious dissenters.[174] Senator Williams objected to the amendment on the grounds that "it creates a cumbersome process whereby the NLRB must certify . . . every employee seeking exemption from joining a union. . . ."[175] Senator Javits, on the other hand, was opposed to the amendment simply because it opened the door to other broadly-based amendments to the National Labor Relations Act and went beyond the scope of the bill it purported to amend, which was limited to employees of health care institutions.[176] Senator Taft also opposed the Dominick amendment on the grounds that it was not germane to the bill under consideration.[177] For the purpose of showing that, in his opinion, the Dominick amendment was not constitutionally re-

---

[171] Labor-Management Relations Act § 19, 29 U.S.C. § 169 (1974).

[172] 120 CONG. REC. 13536 (1974).

[173] 120 CONG. REC. 13537 (1974) (remarks of Mr. Dominick).

[174] 120 CONG. REC. 13536 (1974) (remarks of Mr. Williams).

[175] *Id.*

[176] 120 CONG. REC. 13537-38 (1974) (remarks of Mr. Javits).

[177] 120 CONG. REC. 13540 (1974) (remarks of Mr. Taft).

quired, Senator Taft also mentioned the *Linscott* and other cases on this issue, which he said would be overruled by the amendment.[178] The Dominick amendment was subsequently defeated.

The original House version of the "health care institution employees" bill was also silent with respect to the religious exemption question. An amendment, however, was proposed—by Congressman Erlenborn—that exempted religious dissenters from the requirements of any union security agreement negotiated among health care institution employees.[179] Opposition to this amendment was voiced only by Congressman Thompson. Among other things, he asserted that such an exemption "might eventually seriously undermine the union's ability to perform its bargaining function," [180] which might be construed as the assertion of a "compelling state interest." But the House of Representatives rejected that view, for it approved the amendment! [181] After the "alternative payments" language was added, the Senate too accepted the amendment without any dissent over the religious exemption provision.[182]

Thus far, there has been no significant litigation under the health care institution religious-objectors exemption.

The Antidiscrimination Provisions of the Civil Rights Act of 1964. Title 7 of the Civil Rights Act of 1964 provides that it shall be an unlawful employment practice for an employer

> [t]o fail or refuse to hire or to discharge any individual, or otherwise to discriminate against any individual with respect to his compensation, terms, conditions or privileges of employment, because of such individual's race, color, *religion,* sex or national origin; . . .[183]

---

[178] *Id.*

[179] 120 Cong. Rec. 16914 (1974).

[180] 120 Cong. Rec. 16914 (1974).

[181] 120 Cong. Rec. 16915 (1974).

[182] 120 Cong. Rec. 22574-83 (1974). About the religious exemption provision, Senator Williams, speaking for the Senate conferees, said:

> The only other matter in which there was disagreement concerned the House provision permitting employees of health care institutions with religious convictions to be exempted from having to join or support a labor organization.
> The Senate conferees accepted this provision with an amendment that each individual so exempted could be required to make payments to a nonreligious charitable fund in lieu of periodic union dues and initiation fees.

120 Cong. Rec. 22575 (1974).

[183] 42 U.S.C. § 2000e-2(a) (1974) (emphasis added).

It is also unlawful for a union to cause an employer to discriminate in this fashion.[184] The Act specifically provides:

> The term "religion" includes all aspects of religious observance and practice, as well as belief, unless an employer demonstrates that he is unable to reasonably accommodate to an employee's or prospective employee's religious observance or practice without undue hardship on the conduct of the employer's business.[185]

This raises two questions: First, in spite of the specific authorization of union security agreements by both the Taft-Hartley Act and the Railway Labor Act, does Title 7 nevertheless protect an employee who, for religious reasons, is unwilling to pay an agency shop fee to a labor organization? If so, what would constitute a "reasonable accommodation without due hardship" in this particular context?

The argument that Title 7's prohibition against religious discrimination does not override the normal operation of a union security agreement is founded in the so-called supremacy clause of Section 8(a)(3) of the Taft-Hartley Act. It states that "nothing in this subchapter, or in any other statute of the United States, shall preclude an employer from making" a union security agreement with a labor organization. The Railway Labor Act contains similar language. The argument, thus, is that this provides an exception to Title 7.

In *Cooper* v. *General Dynamics*,[186] the Fifth Circuit Court of Appeals rejected this argument. It construed the "supremacy clause" as pertaining merely to laws in effect at the time Section 8(a)(3) was enacted, and not to subsequent legislation. The court noted that "to go on, as would the Union, to a conclusion that the quoted language is a true supremacy clause, which for all time lifts section 8(a)(3) above the general level of the United States Code to a position comparable to the Constitution, would be a startling measure indeed."[187] As the court also pointed out, giving the "supremacy clause" this effect would require the nullification of the health care employees exception. Finally, the court noted that neither that specific labor act exception nor Title 7 "precludes or trenches in any direct way upon any employer's

---

[184] 42 U.S.C. § 2000e-2(c) (1974).

[185] 42 U.S.C. § 2000e-(j) (1974).

[186] 533 F.2d 163 (5th Cir. 1976), *cert. petition filed,* Oct. 18, 1976.

[187] *Id.* at 169.

making a union security agreement," [188] thus implying that this is what the "supremacy clause" pertains to. These exceptions, however, apply only to the unusual case where the enforcement of another such legal agreement "would run counter to a particular employee's religious conviction, sincerely held, that can be accommodated without undue hardship." [189]

Another explanation for the preeminence of Title 7 over Section 8(a)(3) was suggested by the district court in *Nottelson* v. *A. O. Smith Corp.*[190] The court noted that the union security authorization of the Taft-Hartley Act was designed to protect the collective rights of the majority, through the elimination of the "free rider." But then, quoting from the language of the Supreme Court in *Alexander* v. *Gardner Denver Co.*,[191] the district court further noted that Title 7

> stands on plainly different ground. It concerns not majoritarian process, but an individual's right to equal employment opportunities. Title VII's strictures are absolute and represent a congressional command that each employee be free from discriminatory practices.[192]

Although the courts are thus unanimous in holding that Title 7's religious accommodation requirements provide an exception to the kinds of union security agreements permitted by Section 8(a)(3),[193] the Supreme Court's recent decision in *Trans World Airlines* v. *Hardison*[194] may suggest a contrary conclusion. In that case the Court held that an employer's duty to "accommodate" an employee's religious belief against working on Saturday does not go so far as to require the employer to violate the seniority provisions of the collective bargaining agreement, as would be the case if other employees were forced to take the religious objector's place in performing Saturday overtime work. The Court stated:

---

[188] *Id.* at 170.

[189] *Id.*

[190] 423 F.Supp. 1345 (E.D. Wis. 1976).

[191] 415 U.S. 36 (1974).

[192] 423 F.Supp. at 1347.

[193] *See also* Yott v. North American Rockwell Corp., 501 F.2d 398 (9th Cir. 1974).

[194] 45 U.S.L.W. 4672 (1977).

[W]e do not believe that the duty to accommodate requires TWA to take steps inconsistent with the otherwise valid agreement. Collective bargaining, aimed at effecting workable and enforceable agreements between management and labor, lies at the core of our national labor policy, and seniority provisions are universally included in these contracts. Without a clear and express indication from Congress, we cannot agree . . . that an agreed-upon seniority system must give way when necessary to accommodate religious observances.[195]

The same kind of argument, if not a stronger one, could be made with respect to union security agreements which, unlike seniority provisions, are specifically permitted by the language of the Taft-Hartley Act. Again analogous to the *Hardison* situation, relieving a religious objector from the obligation of paying union dues means that other employees must bear a proportionately higher share of the cost of union representation. On the other hand, the *Hardison* case could be distinguished on the grounds that Title 7 expressly defers to the normal operation of seniority systems,[196] while it does not similarly defer to union security agreements. The issue, thus, would appear to be a close one.

If, however, the "supremacy clause" of Section 8(a)(3) does not totally preempt the "reasonable accommodation" provisions of Title 7, insofar as the operation of union security agreements is concerned, then an additional issue presents itself—whether this aspect of Title 7 is itself unconstitutional. In this regard, the district court in *Yott* v. *North American Rockwell Corp.*[197] held that it does in fact violate the Establishment Clause of the First Amendment for Congress to require an employer to accommodate the religious beliefs of his employees by forcing him to provide an exception to an otherwise valid union security agreement. A contrary conclusion about this aspect of Title 7, although it did not arise in a union security context, was reached by the Sixth Circuit in a decision that was affirmed by an equally divided Supreme Court.[198] In the *Hardison* case, the courts below had also sustained the constitutionality of the religious accommodation requirement, and the Supreme Court had granted *cer-*

---

[195] *Id.* at 4676.

[196] 42 U.S.C. § 2000e-2(h) (1974).

[197] 14 FEP Cases (BNA) 445 (C.D. Cal. 1977).

[198] Cummins v. Parker Seal Co., 516 F.2d 544 (6th Cir. 1975), *aff'd by an equally divided Court,* 429 U.S. 65 (1976).

tiorari on this issue.[199] Because in that case the Court ultimately held that the employer's reliance on the seniority provision of the contract did in fact satisfy the requirement, the Court found it unnecessary to rule on the constitutional issue.

On the assumption that Section 8(a)(3) is not absolutely "supreme" and that the "reasonable accommodation" requirement of Title 7 is constitutional, the next and possibly more difficult question concerns the proper application of the religious accommodation requirement. Insofar as burden of proof is concerned, the *Yott* case suggests that the employee initially "has the burden of proving that he has offered to the employer an accommodation which is acceptable to him." The employer, or the union, then "has the burden of demonstrating that the suggested accommodation will create an undue hardship."

Although the statute itself talks only in terms of "undue hardship on the conduct of the employer's business," both the Ninth [200] and the Fifth [201] Circuits have construed this to mean that hardship to the union is also relevant. As stated by Judge Brown in *Cooper,* "where the asserted religious discrimination grows out of a collective bargaining contract, . . . the Union as a very real party in interest, has the right to demonstrate that accommodation would cause undue hardship to it and its interest." [202] Moreover, Judge Brown also asserted that a union weakened by a loss of financial support from religious objectors could well cause a hardship to the employer, in that such a union would be less able to negotiate effectively and thus more prone to industrial warfare. Apparently conceding the tenuousness of this argument *vis-à-vis* a hardship on the employer, Judge Brown asserted that society has a "legitimate interest in the maintenance of a strong vigorous advocate in this process of bargaining," [203] sufficient to make the union's hardship a relevant consideration in deciding whether Title 7 requires that accommodation be made for religious objectors to union security agreements.

---

[199] Trans World Airlines v. Hardison, 11 FEP Cases (BNA) 1121 (8th Cir. 1975), *rev'd,* 45 U.S.L.W. 4672 (1977).

[200] Yott v. North American Rockwell Corp., 501 F.2d 398 (9th Cir. 1974).

[201] Cooper v. General Dynamics, 533 F.2d 163 (5th Cir. 1976) (Judges Brown and Rives concurring on this point).

[202] *Id.* at 172.

[203] *Id.* at 173.

With respect to the accommodation issue itself, the *Cooper* court indicated that on remand the lower court should consider "all reasonable accommodations of appellants' religious beliefs, including one which permits their nonpayment of union dues or the equivalent while continuing regular work assignments with their employer. . . ." [204] The simple exclusion of religious objectors from the operation of a union security agreement has, however, been rejected by two lower courts. In the words of the *Yott* court, "exemption is not accommodation." [205] This, moreover, would appear to be consistent with the *Hardison* approach.

Similarly, in *Anderson* v. *General Dynamics*,[206] the court stated that "anything less than payment of the equivalent of dues to the Union for charitable purposes would impose an undue hardship on the Union." [207] The court rejected, as a reasonable alternative, the *direct* payment of an equivalent amount to a charity, on the grounds that this would do nothing to eliminate "free riders." Under the court's suggested approach, the money of the religious objector would be paid by the union to a charity, and this would then justify a *pro tanta* reduction of the amount from other employees' dues that would normally be used for this purpose and a *pro tanta* increase in the amount that would be used for noncharitable purposes—all of which eliminates the religious objector as a "free rider" but which also differs from the normal payment of dues only as a matter of bookkeeping theory.

Another accommodation that has been rejected is that the religious objector be put in a job outside the bargaining unit, on the grounds that such exclusion from the coverage of a union security agreement is apt to be only temporary in light of the union's organizing plans.[208] It has also been suggested that the employee accept a cut in pay, with the company apparently reimbursing the union for the lost dues. This was rejected on the grounds that the cut in pay would subject the union to liability for breach of its duty of fair representation, and the proposed payment by the company would violate both state and federal law.[209]

---

[204] *Id.* at 170.

[205] 14 FEP Cases (BNA) at 450.

[206] 14 FEP Cases (BNA) 667 (S.D. Cal. 1977).

[207] *Id.* at 670.

[208] 14 FEP Cases at 450.

[209] *Id.* at 451.

It would thus appear that Title 7's implied exceptions to Section 8(a)(3) of the Taft-Hartley Act are more theoretical than real in that the courts have been unwilling to find any accommodation with religious belief that is reasonable and does not create an alleged undue hardship on either the employer or the union. In addition, the Supreme Court's *Hardison* decision, though not dealing directly with union security agreements, lends considerable support to this interpretation of the statute.

Union Security Deauthorization Elections

Under the original Taft-Hartley Act amendments, an otherwise valid union security agreement could not be negotiated between an employer and a union unless a majority of the employees in the unit had specifically authorized such a provision in an election held for that purpose by the National Labor Relations Board. Between 1947 and 1951, ninety-seven percent of these elections had resulted in the authorization of a union security clause.[210] Consequently, in order to relieve the Board of the duty of supervising so many elections, in 1951 Congress amended the Act to permit the inital negotiation of a valid agreement, but to make it subject to a subsequent *de*authorization election should one be sought by dissident employees. Section 9(e)(1) of the amended Act now reads:

> Upon the filing with the Board, by 30 percentum or more of the employees in a bargaining unit covered by an agreement between their employer and a labor organization made pursuant to section 8(a)(3), of a petition alleging their desire that such authority be rescinded, the Board shall take a secret ballot of the employees in such unit and certify the results thereof to such labor organization and to the employer.[211]

The effect of an affirmative deauthorization election is to void the union security agreement and immediately relieve the employees of all the membership requirements imposed thereby, including the payment of agency shop fees.[212] An illegal union security agreement (in addition to being an unfair labor practice) is, of course, subject to a deauthorization election, the Board feeling that it would be anomalous to treat illegal clauses more

---

210 SIXTEENTH ANNUAL REPORT OF NLRB 54 (1952).

211 Labor-Management Relations Act § 9(e)(1), 29 U.S.C. § 159(e)(1) (1974).

212 Monsanto Chemical Co., 147 N.L.R.B. 49 (1964).

leniently than it treats legal ones.[213] Finally, the Board can
hold only one union security deauthorization election within any
twelve-month period.[214]

Remedies

When an employee has been wrongfully discharged under an
otherwise valid union security agreement, the employee is normally entitled to reinstatement with backpay. In addition, the
union and the employer will be ordered to cease and desist from
their unfair labor practices and to post the appropriate Board
notices to this effect.[215] The employer and the union can be made
"jointly and severally" liable for the backpay,[216] or in an appropriate case the Board may impose primary liability on the most
culpable party and only secondary liability on the other.[217] Where
the union alone is the respondent in an unfair labor practice
case, it can be ordered to notify the employer that it no longer
has any objections to reinstatement [218] and to assume liability for
whatever backpay is due.[219]

When the union security agreement itself is illegal, the parties
will, of course, be ordered to cease and desist from giving it
any effect.[220] For a time the Board was also ordering the refund
of *all* dues and fees collected under such a contract.[221] The Supreme Court, however, found that this was more punitive than
remedial, and in *Carpenters Local 60* v. *NLRB* held that in the
absence of actual proof that specific, individual employees had
been coerced by the illegal agreement into paying dues to the
union, such as across-the-board reimbursement order was not

---

[213] Andor Co., 119 N.L.R.B. 925 (1957).

[214] Labor-Management Relations Act § 9 (e) (2), 29 U.S.C. § 159 (e) (2)
(1974).

[215] *See* Pinkerton's Nat'l Detective Agency, Inc., 90 N.L.R.B. 205 (1950),
enforced, 202 F.2d 230 (9th Cir. 1953) ; Acme Mattress Co., 91 N.L.R.B. 1010
(1950).

[216] *Id.*

[217] NLRB v. Operating Engineers Local 138, 377 F.2d 528 (2d Cir. 1967).

[218] Pen & Pencil Workers Local 19593, 91 N.L.R.B. 883 (1950).

[219] *See* cases cited n. 215.

[220] Plumbers & Pipefitters Local 231, 115 N.L.R.B. 594 (1956).

[221] *Id.*

appropriate.[222] The Board and the courts have subsequently applied this rule in a variety of factual contexts.[223]

Frequently, when an employer has acquiesced in a union security arrangement that is more compulsory than that allowed by the proviso to Section 8(a)(3), this employer's conduct will also be found to violate Section 8(a)(2)'s prohibition against employer assistance to labor organization. Where this is the case, the appropriate remedy is usually to require the employer to cease giving effect to the contract, including the union security provision, and to withdraw all recognition of the union until it is certified by the Board.[224]

CONCLUSION

Prior to 1948, federal law on union security was relatively uncomplicated. Unfortunately, it also allowed for more union coercion than most Americans were willing to tolerate. Consequently, the Taft-Hartley Act Congress imposed substantial limits upon the institution of compulsory unionism, but it did so in such a manner as to render the law virtually incomprehensible. It is clear that Congress did not have an adequate conception of exactly what kind of union security it wanted to allow; and its inartfully drafted statute, with exceptions tacked onto exceptions, is probably an accurate reflection of the muddled intent of Congress at the time.

The task of making some sense out of all this was thus left to the Board and the courts. The judicial process, however, with its seriatim focus on narrow and specific issues, is ill-equipped to provide a comprehensive, internally consistent body of law on union security. Indeed, from this patch-work quilt of decisions, it is only recently—almost thirty years after Taft-Hartley—that any firm consensus has developed about the scope of an employee's obligation under a union security agreement sanctioned by Section 8(a)(3), and certain details remain obscure even at this time.

---

[222] 365 U.S. 651 (1961).

[223] NLRB v. Booth Services, 516 F.2d 949 (5th Cir. 1975); NLRB v. Hi-Temp, Inc., 503 F.2d 583 (7th Cir. 1974); Crown Cork & Seal Co., 182 N.L.R.B. 657 (1970).

[224] Oscherwitz & Sons, 130 N.L.R.B. 1078 (1961); Pacific Intermountain Express Co., 107 N.L.R.B. 837 (1954); Salant & Salant, Inc., 88 N.L.R.B. 816 (1950). *But see* NLRB v. Gaynor News Co., 197 F.2d 719 (2d Cir. 1952); NLRB v. Sterling Furniture Co., 202 F.2d 41 (9th Cir. 1953).

Moreover, the congressional decision to deal with the checkoff in a part of the statute totally removed from Section 8(a)(3), its failure to deal specifically with hiring hall arrangements, and its awkward handling of the religious-objector problem have all contributed to the confusion.

The obscurity of the law on union security is not, however, of merely theoretical concern, for its by-product is something that touches upon the daily lives of millions of American workers who are living under union security agreements that are in actual practice more compulsory than Congress intended. While it may require the expertise of the Board and the courts to figure out exactly what the law does allow, insuring that this information is conveyed to the affected employees could be accomplished quite simply by requiring union security agreements to reflect what the statute means rather than what it literally says. Until this is done, page upon page of abstract legal analysis must, quite frankly, count for very little.

CHAPTER IV

Union Hiring Halls as a Form of Compulsory Unionism

Under the original Wagner Act, it was a common practice in some industries for an employer to agree to hire only those applicants that had been referred to it through the union's hiring hall or, at least, to give preference to such applicants. Quite understandably, the unions frequently refused to refer anyone except their own members, a combination which in practice had the effect of making union membership a condition of initial employment. These arrangements, considered to be quite legal, were merely an adjunct to the closed shop which was itself a legal form of union security under the then existing proviso to Section 8(3).[1]

With the prohibition of the closed shop in 1948, the status of hiring hall arrangements became uncertain. A union could no longer operate a hiring hall solely for the benefit of its members and at the same time include in its collective bargaining agreement a provision whereby the employer was bound to use the hiring hall as the exclusive source of new employees. Such an arrangement would obviously violate the new Act's requirement that union membership not be made a condition of employment until at least thirty days after hire (or seven days in the case of the construction industry).

On the other hand, it is not altogether certain that the Taft-Hartley Congress intended to outlaw completely all hiring hall arrangements without any regard to the circumstances surrounding their use. Senate Report Number 105 merely states:

> It is clear that the closed shop which requires preexisting union membership as a condition of obtaining employment creates too great a barrier to free employment to be longer tolerated. In the

---

[1] *See* J. E. Pearce Contracting & Stevedoring Co., 20 N.L.R.B. 1061, 1071 (1940).

maritime industry and to a large extent in the construction industry union hiring halls now provide the only method of securing employment. This not only permits unions holding such monopolies over jobs to exact excessive fees but it deprives management of any real choice of the men it hires.[2]

It is not clear from this quotation whether what Congress found objectionable was that these hiring halls were merely a means of implementing closed shop agreements, or that employers were being required to surrender substantial control over the employee-selection process. If the former were the sole focus of concern, then this could be cured by simply prohibiting referrals that discriminated in favor of union members, but otherwise allowing the hiring hall to remain the exclusive or preferred source of new employees. On the other hand, if the statement is also to be read as evidencing congressional concern over the delegation of hiring authority to unions, then this would require the elimination of the exclusivity aspect itself which was a violation of Section 8(a)(3)'s broad prohibition against encouragement of union membership, especially at the prehire stages.

Whatever the actual intent of the Taft-Hartley Congress with respect to hiring halls, some Congressmen apparently construed the new Act as prohibiting hiring halls altogether. But since hiring halls, especially in the maritime industry, were also thought to be beneficial to employees and employers alike, shortly after the Taft-Hartley Act, an amendment was introduced to exempt the maritime unions from the prohibitions against the closed shop.[3] The response of Senator Taft, who opposed the change, was that the Taft-Hartley Act did not prohibit all hiring halls and that the requested exemption was therefore unnecessary. His comments, which are frequently cited as evidence of what the Taft-Hartley Act Congress intended, are as follows:

> In order to make clear the real intention of Congress, it should be clearly stated that the hiring hall is not necessarily illegal. The employer should be able to make a contract with the union as an employment agency. The union frequently is the best employment agency. The employer should be able to give notice of vacancies, and in the normal course of events to accept men sent to him by the hiring hall. He should not be able to bind himself, however,

---

[2] LEGISLATIVE HISTORY OF THE LABOR MANAGEMENT RELATIONS ACT, 1947, at 412 (1974).

[3] *See* 96 CONG. REC. 8433, A1802 (81st Cong., 2d Sess., 1950).

to reject nonunion men if they apply to him; nor should he be able to contract to accept men on a rotary-hiring basis. . . .

The National Labor Relations Board and the courts did not find hiring halls as such illegal, but merely certain practices under them. The Board and the court found that the manner in which the hiring halls operated created in effect a closed shop in violation of the law. Neither the law nor these decisions forbid hiring halls, even hiring halls operated by the unions as long as they are not so operated as to create a closed shop with all of the abuses possible under such an arrangement, including discrimination against employees, prospective employees, members of union minority groups, and operation of a closed union.[4]

Although it is readily apparent from the above quotation that Senator Taft did not construe the Taft-Hartley Act as prohibiting all hiring halls, his comments are again somewhat ambiguous with respect to exactly what it is that makes such an arrangement illegal. The first paragraph of the above quotation seems to suggest that hiring halls are illegal whenever, by contract or practice they become the exclusive source of the employer's job applicants. The second paragraph, on the other hand, suggests that the true "ear mark" of an illegal hiring hall is not so much its exclusivity, but it is the union practice of discriminating on the basis of union membership in making referrals, thus achieving the functional equivalent of the closed shop.

By failing to deal specifically with this issue, Congress necessarily left it up to the Board and the courts to define the parameters of hiring hall arrangements and to accommodate that institution with the Act's specific prohibition against certain kinds of compulsory unionism with which hiring halls had been so closely associated in the past. One of the first major issues to arise concerned the precise point on which the legislative history was so ambiguous—the circumstances, if any, under which an exclusive, albeit nondiscriminatory, hiring hall arrangement could be considered legal under the new Act.

THE LEGALITY OF
EXCLUSIVE HIRING HALL ARRANGEMENTS

After some initial vacillation on the issue, the National Labor Relations Board eventually articulated a firm set of criteria for evaluating the legality of exclusive hiring hall arrangements. In

---

[4] S. Rep. No. 1827, 81st Cong., 2d Sess. 13-14 (1950), Committee on Labor and Public Welfare.

the *Mountain Pacific*[5] case, the Board was confronted with an agreement which gave the union the exclusive right for a forty-eight hour period to supply workmen requested by contracting members of the employer association. The Board began with the premise that the Taft-Hartley Act amendments were "not intended to put an end to all hiring halls, but only those which amount to virtual closed shops."[6] The Board also recognized that the membership requirement prohibited as a condition of initial employment was not limited to a formal type of membership:

> [T]he statutory phrase "encourage membership in a labor organization" is not to be minutely restricted to enrollment on the union books; rather, it necessarily embraces also encouragement toward compliance with obligations or supposed obligations of union membership, and participation in union activities generally.[7]

The Board then proceeded to consider whether or not the exclusive hiring hall encouraged such membership as a condition of initial employment, thus rendering it the functional equivalent of the closed shop. The Board concluded that it did have that effect:

> Here the very grant of work at all depends solely upon union sponsorship, and it is reasonable to infer that the arrangement displays and enhances the Union's power and control over the employment status. Here all that appears is unilateral union determination and subservient employer action with no aboveboard explanation as to the reason for it, and it is reasonable to infer that the Union will be guided in its concession by an eye towards winning compliance with a membership obligation or union fealty in some other respect. The Employers here have surrendered all hiring authority to the Union and have given advance notice via the established hiring hall to the world at large that the Union is arbitrary master and is contractually guaranteed to remain so. From the final authority over hiring vested in the Respondent Union . . . the inference of encouragement of union membership is inescapable.[8]

The Board also concluded, however, that the impermissible encouragement could be muted to the point of making a hiring hall legal if the agreement explicitly provided:

---

[5] Mountain Pacific Chapter of the Associated General Contractors, 119 N.L.R.B. 883 (1957).

[6] *Id.* at 896.

[7] *Id.* at 895.

[8] *Id.* at 896.

(1) Selection of applicants for referral to jobs shall be on a nondiscriminatory basis and shall not be based on, or in any way affected by, union membership, bylaws, rules, regulations, constitutional provisions, or any other aspect or obligation of union membership, policies, or requirements.

(2) The employer retains the right to reject any job applicant referred by the union.

(3) The parties to the agreement post in places where notices to employees and applicants for employment are customarily posted, all provisions relating to the functioning of the hiring arrangement, including the safeguards that we deem essential to the legality of an exclusive hiring agreement.[9]

The Supreme Court, however, was subsequently to repudiate the Board in this regard. In *Local 357, Teamsters* v. *NLRB*,[10] the employer and the union had agreed that "casual employees" would be hired exclusively through the union's hiring hall, with priority being given on the basis of seniority. Although the agreement provided that seniority would be computed "irrespective of whether such employee is or is not a member of the Union," the Board held that none of its *Mountain Pacific* requirements were met. The agreement being illegal per se, the Board found that a discharge pursuant to its terms was an unfair labor practice even though the employee who had attempted to circumvent the hiring hall was himself a union member.

The United States Supreme Court reversed this ruling. It began with the proposition that a Section 8(a)(3) and 8(b)(2) violation consists of two coincident elements: (a) That there be "discrimination," and (b) that it "encourage or discourage membership in labor organizations." The Court then conceded that an exclusive hiring hall has the effect of encouraging union membership to the extent that the term *membership* encompasses even mere involvement in union activities. But, the Court said, this was not an encouragement that was the result of discrimination. Since the discharged employee was himself a member of the union, there was no discrimination in that sense. The Court further asserted, with respect to the legality of the instrument itself, that "surely discrimination cannot be inferred from the face of the instrument when the instrument specifically provides that there will be no discrimination against 'casual employees' because of the presence or absence of union mem-

---

[9] *Id.* at 897.

[10] 365 U.S. 667 (1961).

bership." [11] In the absence of any discrimination, no violation was made out.

This aspect of the Court's opinion is unduly narrow in its reading of the statutory term *discrimination*. Concededly, in referring job applicants, the union here did not discriminate on the basis of formal union membership, and the hiring hall agreement did not contemplate that the union should do so. But the Act does not merely prohibit "discrimination on the basis of formal union membership that has the effect of encouraging union membership," [12] which is how the Court seemed to be reading it in this particular case. Rather, the Act broadly proscribes discrimination having such an effect, without express regard to its basis, leaving it up to the Board and the courts to identify the exact bases and circumstances under which discrimination having that effect is actually going to be considered illegal.

Apart from discrimination on the basis of formal membership itself, the next most common form of prohibited discrimination is that based on an employee's participation in union-related activities; *i.e.*, regardless of whether the participant is actually a union member or not. Clearly, that kind of discrimination was involved in the *Local 357* case, where the employer treated job applicants differently, depending on whether or not they had been referred through the union hiring hall. The fact that the union did not discriminate "on the basis of union membership"

---

[11] *Id.* at 675.

[12] As Judge Friendly pointed out in NLRB v. Miranda Fuel Co., 326 F.2d 172 (2d Cir. 1963) (Friendly, dissenting) :

> Congress did *not* say "to *discriminate* in regard to hire or tenure of employment *because* of membership in any labor organization,"—language which, indeed, would not support the result here reached by the Board. Neither did it define the unfair labor practice as being discrimination *in order to* encourage or discourage membership in any labor organization. What Congress forbade was "to encourage or discourage membership in any labor organization" by "discrimination in regard to hire or tenure of employment."

Id. at 181 (emphasis in the original). In that case, the Board had held that union-induced discrimination on a basis that was arbitrary but totally unrelated to union activities was nevertheless a "discrimination" that, if it had the proscribed effect, could be considered within the ambit of Sections 8(b)(2) and 8(a)(3). Although the Second Circuit refused to enforce the Board's order in that case, the *Miranda* doctrine has been accepted in other circuits and has indeed received the tacit approval of the Supreme Court itself. *See* Vaca v. Sipes, 386 U.S. 171 (1967). Judge Friendly's dissenting opinion is frequently cited in this regard.

in making referrals should not have been deemed controlling insofar as the issue of statutory "discrimination" was concerned.

The Court would have been on firmer ground if it had conceded, consistent with its decisions in other areas, that a generally prohibited form of discrimination having a generally prohibited effect was present in this case, but then simply held that Congress nevertheless did not intend to outlaw this particular instance of it—*i.e.*, a hiring hall that was the exclusive source of job applicants but that referred such applicants without regard to the membership or nonmembership in the union —provided the Court did believe that was the intent of Congress. Indeed, this may have been the primary basis of the decision. The Court, as did the Board itself, assumed that Congress did not intend to outlaw hiring halls except to the extent that they amounted to a mere subterfuge for the continuation of the closed shop. But, unlike the Board, the Court felt that the exclusivity aspect alone was insufficient; rather, the functional equivalent of a closed shop would arise in a hiring hall situation only, the Court indicated, where the referral decision itself was predicated, directly or indirectly, on the applicant's formal membership status in the union.

DISCRIMINATORY REFERRALS

Despite the clear language of the statute and the *Local 357* decision hiring hall agreements will still occasionally state explicitly that preference is to be given to union members. The continued existence of such agreements must, however, be attributed to a failure of the Act's enforcement mechanisms rather than to any residual uncertainty as to what the law itself provides, for where such agreements do happen to be the object of unfair labor practice proceedings, they have been uniformly held to be illegal.[13]

On the other hand, a hiring hall agreement that is legal on its face may nevertheless be administered in such a way as to give rise to violations of the Act. The union might refuse to refer any except its own members or give them preference[14] or make the payment of fines or back dues a condition of referral[15]

---

[13] *See generally Legality of Hiring-Hall Arrangement Under Labor Management Relations Act*, 38 ALR 2d 413 (1954).

[14] *See, e.g.*, NLRB v. Local 803, Boilermakers, 218 F.2d 299 (3d Cir. 1955).

[15] *See, e.g.*, NLRB v. Waterfront Employers of Washington, 211 F.2d 946 (9th Cir. 1954) ; Carpenters Local 1437, 210 N.L.R.B. 359 (1974).

or give preference on the basis of length of union membership.[16] Such discrimination—in violation of both the hiring hall agreement itself and the statute—is simply a matter of factual proof, however; and cases of this kind rarely raise difficult questions of law.

Finally, there remains some controversy, and consequent uncertainty, over the criteria that a hiring hall agreement can authorize the union to use in making its referrals. The problem most often arises with respect to criteria which, while seemingly objective on their face, nevertheless operate to give preference to union members.

For example, it is legitimate for a union to condition referrals on the successful completion of a union-administered skills test or apprenticeship program,[17] but not when eligibility to take the test or enter the program is itself conditioned on union membership.[18]

The use of "work experience" as a criteria for referral can also cause difficulties. Generally speaking, an agreement may provide for priority based on the applicant's work experience in the industry or within a particular geographic area.[19] But where, because of the prior operation of an illegal hiring hall, union members would necessarily have the greatest experience and the use of this criteria would thus merely perpetuate the prior discrimination, it has been found to be illegal.[20] Likewise, an agreement may give priority to former employees of the signatory employer or employers, as in the case of a multiemployer bargaining unit.[21] But since collective bargaining agreements frequently contain union security provisions, it has been held that a hiring hall agreement that gives priority to employees who previously worked under a collective bargaining agreement of the signatory union indirectly discriminates in favor of union members and is thus illegal.[22] There is, however, one important exception to this.

---

[16] *See, e.g.,* Local 138, Operating Engineers v. NLRB, 321 F.2d 130 (2d Cir. 1963).

[17] *See, e.g.,* Local 42, Heat Insulators, 164 N.L.R.B. 916 (1967).

[18] *See, e.g.,* Local 99, IBEW, 214 N.L.R.B. 723 (1974).

[19] *See, e.g.,* Romanoff Electric Co., 221 N.L.R.B. 113 (1975).

[20] *See, e.g.,* NLRB v. Local 269, IBEW, 357 F.2d 51 (3d Cir. 1966).

[21] *See, e.g.,* J-M Co., 173 N.L.R.B. 1461 (1968).

[22] *See, e.g.,* Photographers Local 659, 197 N.L.R.B. 1187 (1972); Directors Guild of America, Inc., 198 N.L.R.B. 707 (1972); Nassau-Suffolk Chapter of the National Electrical Contractors Ass'n., Inc., 215 N.L.R.B. 894 (1974).

In *Local 354, IBEW (Interstate Electric Co.)*,[23] the hiring hall agreement gave priority to persons "who have been employed for a period of at least 2 years of the last 4 years under a collective bargaining agreement between the parties to this agreement." Under the principles articulated above and the existing precedent, such an agreement should have been considered illegal.[24] The Board, however, upheld it, in what can at best be described as a cryptic opinion. The Board relied on Section 8(f) of the Act, which provides that in the building and construction industry it shall not be an unfair labor practice to negotiate an agreement which "specifies minimum training or experience qualifications for employment or provides for priority in opportunity for employment based *upon length of service with such employer*, in the industry or in the particular geographical area. . . ."[25]

It has been said that Section 8(f), which was added to the statute in 1959, merely codified, for the benefit of the construction industry, the principles that the Board and the courts had already worked out for hiring halls in general—criteria that legally could be used for referral.[26] The Board, however, seized upon the italicized language of the statute quoted above, construed it as applying not only to the signatory employers to the agreement but also those employers who had "assented" to be bound by it, and thus concluded that the hiring hall arrangement in question was protected by the statute.

This seems to be a complete non sequitur. To say that Section 8(f) allows hiring priority based on work experience with employers other than the signatory employer is not to say that such work experience can also be limited to times when such employer(s) are bound by a contract with the union—especially when, as in this case, the contract contains a union security provision. Those are two very separate issues, and one cannot infer the answer to one from the answer to the other.

Although, as Board Member Jenkins pointed out in his dissent, the *Local 354* case is inconsistent with precedent involving

---

[23] 227 N.L.R.B. No. 291 (1977).

[24] *See* Bechtel Power Corp., 223 N.L.R.B. 925 (1976). Member Fanning's concurring opinion in that case should probably have been taken as a harbinger of things to come.

[25] 29 U.S.C. § 158(f) (1974).

[26] R. GORMAN, BASIC TEXT ON LABOR LAW 668 (1976).

hiring hall arrangements in both the construction industry and elsewhere; the Board expressly overruled only the prior case dealing with a construction industry hiring hall.[27] This, plus the Board's reliance on Section 8(f), suggests that the *Local 354* decision will probably not be applied to any hiring hall arrangements other than those in the construction industry. In itself, however, this represents an important exception to the Board's prior policy of prohibiting this kind of indirect discrimination on the basis of union membership.

Another close case involved the giving of priority to strikers and unemployeds (persons out of work because of someone else's strike or because they had been locked out) over a group of so-called casuals. The Trial Examiner had inferred that such strikers and unemployeds were far more apt to be union members than casuals were, and that this constituted discrimination on an impermissible basis. The Board, however, reversed. It held that there was no hard evidence to show that strikers and unemployeds were predominantly union members. Moreover, the preference for these employees was justified by evidence showing that they were generally more reliable than the casuals, thus tending to negate any possible discriminatory intent on the union's part in using this as a criteria for referral.[28]

Finally, although a union security agreement requiring an employee to become a member of the union can normally be enforced only after the employee has been hired, in one instance the Board has allowed enforcement at the hiring hall level. In *Mayfair Coat and Suit Co.*,[29] an employee was discharged when, after thirty days, he failed to pay the initiation fee as required by the union security agreement between his employer and the union. Immediately thereafter, this individual applied to the hiring hall. The union refused to refer him to an employer in the same multiemployer bargaining unit as the original employer and thus subject to the same union security provision. The Board concluded that this was a valid way of implementing that union security provision and indicated:

---

[27] Nassau-Suffolk Chapter of the National Electric Contractors' Ass'n, Inc., 215 N.L.R.B. 894 (1974).

[28] Pacific Maritime Ass'n, 155 N.L.R.B. 1231 (1965); *compare* Standard Fruit & Steamship Co., 211 N.L.R.B. 121 (1974) (illegal for union to prefer applicants who had previously picketed on behalf of the union).

[29] 140 N.L.R.B. 1333 (1963).

> It would be cumbersome and unnecessary to refer to a member company of an association . . . an individual who has already had his grace period, only to have the union immediately request his discharge by the company, as it would be lawfully entitled to do, for failure to pay his initiation fee.[30]

Subsequently, however, the Board narrowed this holding somewhat. In *Asbestos Workers Local 5*,[31] the Board held that though an attempt to be referred through the hiring hall immediately after discharge amounted to little more than a request of a reconsideration of the discharge itself, a request which the union need not honor, this cannot be said of an application for referral that comes some twenty-one months later. The Board indicated that the union cannot forever refuse to refer an employee who had previously been discharged for nonpayment of fees and dues under a union security agreement. The union can, however, condition this subsequent referral (presumably, to the same employer only) on the employee's immediate payment of the requisite fees and dues, the theory being that this employee's "grace period" has already run.

FEES FOR THE USE OF A UNION HIRING HALL

Although a person certainly cannot be required to become a formal member of a union as a condition of being referred through the hiring hall, the Board and the courts have held that a job applicant who is not a member of the union can be charged a "reasonable fee" for this service; union members are presumed to pay for the service with their normal dues. Typically, a union will charge a fixed amount for each month that a nonmember applicant maintains his name on a referral list. The Board has even held that an applicant who has been repeatedly late in paying this monthly fee can be denied referral altogether on the grounds that "a person's credit standing, which reflects upon his character, may well be reasonably related to his performance as a responsible employee." [32]

The notion that a union can charge a reasonable fee for its hiring hall services, while plausible on its face, is subject to criticism on the grounds that it does in fact permit that which the

---

[30] *Id.* at 1335.

[31] 191 N.L.R.B. 220, *enforced per curiam*, 462 F.2d 1394 (9th Cir. 1972).

[32] Pacific Maritime Ass'n, 155 N.L.R.B. 1231, 1234 (1965).

Act specifically prohibits—namely, an agreement requiring employee "membership" in the union at some time earlier than thirty days (or seven days in the case of the construction industry) after the date of hire. This is especially true in light of the amount that unions have been allowed to charge for this service.

Three determinants of a "reasonable fee" have been advanced. First, it has been suggested that the fee should merely represent the job applicant's pro rata share of the cost of running the hiring hall during the months that he is registered there, and nothing more. Second, it has been argued that the amount should be determined by reference to the applicant's pro rata share of all the union's expenses in negotiating and administering the collective agreement (which would necessarily include its costs in running the hiring hall). And finally, the unions have contended that the fee should reflect the job applicant's pro rata share of all of the union's expenses, which would thus make the fee equivalent to a formal union member's monthly dues.

Initially, the Board took the position that the third approach was the proper one. In *Local 825, Operating Engineers*,[33] where the hiring hall fee charged to nonmembers was roughly equivalent to the union's monthly dues,[34] the Board upheld the fee and noted:

> Apart from the fact that all employees, whether members or nonmembers, receive all the benefits of the Respondent's [the union's] collective bargaining agreement, including welfare and pension payments, it would be a matter of considerable difficulty to distinguish between the costs of operating a referral system that guaranteed to each applicant union wages and conditions of employment and those union costs which might be said to have no relation to the applicant's job opportunities before, during, and after his employment at a particular jobsite.[35]

The Board's position in this regard was, however, subsequently repudiated by a court of appeals. In *Local 138, Operating Engineers* v. *NLRB*,[36] the union had charged nonmember users of

---

[33] 137 N.L.R.B. 1043 (1962).

[34] Nonmembers were charged a $9.00 monthly fee for being registered at the hiring hall. Membership dues were $10.00 monthly, but $1.10 of this was sent to the International—thus making the nonmember hiring hall fee actually higher than monthly dues! On the other hand, members also had to pay a $360.00 initiation fee.

[35] *Id.* at 1044.

[36] 321 F.2d 130 (2d Cir. 1963).

the hiring hall a fee that was the exact equivalent of its monthly membership dues. The Board sustained this, but the court held that a union could not require nonmembers to pay union dues, in effect, under the guise of charging for its *services as an employment agency*." [37] The court thus reversed and indicated:

> The Board should consider on remand what proportion of the fees that were paid were reasonably related to the value of the services provided by the union, having in mind also the cost to the union of performing such service.[38]

Presumably, the term "services" in the quoted language referred to the union's services as an employment agency, which would suggest that the court was taking the first approach articulated above. On remand,[39] however, the union still argued that it was entitled to compensation for *all* the services and benefits, tangible and intangible, that it might render to the user of a hiring hall. The Board's Trial Examiner rejected this view. He indicated:

> The Union's contention that all its expenses redound to the benefit of the permit men as well as to the benefit of the members may well be accurate in a long-range view (although it takes a rather doctrinaire view of labor solidarity to find benefit to nonmembers in such matters as convention expenses, members' death benefits, goodwill contributions to other unions, and litigating this and related cases before the Board), but the only expense for which the Union may lawfully charge the permit men is for "its services as an employment agency" . . . [quoting from the court's opinion]. The other services the Union renders permit men are services it renders as their statutory bargaining representative, and as to this permit men are "free riders," . . . as the union had no union-security clause in its contract which would have required nonmembers to pay the equivalent of dues in return for the Union's services.[40]

Clearly, the thrust of this paragraph is that the hiring hall fee can be used to reimburse the union for neither its purely fraternal activities nor its activities as a bargaining agent, other than those directly related to the operation of the hiring hall itself. But then the Trial Examiner continued:

> However, as appears below, the General Counsel has urged a more lenient view of the Union's liability here and is permitting the

---

[37] *Id.* at 135.

[38] *Id.* at 136.

[39] J. J. Hagerty, 153 N.L.R.B. 1375 (1965).

[40] *Id.* at 1378-79.

Union to claim as allocable to the hiring hall all union expenses except those which are "institutional" in character, *i.e.*, expenses incurred by the Union as an organization rather than in the course of making or policing collective-bargaining agreements.[41]

The Trial Examiner, by acquiescing in the General Counsel's "lenient view," thus ended up taking an approach substantially similar to the second one described above, rather than follow the court's intimation that only the costs of actually running the hiring hall could be attributed to a nonmember user. The Board agreed with this and petitioned the court of appeals for enforcement of its order requiring the union to remit $3.50 of the $10.00 monthly fee it had been receiving from nonunion users of the hiring hall.[42] The union resisted enforcement on the grounds that the approach followed by the Board did not allow it to charge enough. But no one argued on behalf of the individual employees that the amount allowed by the Board was still excessive and, indeed, inconsistent with the court's prior remand. The lack of anyone to argue this particular point may thus explain an apparent anomaly in the court's second opinion.

Responding to the union's argument that it should be allowed to charge nonmembers "the fair value of all services received from the union," the court opined:

> The union clearly misinterprets our earlier opinion. When this case was first before us, we assumed that the permit fees were charged solely for the use of the hiring hall, because that was the only service for which the union had a right to charge the permit men. Thus when we remanded for further findings, ordering the Board to consider what proportion of the fees was reasonably related to the "value of the services provided by the union," we were referring to the value of the hiring hall services. . . . Furthermore, we have no reason to doubt that we were correct in limiting the permit fees to an amount reflecting the value of the hiring hall services only.[43]

The court thus concluded that "the Board's interpretation of our mandate was correct." [44] What the court apparently failed to realize was that the Board had not, in fact, determined the amount in the fashion described by court but had followed the General Counsel's "more lenient view" by allowing the union "to

---

[41] *Id.* at 1379.

[42] NLRB v. Local 138, Operating Engineers, 385 F.2d 874 (2d Cir. 1967).

[43] *Id.* at 876-77.

[44] *Id.*

claim as allocable to the hiring hall all union expenses except those which are 'institutional' in character"—a far different thing from limiting it to expenses which are demonstrably related to the actual operation of the hiring hall itself.

That the court was arguably wrong in accepting the Board's method of computing a reasonable fee for the use of a hiring hall can also be inferred from the reasons that the court itself gave for rejecting the union's argument. The court noted that if a union could charge nonmember users of the hiring hall a fee equivalent to its own formal membership dues (thus including institutional expenses), this would in effect convert it into a union security agreement:

> If the union wants union security, it may bargain for it. It may not short-circuit the system Congress has established by attempting to gain union security through an exclusive hiring hall. The union's interpretation of the Act would render purposeless the proviso to § 8(a)(3).[45]

Since what the union could get under a union security agreement is full membership dues (covering the cost of *both* the union's institutional activities and its collective bargaining activities), what it can get through charging a fee for the use of a hiring hall must necessarily be less. Assuming the logic of the argument generally, it nevertheless contains a dubious premise—namely, that a union can, in fact, use a union security agreement to compel the payment of full membership dues. As has been developed elsewhere,[46] the better current authority seems to be that membership dues under a Section 8(a)(3) union security agreement must be limited to an amount necessary to reimburse the union for the performance of its statutory duties only—namely, collective bargaining and contract administration. If this is so, then the overall logic of the court's argument would now suggest that the hiring hall fee must be related directly to the operation of the hiring hall itself, for to allow all expenses except institutional ones would be to allow what the Act says can be obtained only through a union security agreement, which could not in any event become operative until some time after an employee was hired, not before.

Indeed, one may question whether the Act allows a union to charge a nonmember any fee for the use of its hiring hall, when this is pursuant to an exclusive agreement between that union

---

[45] *Id.* at 877-78.

[46] *See* Chapter VI, *infra.*

and an employer, even when the fee is directly related to the costs of the operation of such a hall. The applicant, it is true, is merely being charged a fee for a specific service. But the same is true of the money that an employee is obligated to pay under a union security agreement; this is supposed to be in return for the benefits of representation that the employee receives from the union. But, with respect to such an obligation generally, Congress has expressly said that it shall not be imposed prior to thirty days after hire (seven days in the case of the construction industry). If that is true with respect to the benefits that the union generally provides, it should be no less true with respect to a specific benefit. Clearly, a union could not, for example, have a union security agreement requiring membership on or after the thirtieth day and also charge a special fee to compensate the union for providing the benefit of representation during the employee's first thirty days of work.[47] It is not clear why the result should be any different when the benefit in question is the operation of a hiring hall.

Nevertheless, under the existing interpretation of the law an employee can, as a condition of initially being referred under a hiring hall arrangement, be required to pay a fee the amount of which is determined by the "costs of the referral system and of collective bargaining and contract enforcement."[48]

CONCLUSION

A primary concern of the law has been that hiring halls not become a cover for de facto closed shop or other forms of otherwise illegal union security arrangements. There are three ways in which this might happen.

First, since Board processes must be initiated through the filing of a "charge," and since many employees are ignorant of their rights and/or fear union reprisal for exercising them, it is probable that many violations of the "legal niceties" simply go unreported and thus unremedied.

Second, there is the danger that seemingly objective criteria for referral under a hiring hall agreement will in fact operate to discriminate against nonmembers of the union. Although the

---

[47] *Compare* NLRB v. Laborers Local 573, 75 CCH Lab. Cas. ¶ 10,568 (7th Cir. 1973) (opinion withheld from publication), *enforcing* 196 N.L.R.B. 440 (1972). ("Working Dues" during first seven days of employment held to be illegal.)

[48] Boston Cement Masons Union 534, 216 N.L.R.B. 568 (1975).

Board and the courts profess to be aware of this danger and have on occasion invalidated such criteria, the decision in the recent *Local 354* case, if taken as a general shift in Board policy, may portend a new tolerance to other indirect forms of discrimination as well.

And third, to the extent that a service fee for the use of a hiring hall merely represents an itemized charge for a benefit which the union provides to those it represents, allowing such a fee is tantamount to allowing a union and a compliant employer to impose exactly the same kind of obligation that is normally imposed under a union security agreement and then only at some time *after* the employee has been hired. The danger that a hiring hall agreement will in this manner effectively provide for an "agency fee as of date of hire" kind of arrangement is not merely potential; that danger is an existing reality, for under the existing Board and court decisions, that is exactly what the law allows.

CHAPTER V

Union Security Agreements Under the Railway Labor Act

The original Railway Labor Act[1] did not rule on the legality of union security agreements.[2] In 1934, however, the Act was amended and all forms of compulsory unionism were prohibited.[3] Oddly enough, the railway unions did not oppose this amendment at this time, being more concerned with the growing incidence of so-called company unions than with obtaining the benefits of the closed or union shop. Fearing that the carrier-employers would use compulsory membership in company-dominated unions and the mandatory checkoff of dues to such unions as a means of destroying the independent unions, the labor representatives decided that a total prohibition against all forms of compulsory unionism was the lesser of two evils. In the words of one labor official, "Our needs at the moment were to prevent carrier abuses which threatened our very existence. . . ."[4]

Later, after the problem of "company unions" had been virtually eliminated, union security again became a matter of priority for the railway unions, and amendments to the Railway Labor Act were eventually introduced into Congress.

The 1950 debates over the union security amendments to the RLA are remarkably similar to the 1948 debates over the Taft-

---

[1] Portions of this chapter originally appeared in Haggard, *A Clarification of the Types of Union Security Agreements Affirmatively Permitted by Federal Statutes*, reprinted with permission from the RUTGERS-CAMDEN LAW JOURNAL, Vol. 5, No. 3, pp. 418-452. Copyright 1974 by Rutgers School of Law-Camden.

[2] Act of May 20, 1926, ch. 347, §§ 1-11, 44 Stat. 577.

[3] Act of June 21, 1934, ch. 291, § 11, 48 Stat. 1185 (repealed 1951).

[4] *Hearings on H.R. 7789, before the House Committee on Interstate and Foreign Commerce*, 81st Cong., 2d Sess. (May 9, 1950) (testimony of George M. Harrison).

Hartley Act—with many of the same arguments being advanced, both for and against compulsory unionism. Yet there was one important difference. Up to this time, many of the railway unions had adhered to racially discriminatory membership practices.[5] Negro labor leaders, however, believed that if union membership were going to be made a condition of employment, as under the union shop, then such membership should also be open to everyone in the bargaining unit; otherwise, union security agreements would become an invidious way of depriving Negro employees of their jobs. Thus, Congress was urged to outlaw membership discrimination directly.[6] But, as in 1947-48, Congress was not yet ready to regulate the membership rules and internal practices of labor unions. This was to come later. Instead, Congress resolved the dilemma by limiting the circumstances under which nonmembership in a labor union could result in an employee's discharge under a union security agreement. In this regard, Congress simply tracked the language of Section 8(a)(3) of the Taft-Hartley Act. As amended, Section 2, Eleventh (a) provides that employers and unions subject to the Act shall be permitted

> to make agreements, requiring, as a condition of continued employment, that within sixty days following the beginning of such employment, or the effective date of such agreements, whichever is the later, all employees shall become members of the labor organization representing their craft or class: Provided, That no such agreement shall require such condition of employment with respect to employees to whom membership is not available upon the same terms and conditions as are generally applicable to any other member or with respect to employees to whom membership was denied or terminated for any reason other than the failure of the employee to tender the periodic dues, initiation fees, and assessments (not including fines and penalties) uniformly required as a condition of acquiring or retaining membership.[7]

Section 2, Eleventh (b), allows this form of union security, provided such checkoff authorizations are "revocable in writing after the expiration of one year or upon the termination date of the applicable collective agreement, whichever occurs sooner."

Finally, Section 2, Eleventh (c), provides that whenever a collective bargaining agreement requires "membership in a labor organization" as a condition of employment, with respect to any employee in the "engine, train, yard, or hostling service," that

---

[5] *See* H. RISHER, THE NEGRO IN THE RAILROAD INDUSTRY 1-72 (1971).

[6] *Id.* at 72-73.

[7] 45 U.S.C. § 152 (1970).

requirement shall be deemed satisfied "if said employee shall hold or acquire membership in any one of the labor organizations, national in scope, organized in accordance with this chapter and admitting to membership employees of a craft or class in any said service."

Most of the litigation under the union security provisions of the Railway Labor Act has focused on the question of which unions, other than the contracting union, an employee can be a member of and still satisfy the requirements of a union security agreement, as provided in subsection (c). Likewise, there is a question about the circumstances under which an employee can opt for such alternative membership. Related to both these matters are the cases construing the checkoff provisions of the Act. The wording of subsection (a) also raises an issue with respect to the kind of membership that is contemplated by the statute, and there is some case law on this matter as well. Finally, the question of how a railway union can spend its union security agreement dues has received considerable judicial attention—and continues to do so. These matters will be discussed in turn.

ALTERNATIVE UNION MEMBERSHIP

One of the unique aspects of union security agreements under the Railway Labor Act is that the statute allows employees to satisfy the requirements of such an agreement through membership in a union other than the one that represents the employee in collective bargaining.

This somewhat unusual provision was written into the statute because of the peculiar conditions of the railroad industry. Traditionally, employees in this industry have organized themselves along craft rather than industrial lines—engineers, firemen, brakemen, conductors, and other so-called operating employees each being represented by a separate union. Moreover, there is also a high degree of craft mobility in the industry. A fireman may be temporarily promoted to engineer, or a conductor might serve as a brakeman for several months. In conjunction, craft organization plus craft mobility pose the following dilemma: Under a union security agreement, an employee will either have to belong to two or more unions or to change unions constantly as he changes jobs. The former alternative would be expensive, and the latter would result in a continuing loss of seniority and union benefits. To resolve this dilemma, Congress chose in writing subsection (c) to allow the affected class of employees to maintain membership in just one union, whether it was the current representative of that employee or not, without thereby risking discharge under a union security agreement.[8]

Although subsection (c) appears clear on its face, two problems of interpretation have arisen, one of which has not yet been authoritatively resolved. The first problem pertains to the kind of union that an employee may be a member of and still satisfy the requirements of a union security agreement. Subsection (c) imposes three requirements: that the union in which the employee maintains his membership be "national in scope," that it be "organized in accordance with the provisions of the Railway Labor Act," and that it "admit to membership employees of a craft or class" covered by the Act.

For the most part, however, an employee is limited to maintaining his membership in one of the so-called standard unions. The union security provisions of the Railway Labor Act do not define the term "national in scope," nor do they expressly provide a means for determining whether a union meets this requirement. Accordingly, in *Pigott* v. *Detroit, Toledo & Ironton Railroad Co.*,[9] the Sixth Circuit Court of Appeals deferred to the administrative processes established by the Act for resolving this issue in another context.

Under the Act, the labor organizations that are entitled to participate in the selection of members to the National Railroad Adjustment Board are limited to those that are national in scope. If a dispute arises with respect to the right of a labor organization to participate, the Secretary of Labor is instructed to investigate the claim, and if he determines that the organization is qualified, he notifies the Mediation Board. The Mediation Board then appoints a panel of three: a representative of the previously qualified unions, a representative of the claimant union, and a third or neutral party. The determination of the panel is final and binding. After the amended Act became effective, the Secretary of Labor certified the existing standard unions; and as a practical matter, they have maintained their monopoly over the selection of members to the National Railroad Adjustment Board.[10]

---

[8] *See* Pennsylvania Railroad Co. v. Rychlik, 352 U.S. 480, 489-90 (1956).

[9] 221 F.2d 736 (6th Cir. 1955), *cert. denied*, 350 U.S. 833 (1955).

[10] *See* Northrup & Kahn, *Railroad Grievance Machinery: A Critical Analysis*, 5 Industrial and Labor Relations Review 365, 370-72 (1952).

Thus, when the court in *Pigott* deferred to these processes, it was adopting, for the purposes of the union security provisions of Section 2, Eleventh, a definition of "national in scope" that is more political than factual in its orientation.

Subsequently the Supreme Court reached essentially the same conclusion. In *Pennsylvania Railroad Co.* v. *Rychlik*,[11] the Court held that the only other union, apart from the bargaining representative itself, that an employee could elect to join under a union security agreement was a labor union that had already been qualified as an elector to the National Railroad Adjustment Board. The Court noted that the only purpose of union security agreements was to eliminate the free rider. Therefore, the alternative membership that the statute allowed should be in a union that itself bore the expenses of the administration of contracts under the Railway Labor Act—to wit, unions that were "qualified electors."

The second problem, as yet not fully resolved, pertains to the circumstances under which an employee can elect to become a member of one of these other unions. Can an employee simply join another qualified union at will? Or is the option more circumscribed? In *Rychlik*, the Supreme Court indicated that subsection (c) was a limited exception to the general rule that an employee must be a member of the union that has negotiated the union security agreement and otherwise represents him in collective bargaining and contract administration. The Court noted:

> [T]he *only* purpose of Section 2, Eleventh (c) was a very narrow one: to prevent compulsory dual unionism or the necessity of changing from one union to another *when an employee temporarily changes crafts.* . . .
>
> Nor was it intended to provide employees with a general right to join unions other than the designated bargaining representative of their craft, *except to meet the narrow problem of intercraft mobility.* . . . In other words, once a union has lawfully established itself for a period of time as the authorized bargaining representative of the employees under a union-shop contract, Congress has never deemed it to be a "right" of employees to choose between membership in it and another competing union.[12]

It would thus appear that when an employee is initially hired, if a union security agreement is in effect, the employee must join the union having jurisdiction over that job. If the employee is subsequently promoted or transferred into another craft

---

[11] 352 U.S. 480 (1956).

[12] *Id.* at 492-94 (emphasis added).

or class, the employee can retain his membership in the original union despite the fact that he would be represented by another union. This, however, would appear to be the only situation in which an employee could avail himself of the subsection (c) option of belonging to a union other than the one that represents him.

This interpretation of the Act was subsequently followed by the Third Circuit in *Rohrer* v. *Conemaugh & Black Lick Railroad Co.*[13] The United Steelworkers had been certified as the collective bargaining representative of all the employees of the railroad regardless of their class or craft. A union security agreement was negotiated, and employee Rohrer had joined this union. Subsequently, however, he terminated his membership in the Steelworkers and joined the Brotherhood of Railroad Trainmen. The Steelworkers sought to have him discharged under the terms of the union security agreement. Rohrer attempted to rely on subsection (c), but the court held it to be inapplicable since the "dilemma of intercraft mobility" was simply not present in Rohrer's situation. The court noted that Rohrer was attempting to do exactly what the *Rychlik* case says an employee is not entitled to do under the Act.

Other courts of appeals, however, have declined to follow the Third Circuit's lead in narrowly construing the scope of subsection (c). In *Birkholz* v. *Dirks*,[14] for example, the Trainmen's Union was the bargaining representative of all the employer railroad's yard employees. From the beginning, a number of these employees had maintained their membership in the Switchmen's Union. This situation continued up to 1966, when the union security agreement was modified to require membership in either the Trainmen's Union or some other union having a contract with the employer. Under the literal terms of the agreement, the Switchmen's Union did not qualify. The Switchmen's Union employees sought to have the contract declared illegal, on the grounds that they had a right under subsection (c) to satisfy the union security agreement by maintaining membership in unions other than those identified by the contract. Since, in this case, the employees' desire to maintain membership in a union other than their collective bargaining representative was not even remotely related to problems of "craft mobility," the

---

[13] 359 F.2d 127 (3d Cir. 1966).

[14] 391 F.2d 289 (7th Cir. 1968).

district court, relying on *Rychlik* and *Rohrer,* denied their request for relief.

The Seventh Circuit Court of Appeals reversed. The court found that the Switchmen's Union met the literal requirements of subsection (c), and was also a "qualified elector." Thus, the statute guaranteed these employees the right to be a member of this union rather than the Trainmen's Union; since the Trainmen's Union security agreement purported to deprive them of this right, it was null and void.

With respect to the broad language of the *Rychlik* decision quoted above, the court merely indicated that "what the Supreme Court said in dictum in that case was with respect to that factual situation." The *Rohrer* case was similarly limited to its facts.

The Second Circuit, on the other hand, has not been quite so direct in its disregard of the Supreme Court's view; in *O'Connell* v. *Erie Lackawanna Railroad Co.,* the court at least attempted to bring the case before it under the umbrella of an intercraft mobility problem, albeit of a kind different from that involved in *Rychlik*:

> [T]here are two aspects to the operation of the proviso reflecting the two situations in which intercraft mobility might lead to the dual unionism problem.
>
> First, when an employee changes crafts his new craft may be represented by a different union. Under the statute the employee clearly does not have to change unions. The second situation in which the problem arises . . . is when so many employees change crafts without changing unions that the bargaining agent for the [new] craft no longer has majority membership in the craft [as where large numbers of engineers move into firemen's jobs, and the engineers' union eventually becomes the bargaining representative]. The second aspect of the operation of Eleventh (c) is to permit these firemen, now a minority, to satisfy the union shop requirement by membership in the craft union, even though it is no longer their bargaining agent.[15]

While the court's hypothetical is an ingenuous, and probably valid, extension of the intercraft mobility rationale, it is difficult to see its relevance to the facts of the *O'Connell* case; the change in unions there was not a result of intercraft migration but was, rather, simply a consequence of the merger of two railroads—a situation hardly unique to the railroad industry.

---

[15] 391 F.2d 156 (2d Cir. 1968) at 162.

Moreover, it is not altogether clear that the Second Circuit even intended to limit the application of subsection (c) to intercraft mobility situations. At one point, the court seemed to suggest that an employee can always transfer his membership from the union that represents him to another union so long as this other union meets the necessary requirements. The court said that this was the implied teaching of the Supreme Court in *Felter* v. *Southern Pacific Co.*,[16] which was decided after *Rychlik*. In that case, an employee simply left the union that represented him and joined another; no aspect of the intercraft mobility problem was involved. When he also attempted to revoke his checkoff authorization to the first union, the company insisted that he follow the terms of the collective bargaining agreement and use a particular form that had been provided by the union and was returnable to the company only through the union. This the employee refused to do, and the company thus declined to honor his revocation request. The only issue before the Supreme Court was whether this requirement could validly be imposed upon an employee under subsection (b); the Court held that it could not. The Second Circuit, however, also read the decision as expressing tacit approval of the employee's right to change union membership under the situation described.

There is other authority for the proposition that the *Rychlik* dicta quoted above is not controlling, and that under the statute an employee can always opt to maintain his membership in an alternative union. This is possible even if his reasons for doing this are not directly related to the dilemma posed by intercraft mobility, so long as this other union meets the requisite qualification. When sitting on the Eighth Circuit Court of Appeals, Mr. Justice Blackmun, now of the United States Supreme Court, indicated that this was how he construed the Act—notwithstanding the broad language of *Rychlik*.[17]

Undoubtedly, the Supreme Court will eventually be called upon to resolve this conflict, and when it is, it will probably adopt the views of the Second and Seventh Circuits. The Court will argue that the purpose of Congress in drafting subsection (c) was to eliminate the danger that union security agreements would necessitate membership in two unions by railway employees. This

---

[16] 359 U.S. 326 (1959).

[17] Brotherhood of Locomotive Firemen v. Northern Pacific Railway Co., 274 F.2d 641, 650 (8th Cir. 1960).

dilemma of dual membership arises primarily because railway employees frequently move from one craft to another, each craft being represented by a different union. There is, however, no specific indication in the legislative history that this particular cause of the dilemma was the exclusive concern of Congress. After rejecting one narrowly drawn proposal, Congress chose to approve an across-the-board authorization of alternative membership, so long as it was in another national union representative of operating employees.[18]

The trouble with this argument is that it ignores the implications of subsection (c), which limits alternative membership to employees in the so-called operating divisions. Other railway employees, though covered by the Act, do not have this option. This is significant because of the fact that intercraft mobility was widespread only among these operating employees. On the other hand, railway employees who are not in an operating division are by no means immune from the dilemma of dual unionism—brought about, for example, by a change in bargaining representatives. But since the option of alternative membership was not made available to these employees, this may suggest that Congress was not concerned with the problem of dual unionism generally, but rather only to the extent that it arises because of the phenomenon of intercraft mobility.

The problem of alternative membership has to a large extent been obviated by the merger of most of the operating unions into the United Transportation Union. Some rivalry over membership still exists, however, between that union and the Brotherhood of Locomotive Engineers.

CHECKOFF AUTHORIZATIONS

Under Section 2, Eleventh (b), a railway union and a carrier are permitted to negotiate checkoff agreements whereby union dues are deducted from the employee's paycheck and forwarded directly to the union. Congress, however, imposed two important limitations. First, employees cannot be compelled to pay their union dues in this fashion, and no checkoff will be made unless the employee has first provided a written authorization to the employer. Second, such an authorization shall be revocable in writing after the expiration of one year.

---

[18] The legislative history of this provision is well summarized in O'Connell v. Erie Lackawanna Railroad Co., 391 F.2d at 159-61.

In *Felter* v. *Southern Pacific Co.*,[19] the Supreme Court was confronted with a collective bargaining agreement that required that the revocation be on a form provided by the union, which would then forward it to the employer. An employee submitted a written revocation to the employer, but refused to use the union's form or to forward it through the union. The employer, consequently, did not honor his request. The Supreme Court ultimately held that the requirements of the collective bargaining agreement went beyond those authorized by the statute, "which are simply that there be a writing, attributable to the employee and fairly expressing a revocation of his assignment, furnished the carrier." [20] One wonders, along with the dissent,[21] whether so trivial an issue was deserving of Supreme Court attention.

On the other hand, the option that an employee has under subsection (c) of maintaining membership in an alternative union has given rise to some legal issues, involving the checkoff, that are considerably more complex.

In *Switchmen's Union* v. *Southern Pacific Co.*,[22] the Switchmen's Union was the certified bargaining representative of the company's switchmen and the Brotherhood of Railroad Trainmen similarly represented the trainmen. Under subsection (c), of course, employees in both classes had the option of being members of either union, in satisfaction of their obligations under the union security agreement. In fact, some of the switchmen were actually members of the Trainmen's Union. The collective bargaining agreement between the Trainmen and the carrier contained a provision which authorized the checkoff of dues to the Trainmen for all its members regardless of whether they were employed as trainmen or as switchmen. The Ninth Circuit Court of Appeals, however, held that the arrangement was illegal under the Railway Labor Act. The court concluded that

> in making the dues check-off agreement with the Trainmen applicable to [employees] for whom the Switchmen's Union was the exclusive representative, the Carrier violated its obligation to bargain exclusively with the Switchmen's Union as to all matters pertaining to [these employees].[23]

---

[19] 359 U.S. 326 (1959).

[20] *Id.* at 335.

[21] *Id.* at 340.

[22] 253 F.2d 81 (9th Cir. 1958).

[23] *Id.* at 84.

Subsequently, in *Brotherhood of Locomotive Firemen* v. *Northern Pacific Railway Co.*,[24] the Eighth Circuit Court of Appeals was confronted with this situation: The Brotherhood had negotiated a checkoff agreement with the carrier, and pursuant to this agreement certain employees had signed written authorizations for the checkoff of their dues to this union. Within a year, one of these employees transferred his membership from the Brotherhood to another qualified union. Upon receiving notification of this, the carrier refused to continue to deduct this employee's dues and pay them to the Brotherhood. The Brotherhood claimed that under the agreement and as authorized by subsection (b), the employee's wage assignment was irrevocable for one year.

The court rejected this contention and in doing so succinctly stated the governing rules regarding checkoff authorizations under the Act:

> [I]f there is to be a checkoff at all, three conditions must be met:
>
> a. The checkoff must be pursuant to an agreement with the bargaining representative which, here, is the Brotherhood;
>
> b. Payment can be made only to that representative, and to no other; and
>
> c. The employee must then be holding membership in that representative.
>
> If any one of these three conditions is not met, there can be no deduction. Further, because the employee has the right to change his membership among qualified labor organizations, he has, in effect, the power to terminate the checkoff in his case, for nothing, says the statute, shall prevent the membership change and, once it is changed, the third of the three conditions is not met. The one year provision as to irrevocability of a written dues assignment, once executed, then necessarily is subordinate to these other provisions and is defeated by an allowable membership change; the one year provision, therefore, can have application only to the situation where the employee's membership in the qualified labor organization, in favor of which he has executed the dues assignment, continues throughout the one year period.[25]

This opinion was written by Judge Blackmun, now of the United States Supreme Court.

---

[24] 274 F.2d 641 (8th Cir. 1960).

[25] *Id.* at 646.

AGREEMENTS AUTHORIZED BY THE RAILWAY LABOR ACT—THE MEANING OF THE TERM MEMBERSHIP

As was indicated earlier, the language that Congress used in authorizing union security agreements under the Railway Labor Act was substantially identical to the language previously used in the Taft-Hartley Act. The RLA thus raises the same problems of construction: Do the terms *members* and *membership* connote, for the purposes of either job retention or the imposition of discipline, a formal type of associational relationship with the union, or is the mere payment of money all that is required? In short, exactly what kind of union security agreement does the RLA authorize?

An Analysis of the Legislative History

As with the Taft-Hartley Act, Congress repeatedly said that its amendments to the RLA were intended to authorize the so-called union shop.[26] But the apparent contradiction between the requirement of membership under a true union shop, on the one hand, and the prohibition against discharge except for nonpayment of fees and dues, on the other, is not specifically referred to in the 1950 debates. Indeed, congressional discussion of the union security provision is rather slim and unenlightening. The various explanations of the amendment do, however, follow a fairly consistent pattern. First, Section 2, Eleventh, authorizes union security agreements which require employees to become members of the union. Second, unions are to have the option of not accepting certain employees as members and of expelling others. Third, it is emphasized that an employee who is denied membership status for any reason other than the payment of dues, fees, and assessments cannot be discharged under the type of agreement authorized by Section 2, Eleventh.[27]

The repeated emphasis upon these three points is consistent with, and, indeed, suggestive of, the union option interpretation of Section 8(a)(3) which is arguably implicit in Chairman

---

[26] S. REP. No. 2262, 81st Cong., 2d Sess. (1950). After describing what the amendments allow, the report concludes that "[t]his type of agreement is what is commonly known as a union shop." *Id.* at 2. *See also* 96 CONG. REC. 15735, 16264, 16268, 16269, 16328, 16331, 17050 (1950).

[27] *See* S. REP. No. 2262, 81st Cong., 2d Sess. (1950); 96 CONG. REC. 15736, 16264, 17058, 17060 (1950).

Miller's dissent in *Hershey Foods*.[28] According to this view, a union security agreement can require formal membership. The union, however, has the option of refusing to accept an employee as a member since Congress did not want to intrude into the internal affairs of such organizations. But when a union exercises this option, the employee's job rights will remain protected so long as he tenders his periodic dues and fees. Except as a response to a union expulsion, the mere tender of money is, however, insufficient to satisfy the requirements of a union security agreement.

Senator Holland's explanation of the amendment is most pointed in this regard. He said that under an agreement authorized by the amended statute, nonunion members would "be required to join the union." He then added, "there would be no exception to that other than the refusal of the union to admit them . . . every man not now a member of the union would be forced to apply for membership and subject himself to that situation, whatever it might be." [29] The testimony of an official of one of the railroad unions before the House and Senate Committees makes it quite clear, moreover, that the unions wanted the union shop in order to achieve disciplinary power over the employees they represented.[30]

Finally, the legislative history of the alternative membership authorization in Section 2, Eleventh (c), strongly suggests here that Congress had in mind "membership" in the colloquial or literal sense (*i.e.,* as meaning something more than the mere payment of money). The whole dilemma of dual membership is predicated on this assumption. Congress was worried that under the union security agreements that it was newly authorizing, railway employees who moved from one craft to another would be required either to bear the expense of membership in two unions or to drop membership in the first union and thereby forfeit certain union benefits. Clearly, the union benefits in question—items such as pension eligibility, insurance benefits, and the like—are available only to actual members rather than to mere agency fee payers.

---

[28] 207 N.L.R.B. at 897-98 (1973).

[29] 96 Cong. Rec. 16331 (1950).

[30] *See Hearings on H.R. 7789 before the House Comm. on Interstate and Foreign Commerce,* 81st Cong., 2d Sess. 11, 38 (1950) (testimony of George M. Harrison); *Hearings on S. 3295 before a Subcom. of the Senate Comm. on Labor and Public Welfare,* 81st Cong., 2d Sess. 28 (1950).

While the legislative history is apparently devoid of any *specific* language which supports an agency shop interpretation of the RLA, more generalized and thus more reliable constructions of congressional intent lean strongly in that direction. First, beyond all doubt, the primary intent of Congress was to bring the union security provisions of the RLA into parity with those of the Taft-Hartley Act.[31] As was seen earlier, while the legislative history of that prior Act was not free from ambiguity, the various objectives of the Taft-Hartley Congress can all be met only under an agency shop interpretation of Section 8(a)(3). Since in amending the RLA, Congress intended to do for the railroad unions what the Taft-Hartley Act had done for other unions, the more extensive legislative history of Taft-Hartley should be incorporated by reference into that of Section 2, Eleventh, of the RLA.

Second, as with the Taft-Hartley Act, the legislative history of the RLA shows that in permitting union security agreements, Congress mainly intended to eliminate the problem of the so-called free rider.[32] It is reasonable, moreover, to assume that Congress intended to move no further from its former position of total prohibition than was necessary to achieve this limited objective. Such an objective is met under a union security provision which requires no more than the payment of the equivalent of periodic union dues and fees. The "elimination of the 'free rider'" rationale cannot, however, justify the requirement that an employee not only pay money to the union but also be subject to the internal discipline of the union as a private contractual association.

Third, although this qualification has subsequently been read into the Taft-Hartley Act by the Board and the courts,[33] in the Railway Labor Act, Congress expressly provided that nonpayment of periodic dues, initiation fees, and assessments" was not meant to include or refer to the nonpayment of "fines and penalties." As was true of the Taft-Hartley Congress, it would appear that the 1950 Congress assumed that the principal manner in which unions enforced their fines was by expulsion from the union. Congress wanted to make clear that an employee who was expelled from union membership for nonpayment of his fines

---

[31] S. Rep. No. 2262, 81st Cong., 2d Sess. (1950) ; 96 Cong. Rec. 15737, 16261, 16265, 16267, 16269, 17047, 17049, 17060 (1950).

[32] 96 Cong. Rec. 16265, 17050, 17058 (1950).

[33] *See, e.g.*, NLRB v. Longshoremen's Local 17, 431 F.2d 872 (9th Cir. 1970) ; Pen & Pencil Workers Local 19593, 91 N.L.R.B. 883 (1950).

was not thereby subject to discharge under the union security agreement.[34] The underlying principle of this statutory exception is that the employee's job rights should be kept separate from his purely internal union obligations. It would be anomalous indeed for Congress to say specifically that a union security agreement cannot make the payment of union fines a condition of continued employment, but at the same time allow such an agreement to impose as a necessary incident to the employment relationship a legal obligation to pay such fines. The inference to be drawn is that an employee's obligation to pay union fines does not arise by virtue of and cannot be enforced by means of the kind of union security agreement Congress envisioned. Only the agency shop agreement meets that requirement.

While the broad thrust of congressional intent is relatively clear, as in the Taft-Hartley Act, the words chosen to implement that intent were unfortunately ambiguous. On the other hand, unlike the Taft-Hartley Act, the RLA's interpretation by the courts is now totally free from ambiguity.

An Analysis of the Case Law

The exact type of union security agreement authorized by Section 2, Eleventh, of the RLA has not been relevant to the issues most frequently litigated under that section. Presumably, the *Union Starch* doctrine of the Taft-Hartley Act would likewise apply to prohibit discharge under a RLA union security agreement for any reason other than nontender of dues and fees.[35] But, as with the Taft-Hartley, there remains the separate issue of whether the Act authorizes compulsory membership for purely disciplinary purposes. On this issue, the courts have answered with an unequivocal no.

In *Railway Employees' Department* v. *Hanson,*[36] the Supreme Court construed the Act as authorizing the union shop, but there is language in the decision which strongly suggests that formal membership was not contemplated by the Court.[37] The Court,

---

[34] *See* 96 CONG. REC. 15736, 16267 (1950).

[35] *Accord,* Higgins v. Cardinal Mfg. Co., 188 Kan. 11, 22-23, 360 P.2d 456, 464-65 (1961). *But cf.* Shiels v. Baltimore & Ohio Railroad Co., 154 F.Supp. 917, 924 (S.D. Ind. 1957).

[36] 351 U.S. 225 (1956).

[37] *But see id.* at 231, n. 3, where the Court defined the "union shop" as a variant of the "closed shop," the difference being the time when membership

for example, noted that the primary purpose of Congress in authorizing union security agreements in the railroad industry was to insure that all of the alleged beneficiaries of union representation contributed to its cost.[38] Thus the Court concluded that "[t]he *only* conditions to union membership authorized by § 2, Eleventh of the Railway Labor Act are the payment of 'periodic dues, initiation fees and assessments.' "[39] The Court also took cognizance of the fact that when an employee "becomes a member of these unions he is subject to vast disciplinary control. . . ."[40] But the Court held that on the facts before it there was no evidence that the union was attempting to use this power in contravention of First Amendment rights.[41] The Court then suggests—admittedly by way of dicta—that such control would be illegal under the Act since "Congress endeavored to safeguard against that possibility by making explicit that no conditions to membership may be imposed except as respects 'periodic dues, initiation fees and assessments.' "[42] The Court also stated that "The prohibition of fines and penalties precludes the imposition of financial burdens for disciplinary purposes."[43] Thus, the contractually required membership that the Act authorizes does not vest union disciplinary control over the employees.

In *Sandsberry* v. *International Association of Machinists*,[44] decided by the Texas Supreme Court shortly after the *Hanson* decision, the limited nature of the type of union security agreement authorized by the RLA was made explicit. Plaintiffs had argued that because of the disciplinary power the union exercised over them by virtue of their compelled membership, their First Amendment rights were being violated, and that Section 2, Eleventh,

---

is required. Clearly, formal membership is contemplated under the closed shop, and, if the only difference between the closed shop and the union shop is the timing of the required membership, then this suggests that formal membership is also required under the union shop. This, however, is probably reading too much into the Court's casual distinction between the closed shop and the kind of union security agreement allowed under the statute.

[38] *Id.* at 231.

[39] *Id.* at 235 (emphasis added).

[40] *Id.* at 236-37.

[41] *Id.* at 238.

[42] *Id.*

[43] *Id.* at 235.

[44] 156 Tex. 340, 295 S.W.2d 412 (1956).

was therefore unconstitutional. The Texas Supreme Court rejected the major premise of this argument:

> Petitioners vigorously urge that the proposed contract makes the absolute requirement that nonunion employees become full union members. But it no more requires full union membership than does the contract in *Hanson* and as expressly held in that case the contract does not compel full union membership.
>
> . . .
>
> [T]he membership requirements of this contract and of the union shop statute are merely formal and fictional aside from the financial obligation. . . .
>
> . . .
>
> The unwilling employee need assume no pledge of conformity nor promise of obedience, nor even make application for membership to retain employment under the union shop contract.[45]

Subsequently, in *International Association of Machinists* v. *Street*,[46] the United States Supreme Court again repeatedly emphasized that the only congressional purpose in authorizing union security agreements was to eliminate the so-called free rider.[47] After reviewing the legislative history, the Court noted:

> The conclusion to which this history clearly points is that § 2, Eleventh contemplated compulsory unionism to force employees to share the costs of negotiating and administering collective agreements, and the costs of the adjustment and settlement of disputes. One looks in vain for any suggestion that Congress also meant in § 2, Eleventh to provide the unions with a means for forcing employees, over their objection, to support political causes which they oppose.[48]

The same could be said of the employee's right to be free from union disciplinary control. Since the purpose was only to eliminate the so-called free rider, it is erroneous to conclude that the union security agreement authorization of Section 2, Eleventh, was meant to provide the unions with a means of forcing employees, over their objections, to comply with the union's purely internal rules.

Finally, in the recent case of *Marden* v. *International Association of Machinists*,[49] a federal district court in Florida held,

---

[45] *Id.* at 344-45, 295 S.W.2d at 414-16.

[46] 367 U.S. 740 (1961).

[47] *Id.* at 750-51, 753, 755, 761, 764.

[48] *Id.* at 763-64.

[49] 78 CCH Lab. Cas. ¶ 11,412 (S.D. Fla. 1976).

specifically and without equivocation, that under the Act an employee can be required to become nothing more than an "agency fee payor." The court recognized that the statute purported to authorize a requirement of membership, but explained this as follows:

> In order to pass constitutional standards, however, the concept of "membership" has been peculiarly defined. As judicially interpreted, the term does not connote formal membership, but refers only to the duty of workers to give financial support to unions legally authorized to act as their collective bargaining agents.[50]

After so holding, the court took one additional and extremely important step. It noted that under the collective bargaining agreement, employees were required to "join the union" and to maintain "membership in good standing." This, the court concluded, "artificially induces uninformed employees to become formal members," since from the language of the agreement "a new employee . . . could draw only the conclusion that formal union membership is a condition of his employment." The court thus held that the agreement violated the Railway Labor Act and required the employer to "provide adequate notice to new employees of the availability of the agency fee payor status," notwithstanding the language of the existing contract.

The holding of the *Marden* court on this issue reflects a proper effectuation of congressional intent and of the Supreme Court decisions previously discussed. Most union security agreements under both the RLA and the Taft-Hartley Act (including the NLRB's so-called model union security agreement) strongly suggest that actual membership is a condition of employment. It is only those employees who happen to be well versed in the nuances of statutory construction that benefit from the law's prohibition of compulsory union membership in the literal sense. Clearly, the *Marden* doctrine should be affirmed; moreover, it should also be applied in the context of the LMRA—a step that the National Labor Relations Board has declined to take.

---

[50] *Id.* at 20,860-61.

CHAPTER VI

Compulsory Dues and Non-Collective Bargaining Purposes

The primary function of a labor union is to represent employees in collective bargaining with their common employer. Historically, labor unions have also engaged in a wide range of other activities on behalf of their members—sponsoring social events, providing insurance and other kinds of group benefits, financing political candidates, publishing newspapers, supporting charities, lobbying on matters of concern to labor, and a myriad of similar undertakings. When labor unions were purely private, voluntary associations, all of these activities were financed with similarly voluntary membership dues. If a member objected either to the union's mode of bargaining or to its choice of political candidates, then he could simply withdraw his financial support of these activities by cancelling his membership.

All of this changed, however, when Congress made majority unions the statutory agent of *all* employees in a given unit and authorized the negotiation of labor agreements requiring membership (in the form of financial support) in the union as a condition of continued employment. Armed with the extraordinary power of legal coercion, unions became more secure in their financial base, which also enabled them to increase the quantity if not the quality of their activities. No longer, however, did the dissident employee have the option of withdrawing his financial support of those activities to which he objected—or so it might have appeared to an employee prior to 1961.

THE USE OF COMPULSORY DUES FOR POLITICAL PURPOSES

The first crack in the apparent authority of unions to spend compulsory dues as they saw fit arose in the context of union political activity. It is understandable how expenditures of this kind could be expected to precipitate challenge among compulsory dues payors. An employee who has voted against the union and who fails to appreciate the employment benefits that the union has supposedly obtained for him will naturally resent paying any money to the union, but when the money is being used to finance political causes which he detests, an especially sensitive nerve is touched. The use of compulsorily obtained monies for such purposes offends our deeply held values of political liberty and freedom of speech.

This, in part, was the contention of the employees in *Railway Employees' Department* v. *Hanson*,[1] who challenged the compulsory unionism provisions of the Railway Labor Act on the grounds, *inter alia,* that money obtained in this fashion was being spent to support political ideas and candidates with which the employees disagreed, in violation of their First and Fifth Amendment rights. In that case, however, the Supreme Court held that there was nothing in trial record to show the extent to which the union was spending its money for political purposes, what those political purposes were, or that the employees in question were in fact opposed to them. The Court, thus, did not reach the issue of the constitutional propriety of using compulsory dues in that fashion. On the other hand, the Court did hold with respect to nonpolitical spending that "the requirement for financial support of the collective bargaining agency by all who receive the benefits of its work is within the power of Congress under the Commerce Clause and does not violate either the First or the Fifth Amendments." [2]

The question that the Court avoided in *Hanson*, however, was to arise again—this time with a full documented record of the union's political activities and of the plaintiffs' objections thereto. In *International Association of Machinists* v. *Street*,[3] the use of compulsory dues for political purposes was again challenged on constitutional grounds. Although in this case the Court did hold that a union cannot, over an employee's objection, spend his money for political causes which he opposes, the Court determined this as a matter of statutory interpretation rather than constitutional law.

---

[1] 351 U.S. 225 (1959).

[2] *Id.* at 238.

[3] 367 U.S. 740 (1961).

There is nothing specific in either the Railway Labor Act (under which this case was litigated) or the Taft-Hartley Act with respect to how a labor union can use the fees it obtains under a union security agreement. In reading such a prohibition into the statute, the Court was clearly influenced by the maxim that "Federal statutes are to be so construed as to avoid serious doubt of their constitutionality" [4]—in most instances, regardless of whether there is any actual legislative intent in this regard. To this extent, the *Street* decision is thus susceptible to a fairly narrow reading. One could argue that it stands for the proposition that the statute only prohibits a union from spending compulsory dues in such a way as would otherwise violate the First Amendment, for example, political or ideological purposes. The specific holding of the case is limited to such spending, and the Court expressly refused to decide whether the statute also proscribes "other union expenditures objected to by an employee and not made to meet the costs of negotiation and administration of collective agreements. . . ." [5]

On the other hand, the remainder of the *Street* opinion serves as an effective rebuttal to the contention that the Court was merely supplying congressional intent so as to avoid constitutional infirmity. The rather lengthy discussion of the legislative history of the union security provisions of the Railway Labor Act suggests that the Court believed that Congress had a specific and narrow purpose in allowing union security agreements, and that the use of compulsory dues for political causes was clearly extraneous to and inconsistent with that congressional purpose:

> The history of union security in the railway industry is marked *first,* by a strong and longstanding tradition of voluntary unionism on the part of the standard rail unions; *second,* by the declaration in 1934 of a congressional policy of complete freedom of choice of employees to join or not to join a union; *third,* by the modification of the firm legislative policy against compulsion, *but only as a specific response to the recognition of the expenses and burdens incurred by the unions in the administration of the complex scheme of the Railway Labor Act.*[6]

The Court proceeded to substantiate those three points in some detail, with particular emphasis being given to the third contention:

---

[4] *Id.* at 749.

[5] *Id.* at 769.

[6] *Id.* at 750-51 (emphasis partially added).

The conclusion to which this history clearly points is that § 2, Eleventh contemplated compulsory unionism to force employees to share the costs of negotiating and administering collective agreements, and the costs of the adjustment and settlement of disputes.[7]

That was the Court's broad theory, from which it followed *a fortiori* that Congress did not intend to authorize the spending of compulsory dues for political purposes—a subsidiary conclusion which the Court documented with specific additional references to the legislative history and which thus formed the literal holding of the Court. Nevertheless, it is submitted that the significance of the case lies not so much in its holding as in the rationale used by the Court to get there.

THE STREET *DOCTRINE AND UNION SECURITY AGREEMENTS UNDER THE TAFT-HARTLEY ACT*

The *Street* decision was rendered under the Railway Labor Act, and the case did not address itself to the specific question of whether the Taft-Hartley Act should be similarly construed. To the extent that *Street* is to be read as a quasi-constitutional decision—as imposing a prohibition against political spending only because the Railway Labor Act would otherwise be unconstitutional—a different result might be reached under the Taft-Hartley Act. This is because the theory that the Supreme Court has used for subjecting RLA-negotiated union security agreements to constitutional scrutiny is a theory that is arguably inapplicable in a Taft-Hartley Act context. Rather, it has been suggested that union security agreements under the Taft-Hartley retain their ostensibly private character and are thus conceptually incapable of even being considered unconstitutional.[8] That being the case, there is no basis for reading such a prohibition into an Act that is otherwise silent on the subject. The Tenth Circuit, in *Reid* v. *McDonnell Douglas Corp.*,[9] adopted this approach in denying that the use of compulsory dues for political purposes, pursuant to a Taft-Hartley Act union security agreement, raised any direct constitutional issues.

On the other hand, to the extent that *Street* can be read, not only as a statement of the minimum limits the constitution re-

---

[7] *Id.* at 763-64.

[8] *See generally* Chapter XI, *infra.*

[9] 443 F.2d 408 (10th Cir. 1971).

quires be imposed but also as a statement of what additional limits Congress did in fact impose upon unions in spending compulsory dues, then the *Street* doctrine is equally germane in a Taft-Hartley Act context. It is clear from the legislative histories of both the Taft-Hartley Act and the 1951 amendments to the Railway Labor Act that Congress intended to allow the same kind of union security agreement under both Acts, and for the same reason—to insure that the recipients of the benefits of union-negotiated and administered collective agreements paid their pro rata share of the expenses of this service.[10] Since the *Street* doctrine flows essentially from this theory, which is as applicable to the Taft-Hartley Act as it is to the Railway Labor Act, it would seem to follow that the doctrine itself is equally applicable to both statutes.

The *Street* doctrine has in fact been applied to the expenditures of unions acting under the aegis of the Taft-Hartley Act. Indeed, in this context the underpinnings of the doctrine have even been expanded somewhat. In the *Reid* [11] case, for example, the court noted that the plaintiffs' claim was "couched in terms of a breach of the UAW's 'fiduciary duty . . . to use [the plaintiffs' dues] for purposes reasonably necessary and germane to collective bargaining only' and that expenditures for political 'doctrines and candidates' opposed by plaintiffs constitutes a violation of that duty." [12] This had reference to the duty of fair representation, which is a well-established doctrine under both the Railway Labor Act and the Taft-Hartley Act, and the court held that a political-spending objection so predicated was at least sufficient to give the district court jurisdiction to hear the suit.

On the other hand, in *Seay* v. *McDonnell Douglas Corp.*,[13] another Taft-Hartley Act case, the court took a slightly different tack. There the court noted:

> The Supreme Court has said as clearly as possible that agency fees exacted from employees under the terms of the bargaining agreement must be limited to use in sharing the costs with other dues of "negotiating and administering collective agreements, and the costs of the adjudgment [*sic*] and settlement of disputes." This limitation is read into the statute under the terms of which the

---

[10] *See generally* Chapters III and V, *supra.*

[11] 443 F.2d 408 (10th Cir. 1971).

[12] *Id.* at 411.

[13] 427 F.2d 996 (9th Cir. 1970).

collective bargaining agreement, with its agency fee provision, was entered into in this case. We find that the limitation asserted here does in fact constitute an implied term of the contract. A provision in the collective bargaining agreement authorizing the expenditure of agency fees for political uses would immediately run afoul of the congressional intent delineated in *Street* and the express holding in both *Street* and *Allen*.[14]

On the basis of these decisions it would thus appear that the *Street* doctrine is fully applicable to union expenditures financed by compulsory dues under both the Railway Labor Act and the Taft-Hartley Act.

THE APPROPRIATE REMEDY FOR A STREET-*DOCTRINE* VIOLATION

One of the issues that the *Street* decision left unresolved was that of framing the appropriate remedy. In this regard, the Court suggested that the lower court might either enjoin the union from spending a proportionate amount of its political activities budget or order that each protesting employee be reimbursed that portion of his agency shop fee that was actually being used for political purposes. Both remedies would have involved a detailed audit of the union's books, and rather than submit to this the unions in the *Street* case simply waived the plaintiffs' obligation to pay the agency shop fee.

Subsequently, in *Brotherhood of Railway Clerks* v. *Allen*,[15] the Supreme Court again addressed itself to the problem of an appropriate remedy and suggested a decree ordering

> (1) the refund to [the plaintiff] of a portion of the exacted funds in the same proportion that union political expenditures bear to total union expenditures, and (2) a reduction of future such exactions from him by the same proportion.[16]

But the Court then went on to recognize the practical difficulties of such judicially administered relief and suggested that unions

> consider the adoption . . . of some voluntary plan by which dissenters would be afforded an internal union remedy. . . . If a union agreed upon a formula for ascertaining the proportion of political expenditures in its budget, and made available a simple procedure

---

[14] *Id.* at 1000-01.

[15] 373 U.S. 113 (1963).

[16] *Id.* at 122. The appropriateness of this remedy was recently reaffirmed in Abood v. Detroit Board of Education, 45 U.S.L.W. 4473 (1977).

for allowing dissenters to be excused from having to pay this proportion of moneys due from them under the union-shop agreement, prolonged and expensive litigation might well be averted.[17]

The unions, however, were slow to respond to the Supreme Court's suggestion, and employees whose agency shop fees were being spent, over their objections, for political causes they opposed were again forced to seek judicial vindication of their rights. In *Seay* v. *McDonnell Douglas*[18] and *Reid* v. *McDonnell Douglas Corp.*,[19] the employees sought an injunction against the union, together with the restitution of that portion of their agency shop fees that had been spent for political activities. After the initiation of these suits, the IAM and the UAW both established internal procedures whereby employees could seek to obtain a rebate on their dues. The unions then asserted that the implementation of an intra-union remedy, as suggested by *Allen*, provided the plaintiffs with all the relief to which they were entitled, and that the cases should thereby be dismissed as moot.

In the *Reid* case, the Tenth Circuit Court of Appeals accepted the union's argument. The court had taken jurisdiction of the case under the theory that the use of agency shop fees for political purposes was a breach of the union's duty of fair representation, and the court proceeded to evaluate the union's rebate plan under the same theory. The court thus concluded that since the plaintiffs had not availed themselves of this remedy or otherwise proved that the plan was "unfair, unreasonable, and unworkable,"[20] no claim of unfair representation had been made out. The district court's summary judgment in favor of the union was thus affirmed.

In the *Seay* case, however, the Ninth Circuit Court of Appeals reached a contrary conclusion on virtually identical facts. The plaintiffs challenged the IAM rebate plan on essentially two grounds. First, they alleged that while under the *Allen* case the union has the burden of proof in establishing the percentage of an employee's fees the union is entitled to retain, under

---

[17] 373 U.S. at 122-23.

[18] 427 F.2d 996 (9th Cir. 1970), *further proceedings*, 371 F. Supp. 754 (C.D. Cal. 1973), *rev'd*, 92 L.R.R.M. 2063 (9th Cir. 1976).

[19] 443 F.2d 408 (10th Cir. 1971), *further proceedings sub nom*, Reid v. Auto Workers Local 1093, 80 L.R.R.M. 2886 (N.D. Okla. 1972), *aff'd*, 479 F.2d 517 (10th Cir. 1973), *cert. denied*, 414 U.S. 1076 (1973).

[20] 479 F.2d at 520.

the IAM procedures the burden was placed on the employee to challenge the amount which the union claims it spends on political activities. And second, in the words of the court, the employees also alleged that

> the union will not fairly and honestly determine the amount of the rebate. Plaintiffs contend that the accounting procedures utilized by the union mask many political expenditures. They also argue that many records have been concealed or destroyed. Thus, they argue that the union cannot be depended upon to fairly determine the amount to which plaintiffs are entitled and that judicial supervision is required.[21]

Apparently impressed by the dilatoriness of the union in establishing the rebate plan in the first place and with its attempt to shift the burden of proof onto the dissenting employees, the court concluded that the district court had erred in its summary disposition of the question of the fairness and adequacy of the intra-union remedy. The district court was thus instructed to hold a hearing on that issue.

In sum, while the Supreme Court in *Street* held that an employee has a statutory (and possibly a constitutional) right not to have his agency shop fees spent on political causes to which he objects, the vindication of that right has been slow and somewhat uncertain. Whether intra-union rebate plans, suggested by the Court in *Allen,* will prove to be an effective and fair remedy remains to be seen.

In all probability, the problem of having compulsory dues used to finance the various political activities of labor unions is a problem that will have to be resolved legislatively, with the government asssuming a prosecutorial role, rather than through the *Street*-type individual suits that are costly, time-consuming, and of dubious efficacy. The existing Federal Election Campaign Act[22] is, however, inadequate to this task; the Act's various exceptions serve as a virtual encouragement to the very kind of political activities the *Street* doctrine was designed to curb.

THE USE OF COMPULSORY DUES FOR NONPOLITICAL PURPOSES

Another issue expressly left open by the *Street* decision was whether compulsory dues could be used to finance union ac-

---

[21] 92 L.R.R.M. at 2067.

[22] 2 U.S.C. §§ 437, 455 (1974).

tivities which, though not political, did not directly involve the negotiation and administration of collective bargaining agreements. The ultimate resolution of that issue may well turn on which of the two rationales advanced in *Street* is deemed the controlling one. The first rationale, which presumes the unconstitutionality only of political expenditures, would tend to suggest that the court was dividing union expenses into two categories: (1) those that are political and thus invoke the spectre of the First Amendment; and (2) all others. Under this view, an agency-fee payor could object only to the union's use of his money for political purposes.

Under the second rationale, which asserts that Congress allowed the compulsory extraction of dues only to the extent of offsetting the union's costs in discharging its statutory duties as the collective bargaining representative, the division would be rather different: (1) expenses to defray the cost of contract negotiation and administration, and (2) all others, including but not limited to politically related expenses.

In the recent case of *Ellis* v. *Brotherhood of Railway Clerks*,[23] a United States District Court in California adopted this latter approach and held that "the Railway Labor Act prohibits the use of fees and dues for non-collective bargaining purposes and activities, over protest from a represented employee."[24] The court then proceeded to list the activities of this union which the protesting employees could not be compelled to support financially:

(1) Recreational, social and entertainment expenses for activities not attended by management personnel of Western Airlines.

(2) Operation of a death benefit program.

(3) Organizing and recruiting new members for BRAC among Western Airlines bargaining unit employees.

(4) Organizing and recruiting new members for BRAC, and/or seeking collective bargaining authority or recognition for:

(a) employees not employed by Western Airlines;
(b) employees not employed in the air transportation industry;
(c) employees not employed in other transportation industries.

(5) Publications in which substantial coverage is devoted to general news, recreational and social activities, political and legislative matters, and cartoons.

---

[23] 91 L.R.R.M. 2339 (S.D. Cal. 1976).

[24] *Id.* at 2343.

   (6) Contributions to charities and individuals.

   (7) Programs to provide insurance, and medical and legal services to the BRAC membership or portions thereof, other than such programs secured for its salaried officers and employees.

   (8) Conducting and attending conventions of BRAC.

   (9) Conducting and attending conventions of other organizations and/or labor unions.

  (10) Defense or prosecution of litigation not having as its subject matter the negotiation or administration of collective bargaining agreements or settlement or adjustment of grievances or disputes of employees represented by BRAC.

  (11) Support for or opposition to proposed, pending, or existing legislative measures.

  (12) Support for or opposition to proposed, pending, or existing governmental executive orders or decisions." [25]

It is submitted that the *Ellis* decision, which draws its validity from the second rationale of the *Street* opinion, represents a sound construction of the Railway Labor Act and should also be extended to the National Labor Relations Act. Under both acts, an individual employee is deprived of his common-law right to negotiate his own terms and conditions of employment; instead, if a majority of his fellow employees so decide, the labor union becomes his statutory agent. The involuntary agency relationship which Congress created was, however, an extremely limited one. The union is the individual's agent only for the purpose of negotiating and administering collective agreements which establish the wages, hours, and working conditions of the employment relationship. Clearly, the union is not the statutory agent of the employee with respect to any of the matters listed by the court in *Ellis*.

When a union negotiates an agency-fee clause with an employer and then uses the extracted money for non-collective bargaining activities, the union has become the de facto agent of the employees for these activities—which is clearly not what Congress intended. Rather, as the Court in *Street* recognized, the amount of money that a union can extract under an agency-fee clause is limited by the scope of the union's statutory agency functions: contract negotiation and administration. To the extent that the union engages in other activities, it does so as a purely voluntary, fraternal organization, and the money that

---

[25] *Id.* at 2342.

it uses to engage in these activities must come from those who choose to associate with the union in that capacity. As was established earlier, however, the Act itself does not compel such membership directly or indirectly.

The *Ellis* case arose under the Railway Labor Act, and thus far this issue has not been specifically litigated under the Taft-Hartley Act. The issue has arisen indirectly in Taft-Hartley Act contexts, and the results here are apparently at odds with the *Ellis* approach.

In *Teamsters Local 959*,[26] the National Labor Relations Board held that a union security agreement could not be used to extract money from employees for the purpose of financing a credit union and building program. The Board held that the payment of money for that purpose could not be made a condition of employment under a Section 8(a)(3) union security agreement because the union was using the money "to accomplish ends not encompassed in its duties as a collective-bargaining agent of the employees."[27] Using an analysis remarkably similar to that used by the Supreme Court in *Street,* the Board noted that Congress had allowed the compulsory payment of union dues only as a means of compensating the union for the performance of its statutory duties on behalf of the employees who allegedly benefit thereby. What the union does in its institutional capacity on behalf of its formal membership, however, is not something for which it can expect compensation from the nonmember employees in the bargaining unit.

The *Local 959* decision was subsequently overruled by the Board. In *Detroit Mailers Union*,[28] the Board noted that "neither on its face nor in the congressional purpose behind this provision [Section 8(a)(3)] can any warrant be found for making any distinction here between dues which may be allocated for collective bargaining purposes and those earmarked for institutional expenses of the union. . . ."[29]

Judicial authority under the Taft-Hartley Act is equally limited, but it too suggests a result contrary to that reached in *Ellis.* In *NLRB* v. *Local 138, Operating Engineers*,[30] the issue was

---

[26] 167 N.L.R.B. 1042 (1967).

[27] *Id.* at 1044.

[28] 192 N.L.R.B. 951 (1971).

[29] *Id.* at 952.

[30] 385 F.2d 874 (2d Cir. 1967).

whether the amount of a hiring hall fee could be equal to the formal membership dues for a month, which would thus compensate the union for both its collective bargaining and its institutional expenses, or whether the amount of such a fee was limited to a pro rata share of collective bargaining expenses alone. The court held the latter to be the case, on the grounds that otherwise this would be tantamount to a union security agreement in violation of the statutory limitations thereof; all of which suggests that, in the view of this court, a true union security agreement could compel the payment of money from employees to finance the non-collective bargaining, institutional activities of unions.

Neither of these cases involved a true *Street*-doctrine cause-of-action because what the Board and the court said about using compulsory dues for non-collective bargaining purposes was within an entirely different legal context, and these cases should have little if any precedent value in a Taft-Hartley Act, *Ellis* type of litigation. Apart from all of that, each of them is arguably wrong!

The issues with respect to union expenditures that are neither political nor for purely collective bargaining purposes remain open under both the Taft-Hartley Act and the Railway Labor Act. The uncertainty of the law on this point was made quite clear in the recent case of *Abood* v. *Detroit Board of Education*.[31] Here, the Court was called upon to apply the *Street* doctrine within the context of union security agreements covering public employees, but what the Court said about *Street* is of universal application.

On the one hand, the Court in *Abood* reiterated the *Street*-decision rationale that "since *only* expenditures related to the union's functions in negotiating and administering the collective bargaining agreement and adjusting grievances and disputes fell within 'the reasons . . . accepted by Congress why authority to make union shop agreements was justified,' "[32] the use of union dues for political purposes was necessarily beyond the scope of what Congress allowed. This suggests that *Street* prohibits all non-collective bargaining expenses regardless of whether they are political or not.

---

[31] 45 U.S.L.W. 4473 (1977).

[32] International Ass'n of Machinists v. Street, 367 U.S. 740, 768 (1961) quoted *Id.* at 4476 (emphasis added).

On the other hand, the Court in *Abood* also seemed to read *Street* as a constitutionally required decision rather than as one mirroring any implied congressional intent to limit the use of compulsory dues to purely collective bargaining purposes. For example, the Court noted that "indeed, *Street* embraced an interpretation of the Railway Labor Act not without its difficulties, . . . precisely to avoid facing the constitutional issues presented by the use of union-shop dues for political and ideological purposes unrelated to collective bargaining." [33] This would tend to suggest that the *Street* doctrine applies only to non-collective bargaining expenses that might violate the First Amendment.

Although there is language in the *Abood* decision to support either view, the Court itself specifically refused to address itself to the issue:

> The appellants' complaints also alleged that the Union carries on various "social activities" which are not open to nonmembers. It is unclear to what extent such activities fall outside the Union's duties as exclusive representative or involve constitutionally protected rights of association. Without greater specificity in the description of such activities and the benefit of adversary argument, we leave those questions in the first instance to the Michigan courts.[34]

---

[33] *Id.* at 4479.

[34] *Id.* at 4480 n. 33.

CHAPTER VII

Section 14(b) and the Scope of Right-to-Work Laws

Congressional reaction against the abuses of compulsory unionism led not only to an affirmative prohibition of the closed shop and the true union shop, but also to an express acknowledgment that the states retained the power to outlaw all of the various forms of union security, even those which Congress chose not to prohibit. This was accomplished in Section 14(b) of the Labor-Management Relations Act:

> Nothing in this Act shall be construed as authorizing the execution or application of agreements requiring membership in a labor organization as a condition of employment in any State or Territory in which such execution or application is prohibited by State or Territorial law.[1]

THE LEGISLATIVE HISTORY

The legislative history of Section 14(b) actually begins with the Wagner Act of 1935. The Wagner Act contained a provision that exempted all forms of union security from the prohibitions of Section 8(3). While the Wagner Act did not contain anything equivalent to the present Section 14(b), the Wagner Act Congress did not intend for Section 8(3) to preempt the states of their power to regulate or prohibit union security agreements. The Senate Report stated that

> the bill does nothing to facilitate closed-shop agreements or to make them legal in any State where they may be illegal; it does not interfere with the *status quo* on this debatable subject but leaves the way open to such agreements as might now legally be consummated.[2]

---

[1] 29 U.S.C. § 164(b) (1970).

[2] S. Rep. No. 573, 74th Cong., 1st Sess. 12 (1935).

Other portions of the legislative history are equally explicit on this point.[3] Apart from imposing the requirement that union security agreements be negotiated by a majority union not dominated by the employer—and in this regard, more permissive state laws would clearly be preempted—Congress chose to adopt a "hands off" attitude and deferred to the various state laws with regard to the legality and enforceability of these agreements. It is against this background that Section 14(b) must be read.

The original version of what was to become Section 14(b) appeared in Section 13 of House Bill 3020.[4] This section, which is somewhat lengthier than the present Section 14(b), states that the Act should not be construed to invalidate any state law which restricts the right of an employer and a union to enter into a union security agreement, and that "such agreements shall, in addition to being subject to any applicable preventive provisions of this Act, be subject to the operation and effect of such State laws and constitutional provisions as well."

The orginal Senate bill was silent in this regard. The Senate conferees, however, apparently agreed with the House that something affirmative should be said about the continued validity of state laws affecting the legality and enforceability of union security agreements. This was deemed necessary because despite the clear intent of the Wagner Act Congress, in 1948 it was said to be an open question whether Section 8(3) of the Wagner Act was totally preemptive of state laws affecting union security.[5] The Supreme Court later answered that in the negative; [6] but in 1947, Congress itself felt constrained to make explicit its continued adherence to the Wagner Act policy of allowing the states virtually unfettered freedom to follow their own policies on imposing legal restrictions on the various types of union security agreements. The House Conference Report, for example, summed it up in these terms:

> It was never the intention of the National Labor Relations Act [the Wagner Act], as is disclosed by the legislative history of that

---

[3] *See* H.R. Rep. No. 969, 74th Cong., 1st Sess. 17 (1935); 79 Cong. Rec. 7570, 7673, 74th Cong., 1st Sess. (1935) (remarks of Senator Wagner); *id.* at 9726 (remarks of Representative Connery).

[4] Legislative History of the Labor Management Relations Act, 1947 at 80 (1974) [hereinafter cited as Legis. Hist. LMRA].

[5] *See* Legis. Hist. LMRA at 335.

[6] Algoma Plywood Co. v. Wisconsin Employment Relations Board, 336 U.S. 301 (1948).

act, to preempt the field in this regard so as to deprive the States of their powers to prevent compulsory unionism. Neither the so-called "closed shop" proviso in section 8(3) of the existing act nor the union shop and maintenance of membership proviso in section 8(a)(3) of the conference agreement could be said to authorize arrangements of this sort in states where such arrangements were contrary to the state policy. To make certain that there should be no question about this, section 13 was included in the House bill. The conference agreement, in section 14(b), contains a provision having the same effect.[7]

For the proponents of Section 14(b), it was apparently enough to argue that this section was merely a continuation of the Wagner Act policy of noninterference with state law. The legislative history reveals no independent reexamination of that policy strictly on the merits. Moreover, it is probable that the proponents of Section 14(b) anticipated or at least hoped that this express invitation to the states would be acted upon, and that this would achieve a broader prohibition of compulsory unionism than could be achieved through Congress directly.

With the possible exception of Senator Morse, the opponents of Section 14(b) were equally abstract in their opposition. It goes without saying that the members of Congress who were opposed to the prohibition of the closed shop were *a fortiori* also opposed to the authorization to the states to prohibit other forms of union security, simply because they, like the proponents of the section, believed that certain states would be encouraged to take advantage of this. Senator Morse expressed this fear quite openly.[8] For the most part, however, the stated objection to Section 14(b) was that this allowance to the states was destructive of a desired uniformity of federal labor policy and that it constituted a dereliction of the federal responsibility for interstate commerce; and this was, moreover, the objection to Section 14(b) which President Truman mentioned in the veto message.[9]

This general outline of the legislative history of Section 14(b) reveals a broad and pervasive policy of deferring to all state prohibitions against the various forms of compulsory unionism. The insights which the legislative history provided on specific legal issues will be dealt with in the context of a discussion of

---

[7] LEGIS. HIST. LMRA at 564; *see also* 335, 371, 412, 564, 1596-97.

[8] LEGIS. HIST. LMRA at 1561.

[9] LEGIS. HIST. LMRA at 665, 920-21, 1561, 1613, 1615.

those issues. In all events, however, these specific issues and the legislative history pertaining to them must be viewed from the perspective of this more general legislative intent.

UNION SECURITY AGREEMENTS AND STATE JURISDICTION

Undoubtedly, one of the most important questions posed by Section 14(b) pertains to exactly what kinds of union security agreements the states are left free to prohibit. The closed shop, the union shop, the agency shop, maintenance-of-membership, preferential hiring, the checkoff, and hiring hall arrangements are all forms of union security or are closely related thereto. But which of these fall within the compass of Section 14(b)?

The Closed Shop

Unlike other, less compulsory forms of union security, the closed shop is affirmatively prohibited by the federal act. The question, however, is whether the states may also outlaw this form of union security. This question arises because as a general matter, state laws are preempted from regulating conduct that the federal act itself affirmatively prohibits. In *Garmon,* the Supreme Court stated this general rule of preemption:

> If the Board decides . . . that conduct is protected by § 7, *or prohibited by § 8,* then the matter is at an end, and the States are ousted of all jurisdiction.[10]

Relying exclusively on the *Garmon* line of preemption cases, the Supreme Court of Iowa thus recently concluded that since

> it is settled beyond argument that a "closed shop" variety of union-security agreement is "outlawed" and prohibited by section 8(a)(3) of the NLRA, . . . Jurisdiction of controversies arising from activities in connection with such agreements is in the exclusive jurisdiction of the NLRB. . . .[11]

The Iowa court's failure to recognize that the *Garmon* doctrine is subordinate to Section 14(b)'s specific relinquishment of exclusive jurisdiction and then to consider the "closed shop" issue from that perspective must be questioned. Literally applied, after

---

[10] San Diego Building Trades Council v. Garmon, 359 U.S. 236, 245 (1959) (emphasis added); *see also* Amalgamated Ass'n of Street Employees v. Lockridge, 403 U.S. 274 (1971).

[11] Walles v. IBEW Local 405, 252 N.W. 2d 701, 710 (Iowa 1977).

the manner of the Iowa court, the *Garmon* doctrine would preempt state jurisdiction over even the modified union shop or agency shop kinds of union security agreements because they are certainly permitted or, to use the *Garmon* language, "protected" by the statute. Obviously, however, Section 14(b) voids the operation of the *Garmon* doctrine with respect to those kinds of agreements; and the critical question is, why does it not also void *Garmon* with respect to the federally prohibited kinds?

This was the conclusion that the Supreme Court of Arizona had reached earlier in *Sheet Metal Workers* v. *Nichols*.[12] The court there conceded that as a general proposition, the *Garmon* doctrine would appear to preempt state jurisdiction over closed shop arrangements. But the court went on to hold that Section 14(b) is a special exception; thus, where the acts prohibited by federal law are also acts prohibited by state right-to-work laws, there is concurrent jurisdiction between the state and federal authorities. According to this line of reasoning, the states could prohibit the closed shop.

The legislative history of Section 14(b) certainly supports this conclusion in its specific language and because of the broad policy of nonpreemption which it evidences. For example, the House Conference Report indicates that the purpose of Section 14(b) was

> to assure that nothing in the act was to be construed as authorizing any *closed shop,* union shop, maintenance of membership, or other form of compulsory unionism in any State where the execution of *such agreement* [*e.g.*, the closed shop] would be contrary to State law. Many States have enacted laws or adopted constitutional provisions to make *all* forms of compulsory unionism [*e.g.*, the closed shop] in those States illegal.[13]

Likewise, Section 13 of the original House Bill, of which the present Section 14(b) is but a condensation, expressly provided that agreements requiring labor union membership as a condition of employment "shall, in addition to being subject to any applicable preventive provisions of this Act [*e.g.*, those which outlawed the closed shop], be subject to the operation and effect of . . . States laws and constitutional provisions as well." [14] In commenting on this, the House Report notes that "by Section 13 the

---

[12] 89 Ariz. 187, 360 P.2d 204 (1961).

[13] LEGIS. HIST. LMRA at 564 (emphasis added).

[14] LEGIS. HIST. LMRA at 81 (emphasis added).

United States expressly declares the subject of compulsory union-ism one that the States may regulate concurrently with the United States. . . ." [15]

On the other hand, the House Conference Report does note that "where State law covering union security agreements is more rigorous than the policy expressed in the bill, such State law shall be unaffected." [16] While this could arguably be con-strued as suggesting that only the "more rigorous" state prohi-bitions were going to be deferred to, it is more plausible to assume that the report was worded in this way to emphasize the fact that the states retained the power to do what Congress itself chose not to do—*i.e.*, prohibit compulsory unionism entirely.

The argument that the states are preempted from prohibiting the closed shop proceeds on the assumption that the scope of Section 14(b) must necessarily be determined by the scope of the Section 8(a)(3) proviso. In other words, under Section 14(b) the states can prohibit only what is affirmatively permitted by Section 8(a)(3); and since the closed shop is not permitted under Section 8(a)(3), the states are without the power to pro-hibit it. The argument purports to be a corollary of the rationale of *Retail Clerks Local 1625* v. *Schermerhorn*, in which the Su-preme Court held that because the agency shop was permitted by the proviso, a state right-to-work law could prohibit it. The Supreme Court, however, did not pass on the converse of that—*i.e.*, if it is not permitted, it is also not prohibitable. Indeed, the Court expressly declined to do so:

> The connection between the § 8(a)(3) proviso and § 14(b) is clear. *Whether they are perfectly coincident, we need not now decide,* but unquestionably they overlap to some extent.[17]

The state legislatures have consistently assumed a power to prohibit the closed shop, as will be revealed by an examination of the various state right-to-work laws, and this power has never been seriously questioned at the federal level.

The True *Union Shop*

Since the Taft-Hartley amendments to Section 8(a)(3) had the effect of outlawing the *true* union shop along with the closed shop, the power of the states under Section 14(b) to prohibit also

---

[15] LEGIS. HIST. LMRA at 325 (emphasis added).

[16] LEGIS. HIST. LMRA at 1586 (emphasis added).

[17] 373 U.S. 746, 751 (1963).

the true union shop is subject to the same preemption argument as was previously advanced with respect to the closed shop. But the argument should be rejected because the scope of Section 14(b) is not perfectly coincident with or determined exclusively by what is permitted under the Section 8(a)(3) proviso; rather, Congress intended to follow a thorough-going policy of nonpreemption even if this resulted in concurrent or overlapping state and federal jurisdiction over certain types of union security agreements.

The Modified Union Shop

Assuming for the sake of argument that the most compulsory form of union security agreement that the federal act itself does not prohibit (which might be called the *modified union shop agreement*) is somehow different than the true "agency shop," if not in its actual effect then in its wording, then this form of union security is clearly within the power of the states to prohibit.

The Agency Shop

Under an agency shop arrangement, an employee is not actually required to become a formal member of the union as a condition of continued employment; he is merely required to pay the equivalent of dues or a service fee. Since Section 14(b) only authorizes states to outlaw "agreements requiring *membership* in a labor organization as a condition of employment," the question arose over whether the states had authority to outlaw an agency shop provision.

This issue was definitively resolved by the Supreme Court in *Retail Clerks Local 1625* v. *Schermerhorn* [18] in 1963. In the companion case of *NLRB* v. *General Motors Corp.*,[19] the Court had held that an agency shop clause was a mandatory subject of collective bargaining because it was a form of union security permitted by the Section 8(a)(3) proviso. The most plausible reading of the *GM* case is to construe it as saying that the only form of membership that can be required under the federal act is the kind of membership that is represented by an agency shop arrangement—namely, the mere payment of money to the union. In *Schermerhorn*, which involved the question of whether a state could outlaw such an agency shop arrangement, the Supreme Court held that "at the very least, the agreements requiring

---

[18] 373 U.S. 746 (1963).

[19] 373 U.S. 734 (1963).

'membership' in a labor union which are expressly permitted by the proviso are the same 'membership' agreements expressly placed within the reach of state law by § 14(b)." [20] The Court held that the kind of union security agreement that is expressly permitted by the Section 8(a)(3) proviso (*i.e.*, the agency shop) is certainly one of the kinds of compulsory unionism that the states can prohibit under Section 14(b), although the Court made it clear that it was not implying that the states could not also prohibit union security agreements that were either more or less stringent than the agency shop arrangement.

This is an undoubtedly correct construction of the term "membership" as it is used in both Section 8(a)(3) and Section 14(b), but the *Schermerhorn* result can also be justified on broader grounds. The agency shop, though not as prevalent at the time of the Taft-Hartley amendments as it was to become, is nevertheless a traditionally recognized form of union security. By providing the union with the funds that are necessary to perform its function, the agency shop arrangement satisfies some of the same objectives as the closed or union shop. Moreover, the agency shop operates as a compulsion upon individual employees to support a union to which they may be personally opposed— one of the evils to which the phrase *compulsory unionism* commonly applies. Since the manifest intent of Congress was not to disturb the historical authority of the states to deal with union security agreements and compulsory unionism, the existence of this intent should alone be sufficient to forestall any judicial finding of preemption—regardless of the specific wording of Section 14(b).

Maintenance-of-Membership

A maintenance-of-membership agreement requires an employee who is a member of the union at the beginning of the contract or who becomes a member to remain so during the term of the contract. Since the membership which an employee is obliged to maintain under such an agreement can be nothing more than the mere payment of money (as under the agency shop),[21] a maintenance-of-membership agreement is one of the "less stringent union security arrangements" [22] the Supreme Court had in mind

---

[20] 373 U.S. at 751.

[21] Marlin Rockwell Corp., 114 N.L.R.B. 553 (1955).

[22] 373 U.S. at 752.

in *Schermerhorn.* The Court there declined to decide whether Section 14(b) authorized the states to prohibit this kind of agreement.

Although there appears to be no direct authority on this point, the opinion of the Supreme Court in *Algoma Plywood Co.* v. *Wisconsin Employment Relations Board* [23] is dispositive of the issue. That case involved a maintenance-of-membership agreement that had been entered into in violation of a state law requiring a prior employee referendum. An employee discharged under this agreement had been ordered reinstated by the state agency. The issue, which was resolved under the terms of the original Wagner Act rather than the Taft-Hartley amendments, was whether such state regulation of compulsory unionism had been preempted by the federal statute. The Court held that there was no preemption here and further indicated that this conclusion was consistent with and reinforced by the subsequent enactment of Section 14(b). The clear implication, therefore, is that the states do have the power to prohibit maintenance-of-membership agreements.

The legislative history of Section 14(b) supports this view. The intent of Congress was to leave the states free to prohibit all kinds of compulsory unionism; and along with the closed shop and the union shop, maintenance-of-membership was several times mentioned as an example of the kinds of union security agreement Congress had in mind.[24]

Checkoff

Although it seems that Section 14(b) authorizes the states to prohibit maintenance-of-membership agreements, the Supreme Court has inadvertently provided a means by which unions can achieve the near equivalent of a maintenance-of-membership agreement, notwithstanding state right-to-work laws. This has been accomplished by means of a total federal preemption of state laws regulating checkoff agreements, whereby employees authorize their employer to transmit the employees' union dues directly to the union.

State power to regulate the checkoff is complicated by two facts. First, the checkoff is not commonly thought of as a tra-

---

[23] 336 U.S. 301 (1948).

[24] *See, e.g.,* LEGIS. HIST. LMRA at 564, where maintenance-of-membership is mentioned twice in conjunction with what Section 14(b) authorizes the states to prohibit.

ditional form of union security, as are the closed shop, union shop, agency shop, and maintenance-of-membership agreements. Second, the most direct federal regulation of the checkoff lies not in Section 8(a)(3), to which Section 14(b) relates, but rather in Section 302 of the Act. Section 302 makes it generally illegal for an employer to pay money to a union, but then lists a number of exemptions, one of which pertains to "money deducted from the wages of employees in payment of membership dues in a labor organization: Provided that the employer has received from each employee, on whose account such deductions are made, a written assignment which shall not be irrevocable for a period of more than one year, or beyond the termination date of the applicable collective agreement, whichever occurs sooner. . . ."

The coincidence of these two facts apparently led one state court to evaluate the state's power to regulate the checkoff solely from the perspective of the normal federal preemption doctrines. The Utah Supreme Court thus held that Section 302 had totally occupied the field, and that state law was preempted.[25] Section 14(b) was not even considered. Subsequently, however, a federal district court in Tennessee found that a checkoff agreement, which was part and parcel of a maintenance-of-membership agreement, was illegal under the state's right-to-work law; the court thus allowed the employer to honor the employees' revocations of their checkoff authorizations even though the contract made such authorizations binding for a year.[26]

Subsequently, in the leading case of *SeaPAK* v. *Industrial Employees, National Maritime Union*,[27] a union sought to enjoin an employer from refusing to deduct the dues of certain employees who had revoked their checkoff authorizations. Under the collective bargaining agreement, the employer was bound to deduct union dues from the wages "of those employees for whom it has valid and enforceable dues deduction authorizations." The employer denied that its actions were in breach of the contract because under the Georgia right-to-work laws, checkoff authorizations were revocable at the will of the employee. The union,

---

[25] Utah v. Montgomery Ward & Co., 120 Utah 294, 233 P.2d 685 (1951).

[26] United Steelworkers v. Knoxville Iron Co., 162 F. Supp. 366 (E.D. Tenn. 1958).

[27] 300 F. Supp. 1197 (S.D. Ga. 1969), *affirmed per curiam*, 423 F.2d 1229 (5th Cir. 1970), *affirmed per curiam*, 400 U.S. 985 (1971); *see also* International Brotherhood of Potters v. Tell City Chair Co., 295 F. Supp. 961 (S.D. Ind. 1968).

on the other hand, construed Section 302 of the LMRA as affirmatively permitting irrevocable authorizations (for no longer than a year), and argued that Section 302 was preemptive of the state law in this respect. The employees' prior authorizations were thus "valid and enforceable," notwithstanding the attempted revocation, and the employer was bound to honor them.

The federal district court adopted the union's position. It found that through Section 302 "the area of checkoff of union dues has been federally occupied to such an extent . . . that no room remains for state regulation in the same field." [28] The court further held that Section 14(b) was inapplicable, since "Congress did not conceive that checkoff of dues for a limited time after an employee's revocation of authorization therefor [*sic*] would amount to compulsory union membership as interdicted by state 'Right-to-Work' laws." [29]

On appeal, the *SeaPAK* decision was affirmed *per curiam* by the Fifth Circuit.[30] The court of appeals, however, adopted as its own the reasoning and opinion of the district court. In turn, the decision of the Fifth Circuit was affirmed by the United States Supreme Court, again without any written opinion.[31] There is, thus, controlling Supreme Court authority for the narrow proposition that Section 302 preempts state laws which purport to make checkoff authorizations revocable at will; and presumably, this is true for the reasons advanced by the district court. Unfortunately, those reasons do not withstand hard analysis.

The stated premise of the court's argument was that the "checkoff of dues for a limited time after an employee's revocation of authorization" does not amount to the kind of compulsory union membership that can be prohibited under Section 14(b). Section 14(b), rather, "leaves unimpaired the right of any state to prohibit union or closed shops." This narrow reading of Section 14(b) is, of course, clearly inconsistent with the Supreme Court's prior decisions in *General Motors* and *Schermerhorn* where it upheld the "obligation to pay initiation fees and regular dues" as "the 'practical equivalent' of an 'agreement requiring membership in a labor organization as a condition of employment' "—*i.e.*, the kind of arrangement which the proviso to Section 8(a)(3) ex-

---

[28] 300 F. Supp. at 1200.

[29] *Id.* at 1200-01.

[30] 423 F.2d 1229 (5th Cir. 1970).

[31] 400 U.S. 985 (1971).

empts from federal prohibition but which is prohibitable by the states under Section 14(b). Since a dues checkoff authorization which is irrevocable for a fixed period is nothing more than an "obligation to pay initiation fees and regular dues," the states should be able to prohibit or regulate this form of compulsory unionism under Section 14(b).

These theoretical objections to the side, the practical impact of the *SeaPAK* decision is to authorize in right-to-work states a form of union security that is, in its critical aspects, closely analogous to a maintenance-of-membership agreement. Under such an agreement, an employee who is a member of the union at the beginning of the contract or who becomes a member during the term of the contract is obligated to remain a member for the duration of the contract. State right-to-work laws can, under Section 14(b), outlaw arrangements of this kind. If, however, dues checkoff authorizations can be made irrevocable for up to a year, this achieves the near equivalent of a maintenance-of-membership arrangement. In both instances, once an employee commits himself to pay dues to the union (which is all that a maintenance-of-membership agreement can require), this obligation becomes a condition of his employment. And this is what union security is all about! It is true that the checkoff and the maintenance-of-membership situations have a different source and duration of obligation (an individual contract *versus* a collective contract) and are enforced in different ways (by not honoring a revocation, on the one hand, *versus* discharge, on the other); but in their critical aspects—that they involve the payment of money to a union as an incident of one's employment—both the irrevocable checkoff and the maintenance-of-membership agreement are similar forms of union security. Yet under the *SeaPAK* decision, state right-to-work laws can prohibit one but not the other.

In the absence of compelling and direct evidence that Congress intended this anomalous result, a more rational construction of Section 14(b) would be one in which irrevocable dues checkoff arrangements are deemed a form of compulsory union membership subject both to the requirements of the federal act and to the more restrictive requirements of the various state right-to-work laws. There is, however, no such evidence. To the extent that it bears specifically on the question, the legislative history of Section 302 suggests that Congress did not intend to override state right-to-work laws. As originally drafted, the section allowed the checkoff of "membership dues . . . *or other periodic payments* to a labor organization *in lieu thereof.*" Senator Goldwater recognized that this would in effect "achieve the equivalent of the type of union security arrangement which is permitted under the Taft-Hartley Act but which it was the intention of Congress in that statute to authorize the States to prohibit [the agency shop] if they so wished." [32] Apparently, Congress agreed with Senator Goldwater's interpretation. "Thus," as one court has put it, "Congress rejected language which . . . would have given tacit congressional sanction to the agency shop in states which had adopted laws prohibiting compulsory union membership." [33] This evidences an intent that Section 302 should not directly supersede state right-to-work laws.

Unfortunately, what Senator Goldwater and Congress failed to appreciate was that the elimination of "other periodic payments" and of "in lieu thereof" was insufficient to accomplish their desired goal. For even with that language omitted, Section 302 still appears to authorize the functional equivalent of another kind of union security agreement that state right-to-work laws are designed to prohibit—the so-called maintenance-of-membership agreements. If Congress had realized that the final draft of Section 302 had this effect, then it most surely would have been corrected, just as a partial attempt was made in the elimination of the periodic payment clause. It would thus appear that *SeaPAK* is inconsistent with legislative intent.

When *SeaPAK* was affirmed on appeal by the Supreme Court, without the benefit of full arguments by the litigants or an opinion from the Court, Mr. Justice Harlan was of the view that the case should have been given more careful consideration. Mr. Justice Harlan was surely correct, for it would appear that the Supreme Court did not fully appreciate the implications of its decision. The matter, thus, should be deemed ripe for reconsideration by the Court.

Union Hiring Hall Arrangements

Under a union hiring hall arrangement the employer agrees to hire only such applicants as are referred to him from the

---

[32] *See* 105 CONG. REC. 7631, 86th Cong., 1st Sess. (remarks of Sen. Goldwater).

[33] Amalgamated Ass'n of Street Employees v. Las Vegas-Tonopah-Reno Stage Line, Inc., 202 F. Supp. 726, 733-34 (D. Nev. 1962).

union hiring hall. Historically, the hiring hall was simply an adjunct to the closed shop; it was an effective means of implementing the exclusive employment opportunities that the closed shop gave to union members.[34] Despite the fact that Congress was well aware of the symbiotic relationship between hiring halls and the closed shop, the Supreme Court has held that Congress did not necessarily intend to outlaw all hiring hall arrangements.[35] A hiring hall is illegal under the LMRA only when the agreement has in fact been used in a discriminatory manner by making membership a requirement of referral and thus achieving a de facto closed shop.

Just as the Supreme Court has sustained the legality of hiring hall arrangements which are neither discriminatory on their face nor applied in a discriminatory manner, so also have the lower courts held that such hiring hall arrangements are not prohibitable by the states under Section 14(b). In *Laborers Local 107* v. *Kunco, Inc.*,[36] the Eighth Circuit of Appeals held that Section 14(b) only allowed the states to prohibit agreements requiring membership in a labor organization. It further held that "[a] hiring hall which, though exclusive, does not require membership does not violate the closed shop prohibition of § 8(a)(3) . . . and thus, *a fortiori*, it is not within the ambit of § 14(b)." [37] Similarly, in *NLRB* v. *Houston Chapter, Associated General Contractors*,[38] the Fifth Circuit Court of Appeals noted that an exclusive hiring hall agreement "does not constitute compulsory unionism so long as the arrangement is not employed in a discriminatory manner." [39] In many of these nondiscriminatory hiring hall arrangements, however, the union charges its users a fee equivalent to its normal union dues, which means that a limited form of union security is being allowed to exist in spite of Section 14(b) and state right-to-work laws.[40]

---

[34] *See* Fenton, *Union Hiring Halls Under the Taft-Hartley Act*, 9 LABOR LAW JOURNAL 505 (1958).

[35] Local 357, Teamsters, 365 U.S. 667 (1961).

[36] 472 F.2d 456 (8th Cir. 1973).

[37] *Id.* at 458.

[38] 349 F.2d 449 (5th Cir. 1965).

[39] *Id.* at 453.

[40] *See* Chapter IV, *supra.*

On the other hand, these decisions[41] clearly imply that a discriminatorily operated hiring hall should be considered one of the "other form[s] of compulsory unionism"[42] which the states were empowered to prohibit under Section 14(b). Otherwise, the states' concurrent jurisdiction over the closed shop would be indirectly but effectively circumvented, contrary to the intent of Congress.[43]

PREEMPTION OF STATE JURISDICTION OVER ILLEGAL AGREEMENTS

While Congress generally adopted a "hands off" policy toward state law regulation of union security agreements, a limited amount of preemption was clearly intended. The Wagner Act and more especially the Taft-Hartley Act either made union security agreements illegal under certain circumstances and/or made some kinds of agreements illegal altogether. While Congress intended to allow the states concurrent jurisdiction to prohibit also these forms of union security, it clearly did not intend to allow state law to validate what the federal act had said was illegal.

The Committee Report on Section 13 of the original House Bill contains the following admonition:

> It goes without saying that no State may invalidate, as to agreements affecting commerce, restrictions or conditions that the amended Labor Act will put upon compulsory unionism.[44]

In accord with this principle is *New Jersey Bell Telephone Co.* v. *Communications Workers*,[45] where the state supreme court held that since under the federal act a union shop is lawful only if freely agreed to by the employer and the union (and then only if authorized by a majority vote of the employees), the compulsory imposition of a union shop, without such agreement or the required vote, by a state board of arbitration was impermissible.

---

[41] *See also* NLRB v. Tom Joyce Floors, Inc., 353 F.2d 768 (9th Cir. 1965).

[42] LEGIS. HIST. LMRA at 564.

[43] *See generally* Wilhoit & Gibson, *Can a State Right-to-Work Law Prohibit the Union-Operated Hiring Hall?* 26 LABOR LAW JOURNAL 301 (1975).

[44] LEGIS. HIST. LMRA at 325.

[45] 5 N.J. 354, 75 A.2d 721 (1950).

WHO MAY ENACT RIGHT-TO-WORK LAWS?

It is an open question whether local governmental bodies such as cities and counties have the power under Section 14(b) to enact right-to-work legislation. There is a division of opinion on this among both the courts and the commentators.[46] In *Kentucky State AFL-CIO* v. *Puckett*,[47] the court held that Section 14(b) pertained only to state or territorial law, but not local law. This conclusion was premised on the assumption that Section 8(a)(3), standing alone, would operate as a total preemption of state laws regulating union security agreements. The court then concluded that Section 14(b)

> makes an exception out of the otherwise full preemption by the Act. The exception should be strictly and narrowly construed because it represents a departure from the overall spirit and purpose of the Act. . . . We think it is not reasonable to believe that Congress could have intended to waive other than to major policy-making units such as states and territories, the determination of policy in such a controversial area as that of union security agreements.[48]

The court's view of the legislative history upon which it premises its conclusion is somewhat questionable. Contrary to the assertions of this court, Congress did not contemplate that the proviso to Section 8(a)(3) would be completely preemptive any more than it contemplated that the proviso to Section 8(3) of the Wagner Act was completely preemptive. Both provisos were merely intended to achieve, in so far as federal law was concerned, a "hands-off" policy toward the kinds of union security agreements that were not otherwise prohibited by federal law. To make this absolutely clear, 14(b) was written, not as a grudging exception to an otherwise dominant policy of preemption, but rather a broad reaffirmation of congressional neutrality toward the lesser forms of compulsory unionism. In Section 8(a)(3) and Section 14(b), Congress was saying, in part, that if these lesser forms of compulsory unionism are going to be deemed illegal, their illegality must flow from some source other than federal law. From this perspective, it is thus totally

---

[46] *Compare* Berke & Brunn, *Local Right to Work Ordinances: A New Problem in Labor and Local Law*, 9 STAN. L. REV. 674 (1957), *with* Finman, *Local "Right to Work" Ordinances: A Reply*, 10 STAN. L. REV. 53 (1957).

[47] 391 S.W.2d 360 (Ky. Ct. of App. 1965).

[48] *Id.* at 362.

irrelevant whether the illegality stems from a state constitutional provision, a state legislative enactment, a local ordinance, or even the judge-made common law of the state.

A more correct conclusion was the one reached by the California court in *Chavez* v. *Sargent*.[49] The court there noted that

> the normal and customary construction of "State Law" encompasses county ordinances. There is nothing in the legislative history of the Taft-Hartley Act or in the Act itself to indicate that Congress left the field open for state legislation but pre-empted it as to county legislation.[50]

It is significant to note, however, that this court went on to hold that the local right-to-work law was invalidated or preempted by a contrary state policy in favor of compulsory unionism. This demonstrates that the inclusion of municipal ordinances within the ambit of Section 14(b) does not deny the preeminence of state policy, which was a concern of the *Puckett* court. As in *Chavez*, the state policy may be contrary to the local policy on right-to-work laws, in which case such laws fail, or the state policy may be to leave this to the local units for determination. In either event, the purpose of Section 14(b) was to let the state policy prevail, and thus Section 14(b) itself should not be read as mandating an automatic exclusion of municipal ordinances.

Related to the problem of whether local right-to-work ordinances are valid under Section 14(b) is the question of the validity of state common-law restrictions on the enforcement of union security agreements. States following the so-called Massachusetts approach, for example, might well be said to prohibit agreements requiring membership in a union as a condition of employment.

Such authority as exists, however, indicates that Section 14(b) does not save these common law doctrines from being preempted by the federal statute. Rather, the term "law" in Section 14(b) has reference only to constitutional provisions and statutory enactments.[51]

---

[49] 329 P.2d 579 (Dist. Ct. of App. Cal. 1958).

[50] 329 P.2d at 582 n. 3.

[51] The Ohio Supreme Court is apparently the only court to have passed on this issue. In Grimes & Hauer v. Pollock, 163 Ohio 372, 127 N.E.2d 203 (1955), the court declined to utilize some old common-law decisions against picketing to obtain a closed shop and held that Section 14(b) only "has reference to a constitutional provision or a legislative enactment."

While this result may be desirable in that it avoids the re-vitalization of what was at best a rather chaotic set of common-law doctrines, it is not an altogether compelling interpretation of Section 14(b). In the first place, the entire legislative history of Section 14(b) leans heavily toward the conclusion that the section should be construed broadly and not narrowly. The inclusion of state common law within the ambit of the section is certainly not an overly broad interpretation of the phrase "State or Territorial law." The Supreme Court has held in a closely analogous context that "the term law in our jurisprudence *usually* includes the rules of court decisions as well as legislative acts," [52] and there is nothing in the legislative history to rebut the presumption that in enacting Section 14(b) Congress intended to use the term in its usual sense.

The only kind of laws that the legislative history specifically mentions were the then-existing state constitutional and statu-tory right-to-work laws.[53] But this is understandable in light of the wide-spread attention these laws were receiving, although at no time did anyone suggest that these were the only forms of state law to which Congress was deferring in the prohibition of compulsory unionism. To the contrary, a strong inference can be drawn that Congress did specifically intend to defer to the state common-law prohibitions.

It must be remembered that the underlying purpose of Sec-tion 14(b) was to continue and make express the very same policy of nonpreemption that was implicit in the old Wagner Act. In determining what kind of state laws the Taft-Hartley Congress intended not to preempt in 1948, it is relevant to look back at the kind of laws the Wagner Act Congress intended not to preempt in 1935. Since in 1935 there were no statutory or constitutional right-to-work laws—the first being passed as a constitutional amendment in Florida in 1944—it necessarily fol-lows that in 1935 Congress intended to defer to the various state common-law prohibitions against compulsory unionism!

---

[52] Warren v. United States, 340 U.S. 523, 526 (1951). In this case a treaty provided that the signatory states could by "national law or regula-tions" make certain exceptions to the duties otherwise imposed by the treaty. The Court held that the federal common law of admiralty was a national law under this treaty, and that the exception the common law recognized was thus a valid one.

[53] *See, e.g.,* Legis. Hist. LMRA at 748, 1543.

This conclusion was implicitly recognized by the United States Supreme Court in the *Algoma Plywood* case. Referring to the Wagner Act, the Court noted:

> The States are free (apart from pre-emption by Congress) to characterize any wrong of any kind by an employer to an employee, whether statutorily created *or known to the common law,* as an "unfair labor practice." At the time when the National Labor Relations Act was adopted, the *courts* of many States, at least under some circumstances, denied validity to union-security agreements. *See 1 Teller, Labor Disputes and Collective Bargaining § 170 (1940)....* Had the sponsors of the National Labor Relations Act meant to deny effect to State policies inconsistent with the unrestricted enforcement of union-shop contracts, surely they would have made their purpose manifest.[54]

Needless to say, the section cited in Teller's treatise contains an exclusive discussion of the various state common-law prohibitions against the enforcement of union security agreements.

Since the Taft-Hartley Congress did not expressly disclaim this particular aspect of the general Wagner Act policy of nonpreemption, it necessarily follows that Congress intended to follow it. Thus the common law of a state can prohibit the enforcement of a union security agreement to the same extent as would be possible under a statute or constitutional provision. Neither the Supreme Court nor even any federal court has passed on this specific issue, but when they do, that conclusion should be deemed inevitable.

STATE POWER TO ENFORCE RIGHT-TO-WORK LAWS

In the second *Schermerhorn* case,[55] the issue was whether the State of Florida, rather than the NLRB, had jurisdiction to enforce the state's right-to-work law. The argument was that exclusive enforcement by the NLRB was necessary in order to achieve uniformity of remedy. The Court, however, held that "Congress . . . chose to abandon any search for uniformity in dealing with the problems of state law barring the execution and application of agreements authorized by § 14(b) and decided to suffer a medley of attitudes and philosophies on the subject." [56]

---

[54] 336 U.S. at 305-06 (emphasis added).

[55] Retail Clerks Local 1625 v. Schermerhorn, 375 U.S. 96 (1963).

[56] *Id.* at 104-05.

Thus, the states under Section 14(b) have the power to enforce their right-to-work laws and to provide a wide range of remedies and sanctions—including injunctions against the enforcement of illegal agreements, damage actions, reinstatement with back pay, and criminal penalties.

The Court in *Schermerhorn* did, however, impose an important limitation on the scope of a state's power to enforce its right-to-work laws:

> [P]icketing in order to get an employer to execute an agreement to hire all-union labor in violation of a state union-security statute lies exclusively in the federal domain . . . , because state power, recognized by § 14(b), begins *only with actual negotiation and execution of the type of agreement described by § 14(b)*. Absent such an agreement, conduct arguably an unfair labor practice would be a matter for the National Labor Relations Board. . . .[57]

That the states should have the power to prohibit the negotiation and enforcement of union security agreements, but not the power to prohibit the exertion of economic force to achieve such agreements, has struck many as being anomalous indeed. The Court itself did not explain its reasoning in this regard. But it has been suggested:

> Perhaps the Court was concerned that certain concerted activity which Congress clearly sought to protect—such as peaceful picketing designed to induce employees to become members, at least when not outlawed by section 8(b)(7), and peaceful informational picketing designed to communicate to the public that a company is non-union—would be too readily outlawed by state courts, particularly when a number of state right-to-work laws are extremely broadly drawn and provide in some instances for severe sanctions (including criminal penalties).[58]

RIGHT-TO-WORK LAWS AND SUPERVISORY EMPLOYEES

Most state right-to-work laws are worded broadly enough to encompass all of the employees of a particular employer, whether such employees be of the rank-and-file variety or occupy supervisory positions. There is nothing on the face of Section 14(b) itself to suggest that state prohibitions against making union membership "a condition of employment" must be limited to a particular class of employees. The companion Section 14(a) does provide, however, that

---

[57] *Id.* at 105 (emphasis in the original).

[58] R. GORMAN, BASIC TEXT ON LABOR LAW 663 (1976).

[n]othing herein shall prohibit any individual employed as a supervisor from becoming or remaining a member of a labor organization, but no employer subject to this Act shall be compelled to deem individuals defined herein as supervisors as employees for the purpose of any law, either national or local, relating to collective bargaining.[59]

Section 14(a) thus raises the question of whether a supervisory employee who is discharged because of his refusal to join a labor union could seek redress under a right-to-work law sanctioned by Section 14(b).

In *Beasley* v. *Food Fair of North Carolina*,[60] an employer discharged some supervisory employees who had joined the labor union that represented other employees in collective bargaining. Because supervisors are not covered by the Taft-Hartley Act, the National Labor Relations Board refused to intercede, and the discharged employees brought suit under a provision of the North Carolina right-to-work statute. As is true in many states, the North Carolina right-to-work statute not only prohibits discrimination against employees who refuse to join a union, but also discrimination against the employees who elect to join. The issue was whether this provision of the state law was preempted by Section 14(a) insofar as it applied to supervisory employees. The United States Supreme Court held that the state law was preempted.

It would appear that the same result might be reached in a converse situation—where a supervisory employee is discharged because of his refusal to join a union. But a close examination of both the legislative history of Section 14(a) and the *Beasley* decision suggests a contrary conclusion.

Prior to the Taft-Hartley Act amendments in 1948, the NLRB had on several occasions found supervisors to be protected under various provisions of the Wagner Act.[61] Congress, however, believed that the Board's position on this matter, more than almost anything else, had "upset any real balance of power in the collective bargaining process."[62] Congress felt that the kind of collective bargaining it wanted to foster would be impossible unless the agents of management (supervisors) owed their un-

---

[59] 29 U.S.C. § 164(a) (1970).

[60] 416 U.S. 653 (1974).

[61] *See, e.g.*, Union Collieries Coal Co., 41 N.L.R.B. 961 (1942); Godchaux Sugars, Inc., 44 N.L.R.B. 874 (1942); Packard Motor Car Co., 61 N.L.R.B. 4 (1945).

[62] LEGIS. HIST. LMRA at 409.

divided loyalty to the employer in both the negotiation and the administration of the contract. Thus in 1948 Congress expressly excluded supervisors from the definition of *employee* under the Act. But that apparently was not enough. In order that this national policy not be subverted by contrary state laws, Congress also enacted Section 14(a).

That, then, is the policy that underlies the *Beasley* decision. Since a state law prohibiting an employer from discharging any supervisor who joins a union would "flout the national policy against compulsion upon employers . . . to treat supervisors as employees." [63] it stands to reason that such a law would be deemed preempted by Section 14(a). But this reasoning does not hold with respect to a law that prohibits an employer (who in most instances would be acting under union pressure) from making union membership a condition of employment for his supervisors. To the contrary, such a law would affirmatively promote the underlying policies of Section 14(a), in that it would tend to preserve the purity of the labor/management distinction by protecting supervisors from being forced into unions of rank-and-file workers. Thus such a state law should not be deemed preempted by Section 14(a), as was implicitly recognized in the *Beasley* decision itself. The Court there noted:

> Section 14(a) does not wholly foreclose state regulations respecting the status of supervisors. . . . [*Hanna Mining* v. *Marine Engineers*] held that "certainly Congress made no considered decision generally to exclude state limitations on supervisory organizing." . . . The Court accordingly held that the Wisconsin anti-picketing statutes—that furthered, not hindered, the Act's limitations—could be applied to activity by a union of supervisors.[64]

The same conclusion should be reached concerning the applicability of a state right-to-work law to supervisory "employees," despite the literal wording of Section 14(a).

EXTRA-TERRITORIAL APPLICATION OF RIGHT-TO-WORK LAWS

When the hiring decision, the performance of the work, and the negotiation and enforcement of a collective bargaining agreement all take place within a state with a right-to-work law, then

---

[63] 416 U.S. at 662.

[64] 416 U.S. at 657, citing Hanna Mining v. Marine Engineers, 382 U.S. 181 (1965).

such a law will clearly operate to void the enforcement of a union security agreement. But when one or more of these activities takes place, in whole or in part, outside the borders of a state having a right-to-work law, then a serious question arises over the applicability of such a law. This is a particularly acute problem for employers who are carriers in interstate commerce.

The Supreme Court, however, has recently provided guidance in the resolution of these problems. In *Oil Workers Union* v. *Mobil Oil Corporation*,[65] a collective bargaining agreement containing an agency shop clause had been negotiated and executed in New York—a state without a right-to-work statute. Subsequently, the contract was re-executed in Texas, which does have such a statute. Pursuant to this contract, employees were hired in Texas to work aboard the company's tankers; but these seamen spent eighty to ninety percent of their working time outside the territorial bounds of Texas. They were required to pay the agency shop fees, and this was ultimately challenged under the Texas right-to-work statute.

The Supreme Court indicated that the applicability of a state's right-to-work law in such circumstances could arguably be determined by reference to one of three tests. First, there was the test adopted by the Fifth Circuit. It determined the sufficiency of the state's interest in applying its right-to-work law by looking to the whole employment relationship and by evaluating the state's contracts from that perspective.[66] On this basis the Fifth Circuit had concluded that the Texas law was applicable to the contract in question.

A second possible test was that adopted by Mr. Justice Stewart in his dissent. He concluded that the controlling state law should be determined by reference to where the hiring takes place, which in this case was Texas:

> In the first place, it seems clear that the State where the hiring actually takes place is the State most deeply concerned with the conditions of hire. The policy of a State such as Texas, which favors unrestricted hiring, will be seriously undermined when union security agreements control the hiring that takes place within its jurisdiction. Moreover, the State where the hiring actually occurs normally provides the bulk of the workforce from which the employees are drawn.[67]

---

[65] 96 S.Ct. 2140 (1976).

[66] *Id.* at 2143-44.

[67] *Id.* at 2153.

A majority of the Supreme Court, however, opted in favor of a third test, one which focuses on the place where the employees actually work. The Court thus held

> that under § 14(b), right-to-work laws cannot void agreements permitted by § 8(a)(3) when the situs at which all the employees covered by the agreement perform most of their work is located outside of a State having such laws.[68]

This was held to be the controlling factor because the Court viewed the entire union security issue—at least insofar as Sections 8(a)(3) and 14(b) are concerned—as focusing upon the kind of post-hiring conditions that can be imposed on an employee. Since post-hiring conditions become operative at the place where the work is performed rather than the place where the employee is hired, the Court concluded that the place of work is the more relevant one insofar as determining the applicable law.[69]

The Court also bolstered its conclusion by reference to two practical considerations. First, it noted that

> the use of a job situs test will minimize the possibility of patently anomalous extra-territorial applications of any given State's right-to-work laws. Use of a job situs test will insure that the laws of a State with a continuing and current relationship with the employees in question will govern the validity *vel non* of any union-shop or agency-shop provision.[70]

The anomalous situation the Court had in mind was that in which a right-to-work statute is applied to an employee who is initially hired in a right-to-work state and is later transferred to and performs his work in a state without such a law. Second, the Court asserted that "under a job situs test, parties entering a collective bargaining agreement will easily be able to determine in virtually all situations whether a union or agency shop provision is valid."[71]

As in many other choice-of-law controversies, the Supreme Court in *Mobil Oil* was faced with the task of choosing between a number of alternatives, each of which could be supported by equally compelling arguments of both the theoretical and the

---

[68] *Id.* at 2144.

[69] *Id.* at 2144-46.

[70] *Id.* at 2146.

[71] *Id.* at 2147.

practical variety. It is not so important which alternative the Court finally chose as it is that the Court made a definite and binding choice, with the specific applications of the Court's test now being left for the lower courts to resolve.

RIGHT-TO-WORK LAWS AND FEDERAL ENCLAVES

A *federal enclave* has been defined as

> a territory which has been transferred by a state through consent or cession to the United States who then acquires exclusive jurisdiction over all activities within the area.[72]

Generally speaking, the enforcement of contracts that are to be performed exclusively on federal enclaves is governed by federal rather than state law. Thus, in *Cooper* v. *General Dynamics*,[73] a federal district court held that an agency shop agreement, valid under federal labor law, could not be voided by the application of the Texas right-to-work statute, since work under this contract was being performed on a federal enclave.

The exclusivity of federal law on federal enclaves is subject to one important exception. The Federal Assimilative Crimes Act[74] incorporates the criminal statutes of the host state and makes them applicable within the federal enclave itself. Since many state right-to-work statutes provide for criminal penalties, an issue thus arises with respect to the applicability of such laws to union security agreements that are enforced on federal enclaves located within right-to-work states.

Although the Texas right-to-work statute contains criminal sanctions, the court in the *Cooper* case did not consider this assimilation argument. In *King* v. *Gemini Food Services*,[75] however, another federal district court did pass on this issue and held that a state right-to-work statute could not be applied on a federal enclave located in Virginia. In so holding, the court relied on the principle that state criminal laws will be applied under the Assimilative Crimes Act only if such laws do not conflict with existent federal law or policy. The court then concluded:

---

[72] Cooper v. General Dynamics, 378 F.Supp. 1258, 1261 (N.D. Tex. 1974), *affirmed on other grounds*, 533 F.2d 163 (5th Cir. 1976), *cert. petition filed*, Oct. 18, 1976.

[73] *Id.*

[74] 18 U.S.C. § 13 (1974).

[75] 81 CCH Lab. Cas. ¶ 13,035 (E.D. Va. 1976).

Such a conflict does arise in the instant case. Virginia law expressly prohibits union shop agreements while federal law expressly permits union shop agreements.[76]

Although what the court said about the respective state and federal laws is obviously true, to characterize the relationship of the laws as a "conflict" is anomalous indeed. The proviso to Section 8(a)(3) of the Taft-Hartley Act was not intended to and does not in fact provide affirmative legal protection to union security agreements. The proviso merely states that such agreements shall not be considered illegal under federal law. Implicit in this, just as it is explicit in Section 14(b), is the federal policy that the state should continue to have the power to outlaw union security agreements within their borders. Moreover, even if Section 8(a)(3) were read as evidencing a federal policy in favor of union security agreements,[77] this policy is expressly limited by Section 14(b). The alleged conflict between permitting and prohibiting union security agreements was resolved by Congress itself in favor of allowing the states to prohibit. That accommodation is the federal policy. To limit the states' exercise of that power through the normal operation of the Assimilative Crimes Act on the grounds that such an exercise would "conflict with federal policy" is, therefore, simply nonsensical.

A rather novel issue involving federal enclaves arose in the recent case of *Vincent v. General Dynamics Corp.*[78] where the defendant employer was in possession of an air force facility under an agreement with the federal government. Only a part of the facility was actually on a federal enclave, and the plaintiffs thus argued that the union security agreement, which did not differentiate between federal territory and state territory, should be deemed totally invalid under the state right-to-work law. The court, however, held just to the contrary and upheld the union security provision even as it might be applied to employees working outside the area designated as a federal enclave. Having concluded that the entire facility constituted but one job

---

[76] *Id.* at 24,106; *see also* Connerton, *Union Shop Agreements in Right-to-Work States*, N.Y.U. 23rd ANN. CONF. ON LAB. 251 (1971).

[77] In Oil Workers Union v. Mobil Oil Corp., 96 S.Ct. 2140 (1976), in a concurring opinion Mr. Justice Stevens stated that he did not join in the majority opinion's "suggestion that federal policy favor permitting union shop and agency shop agreements." *Id.* at 2148. This, in turn, has led some lower courts to read the majority opinion in exactly that fashion, even though such a policy is never expressly referred to therein. *See* Vincent v. General Dynamics Corp., 94 L.R.R.M. 2859, 2865 n. 15 (N.D. Tex. 1977).

[78] 94 L.R.R.M. 2859 (N.D. Tex. 1977).

situs that was incapable of being divided along state-federal boundary lines, the court then relied on the Supreme Court's decision in *Mobil Oil*:

> [T]he law of the federal enclave whereon the vast majority of employees work and the vast majority of facilities and building space are located should control the entire contract.[79]

Since the court had also held, along the lines of the *King* decision, that the Assimilative Crimes Act did not apply, and that the Texas right-to-work law was therefore inoperative on the federal enclave, the union security agreement was upheld in its entirety.

CONCLUSION

For the most part, Section 14(b) has been allowed to accomplish what the framers of the Taft-Hartley Act intended for it to accomplish, despite the erroneous proclivity of some courts to view Section 14(b) as a narrow and grudging exception to the preemption doctrine rather than as a broad statement of a "hands-off" policy on state prohibition of compulsory unionism. Some unnecessary narrowing of the section has, however, occurred, including the states' inability to enjoin strikes to obtain illegal agreements, the exclusion of the irrevocable checkoff and certain hiring hall arrangements from the coverage of right-to-work laws, and the inapplicability of the section on federal enclaves. On the other hand, the states have for the most part been left free to outlaw kinds of union security that would otherwise be permitted by federal law.

---

[79] *Id.* at 2867.

CHAPTER VIII

The State Right-to-Work Laws—A Survey

At the present time, twenty states have comprehensive right-to-work laws.[1] There is, however, no consistency among the various states in the wording or substantive coverage of these laws. Some states have constitutional provisions on the subject, others have only statutes, and still others have both. For the most part, the laws, whether in constitutional or statutory form, are poorly drafted. They all purport to create a "right to work," but they are sometimes indefinite about exactly what the correlative legal duty is and who bears it. Finally, it is apparent that the state right-to-work laws have been drafted, and are frequently construed, without punctilious regard for the federal preemption doctrine or the scope of Section 14(b). Thus some of the statutory provisions and extant state case law are probably invalid and/or not controlling—although, given the confusing and constantly changing nature of that doctrine, it is hard for anyone to determine the efficacy of the states' laws.

EMPLOYEE PROTECTION UNDER RIGHT-TO-WORK LAWS

Compulsory Union Membership

All of the comprehensive state right-to-work laws expressly prohibit membership in a labor union as a condition of employ-

---

[1] ALA. CODE tit. 26§ 375 (1958); ARIZ. CONST. art. XXV (1946); ARIZ. REV. STAT. §§ 23-1301 to 23-1307 (1971); ARK. CONST. amend. 34 (1944); ARK. STAT. §§ 81-201 to 81-207 (1960); FLA. CONST. art. I, § 6 (1944); FLA. STAT. §§ 447.17 (1975 Supp.); GA. CODE ANN. §§ 54-901 to 54-909, 54-9922 (1974); IOWA CODE ANN. §§ 736A.1 to 736A.8 (Supp. 1977); KAN. CONST. art. 15, § 12 (1969); LA. REV. STAT. ANN. §§ 23-981 to 23-987 (1976); MISS. CONST. art. 7, § 198-A (1960); MISS. CODE ANN. § 71-1-47 (1973); NEB. CONST. art. 15, §§ 13 to 15 (1946); NEB. REV. STAT. §§ 48-217 to 48-219 (1968); NEV. REV. STAT. §§ 613.230 to 613.300 (1973); N.C. GEN. STAT. §§ 95-78 to 95-84 (1965); N.D. CENT. CODE §§ 34-01-14, 34-08-02 (1972); S.C. CODE ANN. §§ 40-46 to 40-46.8 (1962); S.D. CONST. art. VI, § 2 (1946); S.D. LAWS §§ 60-8-3 to 60-8-8 (1960 Supp.); TENN. CODE ANN. §§ 50-208 to 50-212 (1966); TEX. REV. CIV. STAT. arts. 5154a, 5154g, & 5207a (1971); UTAH CODE ANN. §§ 34-34-1 to 34-34-17 (1971); VA. CODE ANN. §§ 40.1-58 to 40.1-69 (Cum. Supp. 1974); WYO. STAT. ANN. §§ 27-245.1 to 27-245.8 (1967).

ment. In addition, thirteen of the twenty state right-to-work laws expressly prohibit any requirement that an employee pay union dues and fees or the equivalent thereof as a condition of employment.[2] These states expressly prohibit the agency shop, which the Supreme Court in *Schermerhorn* said the states were empowered to do under Section 14(b). The agency shop, however, is also illegal or apparently illegal in the remaining seven states, either because of a state attorney general opinion, as in two states,[3] or by virtue of a judicial construction of the right-to-work statute in the other five.[4] Only one state right-to-work law,[5] since repealed, has been judicially construed as not prohibiting the agency shop.

In construing the state right-to-work laws as prohibiting not only compulsory union membership of the formal variety, but also the compulsory payment of dues and fees, the courts have adopted a variety of rationale. The first court to hold against compulsory payment simply looked to what it considered to be the intent of the people in passing the right-to-work statute. In *Arizona Flame Restaurant* v. *Baldwin,*[6] the Arizona Superior Court stated:

> [I]t is clear that it was the intent of the electorate to forbid both management and labor from imposing the requirement upon any person, as a condition of his employment, the participation by him in any form or scheme of employee representation. Consequently, it would require a most narrow and unrealistic construction of the existing laws to sanction a contract that would require employees not belonging to a union to contribute an assessment equal to the union dues to obtain or retain employment.[7]

In essence, this is a "lesser evil" type of argument, the larger evil being coerced employee "participation . . . in any form or scheme of employee representation." That, arguably, would include the exclusive representation of such an employee by a majority union. Since the states clearly lack the power to outlaw

---

[2] Alabama, Arkansas, Georgia, Iowa, Louisiana, Mississippi, Nebraska, North Carolina, South Carolina, Tennessee, Utah, Virginia, and Wyoming.

[3] South Dakota and Texas.

[4] Arizona, Florida, Kansas, Nevada, and North Dakota.

[5] Indiana.

[6] 26 CCH Lab. Cas. ¶ 68,647 (Ariz. Super. Ct. 1954), *affirmed on different grounds*, 82 Ariz. 285, 313 P.2d 759 (1957).

[7] 26 CCH Lab. Cas. at 87,172.

such representation, this casts some doubt on the validity of the court's argument. On the other hand, if the court is thought to say that the people intended to go as far as Section 14(b) allows them to go in outlawing the various kinds or degrees of coerced participation in union affairs, then the conclusion is a sound one, even though at the time of this decision it had not been authoritatively determined that the states did have the power under Section 14(b) to outlaw the agency shop.

In a subsequent decision, the Supreme Court of Kansas likewise focused on what it considered to be the intent and purpose of the state legislature and the people in passing a constitutional amendment which guaranteed a right to work, albeit only in terms of a prohibition against compulsory "membership or nonmembership" in a labor organization. In *Higgins* v. *Cardinal Manufacturing Co.*,[8] the court held that this language also prohibited an agency shop agreement where the payment of dues and fees, but not formal membership, was required as a condition of employment. The court first noted that the primary issue in the campaign leading to the adoption of the constitutional amendment was whether workers represented by a union should be allowed to be "free riders" enjoying the benefits of union representation without contributing to the cost thereof. The proponents of the amendment had contended that free rider or not, no worker should be required to give financial support to a union which he opposed. Because the public debate had centered on this issue, the court concluded that the people were fully aware that passage of the amendment would "prevent the payment of forced tribute to any labor organization. . . . by any worker . . .,"[9] and that they therefore intended to outlaw the agency shop.[10]

The court also noted that in drafting the constitutional amendment the legislature must have been aware that as used in the federal Labor-Management Relations Act the term "membership" meant nothing more than the payment of dues and fees. The court then apparently assumed that the kind of compulsory union membership that Congress intended to permit was the same kind of membership that the Kansas legislature intended to

---

[8] 188 Kan. 11, 360 P.2d 456 (1961), *cert. denied*, 368 U.S. 829 (1961).

[9] *Id.* at 24-25, 360 P.2d at 463.

[10] *See also* Amalgamated Ass'n of Street Employees v. Las Vegas-Tonopah-Reno Stage Line, Inc., 202 F. Supp. 726, 736-37 (D. Nev. 1962), *aff'd*, 319 F.2d 783 (9th Cir. 1963).

prohibit under the power reserved to it by Section 14(b). Any other conclusion, the court noted, would be "to declare that the constitutional amendment serves no useful purpose at all." [11] Presumably, what the court meant here was that since everything but the agency shop form of union security agreement was already prohibited by federal law, the constitutional amendment would serve no useful purpose unless it went further and also prohibited the agency shop. [12]

Of all the theoretical arguments (*i.e.*, not based on actual intent of the people or the legislature) for construing right-to-work statutes to include a prohibition of the agency shop, this argument is undoubtedly the most persuasive. It should be noted, however, that the argument of the Kansas court does not attempt to reason directly from federal law to a conclusion about the illegality of the agency shop under state law; rather, from the scope and content of federal law, the court deduces a sensible, albeit hypothetical, intent of the state legislature and then reasons from this intent to the ultimate conclusion. This is an important limitation on the use of federal law, but one which the Supreme Court of Nevada apparently ignored. In *Independent Guard Association* v. *Wackenhut Services, Inc.*,[13] that court reasoned from the *General Motors* and *Schermerhorn* cases as follows: The agency shop is permitted under Section 8(a)(3); Section 14(b) authorizes the states to outlaw any kind of union security agreement that is permitted by Section 8(a)(3); therefore, the Nevada right-to-work statute outlaws the agency shop. The fallacy of the argument lies in the fact that what the states are authorized to prohibit under Section 14(b) does not necessarily correlate with what they actually have prohibited; the latter can be determined only by reference to the state statute and the intent, actual or supposed, that lies behind it.[14] The Nevada Supreme

---

[11] 188 Kan. at 28, 360 P.2d at 466.

[12] *See also* Amalgamated Ass'n of Street Employees v. Las Vegas-Tonopah-Reno Stage Line, Inc., 202 F. Supp. at 735-36: "It would have been an idle act for the people to prohibit only compulsory union membership, for if the agency shop agreement were left valid, the employee would be in the same position he was in before the right-to-work law was passed."

[13] 90 Nev. 198, 522 P.2d 1010 (1974).

[14] *See* Ficek v. Boilermakers Local 647, 219 N.W.2d 860 (N.D. 1974) (Vogel, J., dissenting). Speaking of the *Schermerhorn* and *General Motors* decisions, Vogel correctly noted that "they construe Sections 8(a)(3) and 14(b) of the Taft-Hartley Act, and merely hold that the States can outlaw an agency shop, not that a right-to-work law actually does so." *Id.* at 875.

Court's decision is devoid of any discussion of such matters. Insofar as Nevada law is concerned, the rationale of the Federal District Court in *Amaglamated Association of Street Employees* v. *Las Vegas-Tonopah-Reno Stage Line, Inc.*[15] is to be preferred for the cogency of its analysis, which is essentially the same as that used by the Kansas court in *Higgins*.

In *Schermerhorn* v. *Local 1625, Retail Clerks*,[16] the Florida Supreme Court took a slightly different tack in concluding that the agency shop was prohibited by the right-to-work provision of the state constitution. Rather than construing the term "membership" to include the payment of dues and fees, the court implicitly conceded that what the constitution expressly protected was only the right to join or not to join a union in the formal sense. The court then concluded, however, that an agency shop agreement in effect "requires the nonunion employee to purchase from the labor union a right which the Constitution has given him,"[17] and that such an agreement is therefore inconsistent with the constitutional provision.

The court's reasoning is of doubtful validity. Conceptually, in order to represent a "tax" on the exercise of a right, the requirement in question must force the person who exercises the right to do something that the person who does not exercise the right is not forced to do. With respect to the constitutional right not to become a member of a union, the requirement that such a person pay the equivalent of dues and fees cannot be considered a tax on the exercise of that right since people who do not exercise the right (or who exercise the converse right of joining the union) are subject to the very same requirement. Since the requirement flows from both the exercise and the non-exercise of the right, the requirement can hardly be thought of as a tax on the exercise of that right. Indeed, if the court's reasoning were correct, then the requirement that workers who join the union pay union dues would be equally invalid, since this too could be conceptualized as a tax on the exercise of a constitutional right, in this case the right to join a union.

In *Ficek* v. *Boilermakers Local 647*,[18] the most recent state supreme court decision on this issue, the Supreme Court of

---

[15] 202 F. Supp. 726 (D. Nev. 1962).

[16] 141 S.2d 269 (Fla. 1962).

[17] *Id.* at 273.

[18] 219 N.W.2d 860 (N.D. 1974).

North Dakota adopted by reference most of the varying rationale discussed above. In addition, the court stated that "we agree with the reasoning of the United States Supreme Court in the *General Motors* and *Schermerhorn* cases, *supra,* when such Court held that an agency shop provision which required employees to pay union fees as a condition of employment was the 'practical equivalent' of an 'agreement requiring membership in a labor organization as a condition of employment.' " [19] Presumably, what the court meant was that it agreed with that conclusion, for the reasoning of the Supreme Court in those cases was predicated on a reading of the convoluted language of the proviso to Section 8(a)(3), rather than on just the term "membership" standing alone, and thus such reasoning is obviously inapplicable within the context of the simpler language of the North Dakota right-to-work statute.

More persuasive is the court's argument from public policy. The court determined that the statute should be construed in such a way as to effectuate the intent of its framers rather than in a literal fashion. The court then noted that the public policy which the framers of the statute were attempting to implement was that "a person has a right to work free of any interference, restraint or coercion by either employer or labor organizations." [20] While such a policy could arguably extend to things which the state lacks the power to regulate, in this instance the court determined, and correctly so, that it did have the power to prohibit the agency shop, and that the agency shop would restrain an employee in the exercise of his right to work. The statute, the court thus concluded, should be construed as prohibiting this form of restraint.

The only decision to construe a state right-to-work law as not prohibiting the agency shop is that reached by the Indiana Supreme Court in *Meade Electric Co.* v. *Hagberg.*[21] This was the first court to address the issue. The court there emphasized that the Indiana statute was penal in nature and that under commonly recognized canons of interpretation, "penal statutes will be strictly construed, and not construed to include anything beyond its letter, though within its spirit. . . ." [22] Since the

---

[19] *Id.* at 871.

[20] *Id.*

[21] 159 N.E.2d 408 (Ind. 1959).

[22] *Id.* at 412.

statute spoke only in terms of membership, and since actual union membership is not required under an agency shop agreement, the court concluded that the statute did not prohibit that kind of contractual arrangement. The Indiana right-to-work statute was subsequently repealed.

In Arizona, Florida, Kansas, and Nevada, the right-to-work statutes do not contain penal provisions, and the courts in those states distinguished the *Meade* decision on that basis. In two states, South Dakota and Texas, there has been no judicial determination of whether the statutory prohibition against compulsory union membership also includes a prohibition against the agency shop. Although the attorneys general of both states have ruled that the agency shop is prohibited by their statutes,[23] the Texas right-to-work statute contains penal provisions. Whether the courts of that state will thus follow the *Meade* approach or distinguish the case on a different basis remains to be seen. If, however, what the *Meade* court was concerned with was adequate notice, the Texas attorney general's opinions are quite express that such notice has been adequately given. In the labor union context at both the federal and state levels, as the post-*Meade* decisions suggest, the term *membership* has become a term of art which encompasses both literal membership and membership in the form of the payment of money. It is not unreasonable to expect those affected by this statute in labor unions and management to be on notice of the widely accepted meaning of the statutory term.

Fixed-Term Checkoff Authorizations

As was seen earlier, a checkoff authorization that is irrevocable for a fixed term achieves the same effect as an agreement that requires an employee who becomes a member of the union to maintain that membership for a fixed term. Since all of the state right-to-work statutes prohibit membership in a union as a condition of employment, and since in all the states membership has been construed to include the mere payment of money, it necessarily follows that fixed-term checkoff authorizations are implicitly prohibited by all of the state right-to-work laws.

The case against fixed-term checkoff authorizations is even stronger in those states where the agency shop has been ex-

---

[23] Texas, OP. ATTY. GEN., WW-1018 (1961); South Dakota, OP. ATTY. GEN. Report 1957-58, p. 236 (1958).

pressly outlawed. Most of the provisions having that effect are worded in such a fashion as to prohibit employers from requiring employees, as a condition of employment, to pay dues, fees, or other charges of any kind to any labor union. Whenever an employer refuses to honor the revocation of a checkoff authorization, that employer is literally making the payment of money to the union a condition of employment and has thus violated the statute.

Finally, two of the right-to-work states have provisions which expressly make checkoff authorizations revocable, "at will" in Georgia and on thirty days notice in Iowa.

State prohibition of fixed-term checkoff authorizations, whether such prohibition is achieved directly or indirectly, is, however, preempted by Section 302 of the Labor-Management Relations Act which permits checkoff authorizations to be irrevocable for no longer than a year—or so the Supreme Court held in *SeaPAK*.

Hiring Hall Arrangements

Although none of the state right-to-work laws refer expressly to hiring hall arrangements, several of them have been construed as prohibiting such arrangements irrespective of the preemptive federal law on the subject. For example, the Arkansas right-to-work statute prohibits labor contracts which "exclude from employment . . . persons who are not members of, or who fail or refuse to join *or affiliate with,* a labor union. . . ." In *Kaiser* v. *Price-Fewell, Inc.,*[24] the Arkansas Supreme Court struck down an exclusive but nondiscriminatory hiring hall agreement on the grounds that such an agreement required employees to affiliate with a labor union in violation of the statute.

Subsequently, the Arkansas Supreme Court reaffirmed its *Price-Fewell* decision, but held that an agreement whereby "the Union will furnish at the request of the contractor duly qualified workmen" did not compel involuntary affiliation as a condition of employment, since the agreement did not require the employer to make such a request.[25] The Eighth Circuit Court of Appeals

---

[24] 235 Ark. 295, 359 S.W.2d 449 (1962).

[25] Williams v. Arthur J. Arney Co., 240 Ark. 157, 398 S.W.2d 515, 517 (1966) ; *accord,* Ketcher v. Sheet Metal Workers' International, 115 F. Supp. 802 (E.D. Ark. 1953).

later held that the *Price-Fewell* decision was preempted by contrary federal law.[26]

In *Building Trades Council of Reno* v. *Bonito*,[27] a Nevada case, a collective bargaining agreement required the employer to request craftsmen from the union, but allowed him to hire them from other sources if the union could not supply such craftsmen within forty-eight hours. The Nevada Supreme Court simply assumed that the union would supply only union members, and that so long as the union could supply such craftsmen, "those not union members would be deprived of opportunity to obtain employment because of their non-membership";[28] thus, the union would be in violation of the state's right-to-work law. The court held that a hiring hall or referral arrangement that discriminates on the basis of union membership is prohibited under the law.

In *Painters' Local 567* v. *Tom Joyce Floors, Inc.*,[29] however, a Nevada trial court went beyond this and, in an unreported decision, held that even a nondiscriminatory hiring hall arrangement violated the state right-to-work law. On appeal, the Nevada Supreme Court declined to pass upon the legality of such an agreement under state law, but reversed the lower court on other grounds. Subsequently, the Ninth Circuit Court of Appeals accepted the trial court's decision as the controlling state law on the subject, but then held that such law was preempted by federal law.[30] The federal court's decision on the preemption matter was, however, limited to nondiscriminatory hiring hall arrangements. The *Bonito* case would thus appear to be good law in Nevada still.

In *Branham* v. *Miller Electric Co.*,[31] it was alleged that an employer and a union had an agreement whereby the employer would hire only such persons as were cleared through the union. The defendant employer demurred to the complaint, arguing *inter alia* that it did not state a violation of the South Carolina right-to-work law. The South Carolina Supreme Court disagreed. The court noted that under such an arrangement, "it

---

[26] Laborers Local 107 v. Kunco, 472 F.2d 456 (8th Cir. 1973).

[27] 71 Nev. 84, 280 P.2d 295 (1955).

[28] *Id.* at 86, 280 P.2d at 297.

[29] 81 Nev. 1, 398 P.2d 245 (1965).

[30] NLRB v. Tom Joyce Floors, Inc., 353 F.2d 768 (9th Cir. 1965).

[31] 237 S.C. 540, 118 S.E.2d 167 (1961).

would be certain, as a practical matter, that only union members in good standing would be employed." [32] While in that particular instance it is true that the union had refused to refer the plaintiff because he was not a member in good standing with the union, it is questionable whether the court was justified in simply assuming that the referral arrangement would always be operated in a fashion that discriminated on the basis of union membership.

On the other hand, rather than holding that all union referral arrangements inevitably discriminate on the basis of union membership, the court may have been holding that all such arrangements violate the statute, whether discrimination on the basis of union membership is present or not. This is so because at one point the court noted without limitation that under the statute neither hiring nor firing could "be grounded or conditioned upon union membership or non-membership, referral or non-referral, approval or non-approval." [33] Moreover, the section of the statute which the court said was violated was that which prohibits the creation of an "employment monopoly." Such a monopoly could be said to exist whenever the union becomes the exclusive source of employees, whether or not its referral practices are discriminatory on the basis of union membership.

In *Sheet Metal Workers Local 175* v. *Walker,*[34] an employer had agreed to hire "none but journeymen sheet metal workers and registered apprentices whose qualification as such are recognized by the Union," and the union had agreed to supply such workers. In the event the union was unable to do so within forty-eight hours, the employer was free to hire workers from other sources, provided such workers "comply with the requirements of membership of the Union." [35] A Texas court of appeals held that on its face such a contract "provides for a closed shop, contrary to the laws of Texas." [36] Thus, again, a hiring hall or referral arrangement that discriminates on the basis of union membership was held to violate a state right-to-work law.[37]

---

[32] *Id.* at 547, 118 S.E.2d at 170.

[33] *Id.* at 548, 118 S.E.2d at 171.

[34] 236 S.W.2d 683 (Tex. Ct. of Civ. App. 1951).

[35] *Id.* at 684.

[36] *Id.* at 684-85.

[37] *See also* Finchum Steel Erection Corp. v. Local 384, Ironworkers, 202 Tenn. 580, 308 S.W.2d 381 (1957); a contract under which the union agreed to furnish "union labor" was held to violate the state right-to-work law.

Compulsory Union Representation

Under the federal-law doctrine of exclusive representation, a union that is selected by a majority of the employees in an appropriate unit becomes the exclusive bargaining representative of all the employees in the unit. This operates in derogation of the individual's freedom to work under terms and conditions that are agreeable to him and the employer. Since the underlying philosophy or thrust of the right-to-work statutes is to enhance the individual's freedom to work—free from interference by unions—it is not surprising that some of the right-to-work statutes are phrased in such a way, it can be argued, as to prohibit exclusive representation arrangements, even though this is preempted by federal law.

For example, the Arkansas statute provides that "freedom of organized labor to bargain collectively, and *freedom of unorganized labor to bargain individually* is declared to be the public policy of the State. . . ." [38] Somewhat more ambiguous, but nevertheless susceptible of being construed as prohibiting compulsory representation, the North Dakota statute guarantees the individual worker the full freedom "to decline to associate with his fellows" [39] in a labor context. A similarly worded Wyoming statute was construed by the supreme court of that state as prohibiting compulsory representation. One section of the Wyoming right-to-work statute provides that "no person is required to have any connection with . . . any labor organization as a condition of employment or continuation of employment." [40] In *Local 415, IBEW* v. *Hansen*,[41] the court held that when an employer recognized a union as the exclusive bargaining representative of all his employees, this necessarily required his employees to have a "connection with" the union as a condition of employment. The court, however, held that, so construed, the provision was preempted by Section 9 of the Labor-Management Relations Act, which specifically authorizes the exclusive representation arrangement.

The Louisiana right-to-work statute at one time provided that "the right of a person or persons to work shall not be denied or abridged on account of membership or nonmembership in any

---

[38] ARK. STAT. § 81-201 (1960) (emphasis added).

[39] N.D. CENT. CODE § 34-08-02 (1972).

[40] WYO. STAT. ANN. § 27-245.2 (1967).

[41] 400 P.2d 531 (Wyo. 1965).

labor union or labor organization." [42] In *Piegts* v. *Amalgamated Meat Cutters Local 437*,[43] the Louisiana Supreme Court held that when an employee, without his agreement, is represented by a labor organization, that employee's right to work is "abridged" in violation of the statute. The court noted:

> There are instances where the union demands higher hourly wages and shorter hours. In order to be gainfully employed to support his family, a non-union man might be willing to make concessions. Liberty of contract is the non-union man's prerogative.[44]

When that liberty is taken away from him, his right to work is "diminished, reduced, curtailed, or shortened." [45]

The right-to-work statute under which this decision was rendered was subsequently repealed, but an identically worded statute (in relevant part) was passed which pertained only to agricultural workers.[46] Since such workers are not covered by the Labor-Management Relations Act, the federal preemption doctrine would not apply, and it would appear that the *Piegts* case is still good law in that limited context. It is thus unlawful under the Louisiana right-to-work law for an employer to recognize a union as the exclusive bargaining representative of a group of agricultural workers unless each individual worker has agreed to such representation. This, in essence, mandates members-only collective bargaining. The new Louisiana right-to-work statute, although it does not contain the word *abridge*, could nevertheless be similarly construed but for the federal preemption doctrine.

Compulsory Nonmembership in a Labor Union

Although not expressly authorized by Section 14(b) and undoubtedly preempted by Section 8(a)(3) of the Labor-Management Relations Act,[47] state prohibitions against the so-called yellow dog contract (and other forms of discrimination against union members) exist in most of the states with com-

---

[42] 1914 La. Acts, No. 294, § 1, 2.

[43] 228 La. 131, 81 S.2d 835 (1955).

[44] *Id.* at 140, 81 S.2d at 838.

[45] *Id.*

[46] LA. REV. STAT. ANN. §§ 23-881 to 23-889 (1964).

[47] *See* Leiter Mfg. Co. v. International Ladies' Garment Workers Union, 269 S.W.2d 409 (Tex. Ct. of Civ. App. 1954).

prehensive right-to-work statutes and in a large number of other states as well.

These prohibitions are, however, rarely enforced by state law, and the cases construing these provisions are few. Two states, North Carolina and North Dakota, have construed their statutes as having the same burden of proof on the discrimination issue. In *Willard* v. *Huffman*,[48] the Supreme Court of North Carolina held that an employee who is allegedly discharged in violation of the state law for union activity has the burden of showing "by competent evidence, and by the greater weight thereof, that he was discharged solely by reason of his participation in the discussions with his fellow employees in connection with their proposed plan to join a labor union or that such participation therein was the 'motivating' or 'moving cause' for his discharge."[49] This would appear to be a heavier burden than must be met in proving an analogous violation of the federal statute.

In determining what kinds of conduct these laws prohibit, however, the courts, as they have done for prohibitions against compulsory union membership, have tended to look to the broad intent of the legislature and not be bound by the literal language of the statute. In *Lunsford* v. *City of Bryan*,[50] the Texas Supreme Court held that a statute providing that "the right of persons to work shall not be denied or abridged on account of membership . . . in any labor union" encompassed a prohibition against the discharge of an employee who was not yet a member of the union but who was in the process of becoming one.

RIGHT-TO-WORK VIOLATIONS AND STATUTORY PROHIBITIONS

The central thrust of the right-to-work laws is that if an employee is otherwise qualified for a job, he should not be denied that job merely because of his membership or nonmembership in a labor organization. An employee, however, can be deprived

---

[48] 247 N.C. 523, 101 S.E.2d 373 (1958); *accord*, Sand v. Queen City Packing Co., 108 N.W.2d 448 (N.D. 1961).

[49] 101 S.E.2d at 376. *Likewise*, in Local 324, IBEW v. Upshur-Rural Electric Cooperative, 261 S.W.2d 484 (Tex. Ct. of Civ. App. 1953); although the "true motive" of the employer was never really established, there were a number of legitimate reasons for firing the employee in question, and the court held that the employee had not met his burden of proving that the discharge was related to or a consequence of his union activities.

[50] 156 Tex. 520, 297 S.W.2d 115 (1957).

of a job for these reasons in a variety of ways. As described above, the right to work could have a number of corollary duties. The kinds of conduct which the states most often proscribe are discussed below.

Requiring Union Membership as a Condition of Employment

All of the states with comprehensive right-to-work laws prohibit collective bargaining agreements between an employer and a union which require membership in a labor organization as a condition of employment. The central, but by no means exclusive, purpose of Section 14(b) was to authorize the states to prohibit this particular method of violating the right to work. A provision of Mississippi's right-to-work law is typical in this regard:

> Any agreement or combination between any employer and any labor union or labor organization whereby any person not a member of such union or organization shall be denied the right to work for an employer, or whereby such membership is made a condition of employment or continuation of employment by such employer, or whereby any such union or organization acquires an employment monopoly in any enterprise, is hereby declared to be an illegal combination or conspiracy and against public policy.[51]

Under such a provision, both the employer and the union have a legal duty not to enter into such an agreement, and for the breach of this duty both will be subject to whatever liabilities the act imposes.

Causing the Discharge of a Nonunion Employee

Originally, unions achieved the union security that they desired, not through the enforcement of a collective bargaining agreement making union membership a condition of employment, but rather through the imposition of direct sanctions (boycotts and picket lines) against any employer who hired other than union members. As was seen earlier, a number of states found such union conduct to be actionable at common law, and it was this nonstatutory variety of right-to-work law that the Wagner Act Congress originally intended not to preempt, an intention subsequently expressed in Section 14(b) of the LMRA. In any event, several of the right-to-work statutes expressly codify the

---

[51] MISS. CODE ANN. § 71-1-47(a) (1973).

common law on the subject. Typical in this regard is a provision of the Nevada statute:

> Any combination or conspiracy by two or more persons to cause the discharge of any person or to cause him to be denied employment because he is not a member of a labor organization, by inducing or attempting to induce any other person to refuse to work with such person, shall be illegal.[52]

Similarly, the Wyoming right-to-work statute broadly declares that "no person is required to become or remain a member of any labor organization as a condition of employment or continued employment," [53] and then additionally provides:

> Any person who . . . engages in any . . . strike, work stoppages, slow down, picketing, boycott or other action or conduct, a purpose or effect of which is to impose upon any person, directly or indirectly, any requirement or compulsion prohibited by this act, is guilty of a misdemeanor and shall also be liable in damages to any person injured thereby.[54]

Under this type of right-to-work provision, the corollary duty is upon the union not to induce the discharge of nonunion employees, and the breach of this duty will subject the union to the appropriate liability.

Some state right-to-work statutes neither contain express provisions similar to those quoted above nor even ambiguous provisions susceptible of being construed as imposing a statutory liability on unions who induce the discharge of nonunion employees. The right-to-work provision of the Kansas constitution is of this kind. Yet in *Taylor* v. *Hoisting & Portable Engineers Local 101*,[55] a union caused an employee to be fired because he was not a member of the union, and the employee sued for damages. The Kansas Supreme Court held that the employee had properly stated a course of action under the "common law of Kansas, aided and fortified by the recent 'right to work' constitutional amendment." [56] A similar approach could easily be followed in all of the other right-to-work states.[57]

---

[52] Nev. Rev. Stat. § 613.280 (1973).

[53] Wyo. Stat. Ann. § 27-245.2 (1967).

[54] *Id.* at § 27-246.6.

[55] 189 Kan. 137, 368 P.2d 8 (1962).

[56] *Id.* at 141, 368 P.2d at 11.

[57] *See* Dukes v. Painters Local 437, 191 Tenn. 495, 235 S.W.2d 7 (1950); Large v. Dick, 207 Tenn. 664, 343 S.W.2d 693 (1960).

Unilateral Employer Discrimination Against Nonunion Employees

All of the major right-to-work states, either directly or indirectly, prohibit employers from unilaterally making union membership a condition of employment even where a collective bargaining agreement does not require it, and a union has not otherwise induced an employer to accept this posture. Typical of the states having an express provision in this regard is South Carolina. A section of that state's right-to-work statute provides:

> It shall be unlawful for any employer . . . to require any employee, as a condition of employment . . . to be or become or remain a member or affiliate of any labor organization or agency.[58]

Under a provision of this kind, the legal duty rests solely upon the employer.

REMEDIES AND SANCTIONS UNDER THE STATE RIGHT-TO-WORK LAWS

The remedies and sanctions that are available under the various state right-to-work laws vary appreciably from state to state. In all of the states (except Kansas, its law being totally silent) which have comprehensive right-to-work laws, however, one or more of the remedies/sanctions discussed below is expressly provided for.

Voidness of the Contract

Although it is certainly implicit in all the statutes which outlaw union security contracts, several of the statutes expressly provide that such contracts shall, as in the case of North Dakota, be deemed invalid, void, and unenforceable.

Damages

A substantial number of the right-to-work statutes expressly provide for the recovery of the actual damages that an employee suffers as a consequence of the violation of the right-to-work statute. In addition, several states allow for the recovery of punitive damages, costs, and attorneys' fees. For example, the South Carolina statute provides that upon proof of a violation of the statute the court

---

[58] S.C. CODE ANN. § 40-46.2 (1) (1962).

may determine and award, as justice may require, any actual damages, costs and attorneys' fees which have been sustained or incurred by any party to the action, and, in the discretion of the court or jury, punitive damages in addition to the actual damages.[59]

Injunctive Relief

Approximately one-half of the right-to-work statutes authorize the courts to issue injunctions against violations of the statute. For example, the Iowa statute provides that "any person . . . may be restrained by injunction from doing or continuing to do any of the matters and things prohibited by this chapter. . . ." [60] Injunctions are most often issued against three kinds of conduct: (1) union picketing to obtain an illegal union security agreement; (2) union picketing to cause the discharge of all non-union employees; and (3) the enforcement of an illegal union security agreement. As was seen earlier, injunctions under the first two categories have for the most part been preempted by federal law. At the present time, thus, injunctions are most often used to prevent threatened discharges or to obtain the reinstatement of an employee who has already been discharged.

Criminal Penalties

In most states, a violation of the right-to-work statute is a misdemeanor, punishable by fines up to $5,000 and/or jail terms of as long as twelve months. In some states, this is the only penalty that the statute provides. In North Carolina, although the statute only provides for damages, the supreme court of that state held that a violation of the statute was also a misdemeanor.[61]

"PARTIAL" RIGHT-TO-WORK STATUTES

A number of states which lack a comprehensive right-to-work statute nevertheless guarantee a right to work in one or more of the particular senses discussed above, give the right to a specific class of employees, or otherwise attempt to regulate union security agreements.

---

[59] *Id.* at § 40.46.8 (1962).

[60] IOWA CODE ANN. § 736A.7 (1977).

[61] State v. Bishop, 228 N.C. 371, 45 S.E.2d 858 (1947).

For example, eighteen states,[62] none of which prohibit making union membership a condition of employment, outlaw the so-called yellow dog contract which attempts to make nonunion membership a condition of employment. Likewise, several states either prohibit the checkoff of union dues altogether [63] or make checkoff authorizations revocable at will or on thirty days notice.[64] In two states, checkoffs are valid only if a majority of the employees in the unit expressly approve.[65]

On the other hand, a provision of the New York statute, which applies only to race track employees, is substantially similar to the federal act's authorization of union security agreements, except that under the state act an employee can be required to join the union within fifteen, rather than thirty, days after being hired.[66]

The Massachusetts labor act makes it illegal for an employer to discharge an employee under a contract calling for union membership as a condition of employment, unless the union certifies that certain conditions exist and certain procedures have been exhausted.[67] It is apparent that the Massachusetts statute contemplates formal union membership, and its effect would be to allow discharge in more instances than is allowed by the federal statute. To the extent that the statute has that effect, it is, of course, preempted.

---

[62] CAL. LABOR CODE § 921 (1971); COLO. REV. STAT. § 8-3-119 (1974); CONN. GEN. STAT. § 31-90 (1972); IDAHO CODE § 44-901 (1948); ILL. ANN. STAT. ch. 48, § 2b (1969); IND. STAT. ANN. § 22-6-1-3 (1971); LA. REV. STAT. ANN. § 23-823 (1964); ANN. CODE OF MD. art. 100, § 64 (1964); MASS. GEN. LAWS ANN. ch. 149, § 20 (1971); MINN. STAT. ANN. § 179.60 (1966); N.H. REV. STAT. ANN. ch. 275, § 2 (1966); N.J. STAT. ANN. § 34:12-3 to 34:12-5 (1965); N.M. STAT. ANN. § 59-13-4 (1974); N.Y. CIVIL RIGHTS LAW § 17 (1948); PAGE'S OHIO CODE ANN. § 4113.02 (1973); ORE. REV. STAT. § 662.030 (1953); GEN. LAWS OF R.I. § 28-7-13 (1969); WIS. STAT. ANN. §§ 103.46, 103.52 (1974).

[63] VERNON'S ANN. MO. STAT. § 432.030 (1971) provides that "all assignments of wages, salaries, and earnings, not earned at the time of assignment is made, shall be null and void."

[64] COLO. REV. STAT. § 8-3-108(1)(i) (1974) (revocable on 30 days notice); IND. STAT. ANN. § 22-2-7-2 (1971) (revocable at will); IOWA CODE ANN. § 736A.5 (1973) (revocable on 30 days notice).

[65] PENN. STAT. 43 § 211.6(f) (1964); GEN. LAWS OF R.I. § 28-14-3 (1969); COLO. REV. STAT. § 80-4-6(1)(d) (1973); see Communication Workers of America v. Western Electric Co., 551 P.2d 1065 (Colo. 1976).

[66] (1966) 2 LABOR LAW REPORTER—STATE LAWS (CCH), N.Y. ¶ 41,025 (N.Y. UNCONSOLIDATED LAWS § 7610-a).

[67] MASS. GEN. LAWS ANN. ch. 150A, §§ 4(6), 6A (1971).

On the other hand, in both Colorado and Wisconsin a union security agreement is invalid unless it has been approved by an affirmative vote of either three-fourths (in Colorado)[68] or one-half (in Wisconsin)[69] of the employees in the unit. In both these states the employee's duty to become a union member (*i.e.*, pay the equivalent of dues and fees, which is all the federal law allows) is conditioned upon the employee not being unreasonably refused membership (presumably of the formal variety) in the union.[70] Thus if an employee were unreasonably refused membership in the union, this employee would be relieved of his obligation to pay agency shop fees; at least one Federal Court of Appeals has construed the federal act as having the same effect.[71]

Finally, and somewhat curiously, while both the Colorado and the California statutes do not generally prohibit union security agreements between an employer and a union (calling for membership in the union as a condition of employment), they do prohibit such a contract between an employer and an individual employee.[72]

---

[68] COLO. REV. STAT. § 8-3-108(1) (c) (1974).

[69] WIS. STAT. ANN. § 111.06(1) (c)1 (1974).

[70] WIS. STAT. ANN. § 111.06(1)(c)1 (1974); COLO. REV. STAT. § 8-3-108 (1)(c) (1974).

[71] Local 1104, Communication Workers v. NLRB, 520 F.2d 411 (2d Cir. 1975), *cert. denied*, 96 S.Ct. 778 (1976).

[72] COLO. REV. STAT. § 8-3-108 (1974); CAL. LABOR CODE § 921 (1971).

CHAPTER IX

Union Security in the Context of Labor Arbitration

Federal law itself does not directly require employees to become members of labor organizations. Rather, the law permits an employer and a labor union to enter into a contract whereby the employer agrees to require union membership of his employees as a condition of their continued employment.

As a part of a collective bargaining agreement, such union security agreements are thus frequently subject to arbitration. Indeed, insofar as union security is concerned, arbitration is the most common means for determining the scope of the rights and obligations of the employees, the employer, and the union alike. Despite the large number of arbitration decisions on this subject, however, it must be borne in mind that many contractual violations of union security agreements go unremedied simply because employers too often acquiesce to the union's demands, and because the individual employees lack either the financial resources or the legal right to process a grievance themselves. What this means is that the only cases that are apt to go to arbitration are those in which the interests of the employee happen to coincide with those of the employer. What effect, if any, this natural selection of cases has upon the resulting arbitration case law is impossible to determine, although one must suspect that an effect is there.

Many of the union security issues which labor arbitrators are called upon to resolve are substantially similar to those which arise before the Board and the courts. Consistent with the general divergence of practice on this point, most arbitrators will concern themselves with problems of statutory interpretation, while a few limit their decisions strictly to a construction of the contract.[1] In either event, of course, the precedent value of the

---

[1] *Compare* Union Pacific Railroad Co., 22 LAB. ARB. 20 (1954) (Warren, Arb.) *with*, *e.g.*, Globe-Democrat Publishing Co., 41 LAB. ARB. 65, 71-72 (1963) (Smith, Arb.) and Buckstaff Co., 40 LAB. ARB. 833 (1963) (Young, Arb.).

decision is limited to the contract under which the arbitration is brought, which may account for the diversity of views that one can find on the various union security issues that have confronted arbitrators.

ACTUAL MEMBERSHIP OR THE MERE PAYMENT OF DUES?

The question of what kind of union security agreement federal law actually permits has been a recurring issue before both the NLRB and the courts. The matter, however, has also come up in the context of arbitration.

Pan American World Airways [2] and *Crown Zellerbach Corp.* [3] both involved the question of whether an employee could satisfy the requirements of a union security agreement by merely tendering dues and fees while refusing to acknowledge membership in or even a willingness to become a member of the labor union in question. In arguing that such a tender would satisfy the provisions of a union security agreement under either the Railway Labor Act or the Taft-Hartley Act, the employees and the employer relied heavily on the statutory prohibition against the discharge of a nonunion employee if the employer "has reasonable grounds for believing that membership was denied or terminated *for reasons other than the failure of the employee to tender the periodic dues and the initiation fees uniformly required as a condition of acquiring or retaining membership. . . .*" [4] Both arbitrators, however, rejected this argument.

In the *Pan American* case, Arbitrator Horvitz construed the statutory language as follows:

> In my view the protection afforded by this language cannot be claimed until the employee has applied for union membership. Literally this is because until he has applied for membership he cannot have been "denied" membership. An employee has not applied for union membership until he has given some outward manifestation of his desire or intent to join the union. [5]

Similarly, in the *Crown Zellerbach* case, Arbitrator Peck noted of the statutory language that the protection

---

[2] 20 Lab. Arb. 312 (1953) (Horvitz, Arb.).

[3] 45 Lab. Arb. 1009 (1965) (Peck, Arb.).

[4] *See* 29 U.S.C. § 158(a)(3) (1974) (emphasis added).

[5] 20 Lab. Arb. at 314.

goes only to an employee who tenders the dues and fees "required as a condition of acquiring or retaining membership." Thus, the protection does not extend to one who tenders the fees and dues for some purpose other than that of acquiring or retaining membership.[6]

It is apparent that both of these arbitrators were adopting what has previously been referred to as the *union option* interpretation of the statute. Because this interpretation has subsequently been rejected by the Board and the courts,[7] these decisions have little value. On the other hand, their references to the legislative history and interpretations of the then-existing case law do make as persuasive an argument as has ever been advanced for that particular construction of the statute.

UNION SECURITY AND RELIGIOUS FREEDOM

In several cases labor arbitrators have been confronted with the claim that a union security agreement should not be enforced against an employee whose religious beliefs prohibit membership in or even financial contributions to labor organizations. While some union security agreements make such allowances for religious objectors,[8] arbitrators are not inclined to honor such claims in the absence of an express exception. For example, in *Union Pacific Railroad Co.*,[9] the arbitrator held that the employee simply had not complied with the clear and unambiguous language of the contract, which made no allowance for religious objectors. This arbitrator, moreover, refused to concern himself with the constitutional and statutory issues. On the other hand, in *Benson Shoe Co.*,[10] the arbitration panel engaged in a rather extensive discussion of the First Amendment issue. The panel, however, held that the union security provision, which called for an agency shop, did not violate the individual's freedom of religion. In reaching this conclusion, the panel relied heavily on the decision of Judge Wyzanski in *Linscott* v. *Millers Falls Co.*[11] The arbitra-

---

[6] 45 LAB. ARB. at 1013.

[7] *See* Chapter III, *supra*.

[8] *See* (1976) 2 COLLECTIVE BARGAINING NEGOTIATIONS & CONTRACTS (BNA) 87:102.

[9] 22 LAB. ARB. 20 (1954) (Warren, Arb.).

[10] 62 LAB. ARB. 1020 (1974) (Mass. State Board of Arbitration).

[11] Linscott v. Millers Falls Co., 316 F. Supp. 1369 (D. Mass. 1970), *aff'd,* 440 F.2d 14 (1st Cir. 1971), *cert. denied,* 404 U.S. 872 (1971).

tion panel understood the court in that case to have conceded that a *prima facie* violation of the First Amendment was made when a religious objector was forced to join a union, but then the panel concluded that in the matter at hand, the infringement was "minimal" and was "far outweighed" by the "governmental interests sanctioning union security arrangements." [12]

CONDITIONS OF DISCHARGE OF THE EMPLOYEE

Frequently, before an employee can be discharged for nonmembership in a labor organization, the employer and/or the union are required to meet certain conditions. Where these conditions are specifically spelled out in the contract, labor arbitrators tend to enforce them strictly. For example, in *Florida East Coast Railway Co.*,[13] the union security provision of the contract required the union to notify the employer of an employee's dues delinquency on a special form. Upon receipt of this form, the employer was to notify the employee and, if the deficiency were not corrected within a certain period, to discharge the employee. In this case, however, the union used a slightly different form. The arbitrator held that the employer was under no obligation to effectuate the discharge and, indeed, could not do so until proper notification was received from the union; the arbitrator rejected the union's argument that the form of the notice was merely a procedural nicety, and that the employees were not disserved because a different form was used.

A condition precedent that arbitrators will impose, even where the contract does not specifically require it, is that the employee be on notice of his breach of the union membership obligation. In *Westinghouse Electric*,[14] the arbitrator noted that a union which is seeking the discharge of an employee has "a fiduciary duty to deal fairly with him" and required "at the minimum 'that the union inform the employee of his obligations in order that the employee may take whatever action is necessary to protect his job tenure' . . . [and] give reasonable notice to an employee that he will lose his job for non-payment of dues." [15]

---

[12] 62 LAB. ARB. at 1022.

[13] 45 LAB. ARB. 6 (1965) (Seibel, Arb.).

[14] 56 LAB. ARB. 588 (1971) (Wolff, Arb.).

[15] *Id.* at 589-90, quoting from NLRB v. Local 182, Teamsters, 401 F.2d 509 (2d Cir. 1968), *cert. denied,* 394 U.S. 213 (1969).

Whether an employee who is delinquent in his union dues has the right to make a "belated tender" and thereby save his job is another issue frequently faced by arbitrators. In *Schulze & Burch Biscuit Co.*,[16] the arbitrator upheld the discharge of such an employee on the grounds that a tender of dues after the union has already demanded discharge comes too late; the employer is required to honor the union's demand. The basis of the arbitrator's decision was that a discharge under such circumstances does not violate the Taft-Hartley Act;[17] apparently, the arbitrator was willing to assume that the parties intended to require the discharge of an employee under any and all circumstances permitted by law. In contrast to that approach, many other arbitrators have allowed employees to retain their jobs by merely tendering the unpaid dues within a designated period after the arbitration decision itself[18]—a "belated tender" which statutory law clearly does not require the union to accept or the employer to recognize insofar as discharge is concerned.

Another right that employees who are delinquent in their dues frequently rely upon is that of being treated impartially by the union. Labor arbitrators generally allow labor unions to exercise some discretion and leniency with respect to one employee's dues delinquency without thereby waiving the right to enforce the membership obligation altogether with respect to other employees. This obviously disparate treatment of employees may prevent a discharge,[19] especially when it is apparent that the union may be motivated by considerations other than the employee's failure to pay the required dues.[20]

Finally, even when a discharge is proper under a union security agreement, an issue can arise over the employee's entitlement to severance pay. In *New York Times*,[21] the contract provided that

---

[16] 42 LAB. ARB. 280 (1964) (Solomon, Arb.).

[17] *Compare* S.S. White Dental Mfg. Co., 26 LAB. ARB. 428 (1956) (Gamser, Arb.), in which the arbitrator deferred to what was at that particular time the NLRB's policy of allowing belated tender at any time prior to actual discharge.

[18] *See, e.g.,* Westinghouse Electric Corp., 56 LAB. ARB. 588 (1971) (Wolff, Arb.); Midwest Mfg. Co., 44 LAB. ARB. 1163 (1965) (Teple, Arb.).

[19] Union Pacific Railroad Co., 23 LAB. ARB. 234 (1954) (Leary, Arb.); Southern Pacific Co., 21 LAB. ARB. 471 (1953) (Osborne, Arb.).

[20] *Cf.,* Schulze & Burch Bisquit Co., 42 LAB. ARB. 280 (1964) (Solomon, Arb.).

[21] 48 LAB. ARB. 157 (1967) (Bailer, Arb.).

"a discharged employee shall be entitled to receive in a lump sum a cash severance payment equal to two weeks pay" except where the discharge was for "dishonesty, gross neglect of duty, gross insubordination or repeated drunkeness. . . ." [22] An employee who had been discharged for failing to join the union sought the severance pay to which he thought he was entitled. The arbitrator, however, held that an employee who is terminated because of his refusal to join a labor union in compliance with a union security agreement must be regarded as a "voluntary quit" and, thus, not entitled to severance pay.

SPECIAL PROBLEMS WITH MAINTENANCE-OF-MEMBERSHIP AGREEMENTS

More arbitration decisions on maintenance-of-membership agreements have been rendered than have been on all of the other kinds of union security combined. This is undoubtedly due, in part, to the popularity of this form of union security, especially during the early days of the Taft-Hartley Act. It can however, also be attributed to the poor draftsmanship that is often displayed in such agreements. By its very nature, a maintenance-of-membership agreement imposes obligations that are difficult to define verbally, and many labor agreements tend to leave the details of the obligation obscure, necessitating a great deal of arbitral interpretation and construction. Also, it should be borne in mind that while the membership which must be maintained under a maintenance-of-membership agreement is limited by federal law to the mere payment of dues and fees, labor arbitrators tend to lose sight of this fact, adding yet another complicating factor.

Determining Who is a Member

A maintenance-of-membership agreement typically provides that an employee who is a member of the union or who has applied for membership at the time the collective bargaining agreement is signed, or who becomes a member during the term of the contract, must remain a member for the duration of the contract. Such an agreement thus raises the problem of determining exactly who is a member at the relevant time and/or what represents an application for membership.

---

[22] *Id.* at 158.

This problem frequently arises where, in a prior organizational campaign, the union has used "authorization cards" as a means of obtaining an NLRB election and/or a possible bargaining order; subsequently, the union negotiates a maintenance-of-membership agreement and then seeks to require all of the employees who signed an authorization card to maintain their membership in the union. Whether the union is successful in this claim often depends upon the wording of the authorization card itself and the circumstances surrounding its solicitation. In *Roberts Wholesale Co.*,[23] during an organizational campaign some employees signed an authorization card that read, "For purposes of collective bargaining . . . I, the undersigned, hereby accept membership and authorize [the union] to represent me." The union subsequently negotiated a collective bargaining agreement which provided that employees who are or become members of the union "shall remain members in good standing," and the union proceeded to define such membership in terms of the periodic tender of dues. In spite of the literal wording of the authorization card, the arbitrator held that the employees in question were not members of the union at the time the contract was signed. He noted that the employees had never paid any dues, that the employees had never been formally "inducted" into membership, and that during the nine months since the contract was negotiated, these employees had had no contact with the union, had attended no meetings, and had even crossed the union's picket line. Additionally, and perhaps more important, the arbitrator credited the testimony of the employees to the effect that when they signed the cards they were told that this would merely enable the union to come into the plant and would not actually require them to become members.

On the other hand, in *Pizza Co.*,[24] the authorization card merely said that "I . . . hereby authorize the [union] to represent me for purposes of collective bargaining." The subsequent contract required employees who had applied for membership or who were hired after a certain date to become and remain members of the union. In holding that these employees could be required to maintain their membership in the union, the arbitrator noted that "authorizing a particular union to represent an individual for the purpose of collective bargaining *is* indica-

---

[23] 49 LAB. ARB. 395 (1967) (Krinsky, Arb.).

[24] 55 LAB. ARB. 1033 (1970) (Gross, Arb.).

tive of membership in the union." [25] Although that conclusion
standing alone may be somewhat dubious, in that desiring representation and desiring membership are two different and not
necessarily simultaneous states of mind, the arbitrator also found
that at the time the employees signed the cards, they did in fact
intend to join the union, and that signing the card was thus
tantamount to an application for membership.

An even easier case is presented by the facts of *Midwest Manufacturing Co.*[26] There, the authorization card read as follows:
"Desiring to become a member of [the union] . . . , I hereby
make application for admission to membership and authorize such
organization to be my exclusive collective bargaining representative." The collective bargaining agreement later provided that
all employees who apply for membership shall become and
remain members. Although the employees testified that they
thought the cards would be used only to get an election, the arbitrator found that the union had engaged in no misrepresenta-
tions and that the employees who signed them were therefore,
obligated to become and remain members in good standing.

Resignations or attempted resignations from the union prior to
the date of the maintenance-of-membership agreement also pose
a number of problems for labor arbitrators. For example, in
Bay State Optical Co.,[27] an employee had been a formal member
of the union, but submitted a written resignation prior to the
effective date of the contract. The union contended that since its
constitution, which the employee had subscribed to when he became a member, did not expressly provide for resignations, the
employee was a member of the union at the time the contract was
signed and was required to remain one. The arbitrator, however,
held that union members in good standing have an implied right
to resign, and that the employee in this case had validly exercised
that right.

Less formal resignations, as through the mere discontinuance
of the payment of dues, have not fared so well, however. For
example, in *S.S. White Dental Manufacturing Co.*,[28] the employee
was delinquent in his payment of dues at the time the maintenance-of-membership agreement was signed. But he had submitted

---

[25] *Id.* at 1037.

[26] 44 LAB. ARB. 1163 (1965) (Teple, Arb.).

[27] 13 LAB. ARB. 474 (1949) (Myers, Arb.).

[28] 26 LAB. ARB. 428 (1956) (Gamser, Arb.).

no letter of resignation nor even communicated to the union his belief that he was no longer a member. The arbitrator construed the union constitution as categorizing this employee as a "suspended member" and thus held that he was covered by the maintenance-of-membership agreement.[29]

Employee Versus *"New Hire"*

When a union is selected as the collective bargaining representative of the employees in a particular unit, the first collective bargaining agreement frequently make special allowance for existing employees, insofar as their union security obligations are concerned; that is, existing employees will sometimes be subject only to a maintenance-of-membership requirement (in which case, an existing employee who is not a member of the union will not be required to become one), while all new employees are required to become members as a condition of employment. The following is a typical contract provision of this kind:

> Each regular employee who is a member of the Union on the date of ratification or approval of this agreement . . . or who later becomes a member of the Union, and *all regular employees hired on or after that date*, shall as a condition of employment, pay or tender to the Union such amounts equal to the periodic dues applicable to members. . . .[30]

Under this kind of union security provision, a question frequently arises about the person who was an employee of the company on the date of the contract, but who worked in another unit of the plant and who was later transferred into the unit covered by the union security provision. Is such a person an employee who is required only to maintain his membership? Or is he a "new hire" whose obligation to become a member is unconditional?

The weight of authority is that such a person is a "new hire" for the purposes of the union security agreement.[31] The reasoning behind this is that the coverage of a collective bargaining agree-

---

[29] *See also* Freeport Area School District, 58 LAB. ARB. 1276 (1972) (Duff, Arb.) ; Bay State Optical Co., 13 LAB. ARB. 474 (1949) (Myers, Arb.).

[30] Southern New England Telephone, 61 LAB. ARB. 184, 185 (1973) (Zack, Arb.).

[31] *See, e.g.,* Southern New England Telephone, 61 LAB. ARB. 184 (1973) (Zack, Arb.) ; Sargent Engineering Corp., 43 LAB. ARB. 1165 (1964) (Mc-Naughton, Arb.) ; F. P. Rosback, 19 LAB. ARB. 85 (1952) (Davis, Arb.).

ment is limited strictly to a particular bargaining unit; thus, when an agreement speaks of "employees," it generally means "employees within the bargaining unit," and "hired" likewise means "hired into a job within the unit." Moreover, it has been suggested that the purpose of this kind of union security agreement is best served by such an interpretation. In *Pacific Telephone & Telegraph,*[32] the arbitrator explained it in this fashion:

> What is in operation here is a "grandfather clause," which is a provision designed to cover a specific situation. It is defined by Webster's as "a clause exempting a class of persons because of circumstances applying before the clause takes effect." The "class of persons" involved here are those who were in the bargaining unit before the modified agency shop provisions, found in Article 26.01, was adopted. At the time these employees entered the unit, it was with the understanding that they would not be required to pay Union dues unless they chose to do so. Many Employers believe it would be unfair to later impose such payments as a new condition of employment in the unit. The grandfather provision carries out the Employer's objective of preserving the right of such employees, many of whom have long years of service in the unit, to decide themselves whether or not they wish to assume the obligation of paying periodic dues to the Union. That would appear to be the purpose of the grandfather clause that is included in Article 26.01.
>
> In the Arbitrator's opinion, however, the extension of such option to transferred employees is unwarranted because their situation is not at all the same. The transfer of an employee from one department to another inevitably involves changes, often substantial changes, in the employee's conditions of employment. For example, there may be new tasks to perform, changed hours of work, a different compensation schedule, and so forth. The payment of periodic dues is just another one of the conditions that goes with the new job. The transferee has the right to accept or reject the new position, but she does not have the right to be exempted from any of these new conditions—including the requirement to pay Union dues.[33]

There are, however, a few cases, involving special fact situations, where arbitrators have deviated from the general rule. In *Lord Manufacturing Co.,*[34] an employee joined the union, withdrew during the first available escape period, was transferred out of the unit, and was then transferred back in. Under this

---

[32] 61 Lab. Arb. 368 (1973) (Block, Arb.).

[33] *Id.* at 371-72.

[34] 55 Lab. Arb. 1005 (1970) (Keller, Arb.).

particular contract, if her transfer back into the unit was the equivalent of being hired, then she would have to rejoin the union until the next available escape period. There, however, the arbitrator construed the word "hired" in its literal rather than its specialized labor-law sense, which meant that as an existing employee on the relevant contract date she only had to maintain whatever membership she had in the union—which was none. *Chrysler Corp.*[35] is another case where employees were given the benefit of a "grandfather clause," even though they were not in a bargaining unit covered by the agreement on the relevant contract date. Here, all of the employees in a newly created bargaining unit were suddenly brought under the coverage of a previously negotiated master agreement which contained a union security provision similar to that quoted above. The arbitrator held that these employees were not "new hires" and were thus entitled to refrain from joining under the maintenance-of-membership provision of that agreement.

"Escape Periods"

Under a maintenance-of-membership agreement, an employee who is or becomes a member of the union is required to maintain that membership for the duration of the contract. Implicitly, such an agreement gives the employee the right to resign from membership at the termination of the contract. But when a labor contract is automatically renewed or there is no hiatus between the effective dates of successive contracts, then this right to resign is effectively denied. Thus, many maintenance-of-membership agreements provide for an "escape period" within which an employee who is a member of the union can resign from the union and thus avoid the requirement of continuing to maintain his membership as a condition of employment.

Typically, the escape period comes either just before or after the anniversary date of the contract. Where this term is used in conjunction with contracts of more than a single year, however, some difficulties of construction often result.

In *Springtrol Inc.*, for example, the collective bargaining agreement, which was for a term of three years, required employees who were or became members of the union to remain members

> provided that no more than 15 days prior to each anniversary date of this agreement a member may serve notice upon the Union and

---

[35] 21 LAB. ARB. 45 (1953) (Wolff, Arb.).

the company that he no longer desires to be a member in which case his resignation . . . shall be effective the day following the expiration of this agreement.[36]

The company contended that this provided for an annual escape period (fifteen days prior to *each* anniversary date), while the union contended that employees could withdraw only during the fifteen days prior to the end of the three year term. The arbitrator held that the employees could serve notice of withdrawal fifteen days prior to any of the three anniversary dates, but that such withdrawal would not be effective until the termination of the contract.

Employee "Escape"—A Notice Requirement

Maintenance-of-membership agreements with escape clauses almost always require some kind of notice to the union as a condition of an effective resignation from union membership during the escape period. As one arbitrator put it, though, "Withdrawal is a limited privilege, and the burden rests upon the employee-member to show that he has exercised this privilege substantially in the manner prescribed." [37] Thus, in *International Harvester Co.*,[38] an employee whose letter of resignation was returned to him because it was inadequately addressed and who made no other attempt to contact the union was held not to have effectively resigned from the union.[39]

Although a union is entitled to be put on actual notice of an employee's resignation, the form and timing of this notice in the absence of additional contractual requirements [40] will not be dictated by an arbitrator. In *Hercules Powder Co.*,[41] for example, a group of employees all signed the same letter of resignation. Although recognizing, at least for the purpose of argument, that "a mass petition easily lends itself to ill considered action by the signatories," the arbitrator felt that he had no right to require

---

[36] 59 LAB. ARB. 1307 (1972) (Mueller, Arb.).

[37] International Harvester Co., 25 LAB. ARB. 1, 7 (1955) (Smith, Arb.).

[38] *Id.*

[39] *Contra,* Adams-Millis Corp., 15 L.R.R.M. 2647 (1944) (Dwyer, Arb.).

[40] Registered mail is frequently required as a means of obviating the problem of proof of the actual receipt of the required notice. *See* International Harvester Co., 25 LAB. ARB. 1 (1955) (Smith, Arb.).

[41] 45 LAB. ARB. 270 (1965) (Knowlton, Arb.).

anything more than what the contract itself required—which was that the resignation be in writing. Similarly, in *Carson Manufacturing Co.*,[42] the union had refused to honor resignations that were signed and received prior to the designated escape period. The arbitrator, however, held:

> The writing of a letter of resignation is a matter of intent. The resignation then becomes effective *on the first possible date.*[43]

SPECIAL PROBLEMS INVOLVING CHECKOFF AGREEMENTS

A checkoff arrangement, whereby an employee's union dues are deducted from his paycheck by the employer and forwarded directly to the union, is a convenient way for the employee to discharge his obligations under any of the various forms of union security agreements. The agreement between the employee, the union, and the employer that underlies a checkoff arrangement has, however, proved to be a fruitful source of dispute and misunderstanding and thus the subject of an inordinately large number of arbitration decisions. The special problems that have arisen in this context will be considered separately.

Legality in Right-to-Work States

As is also true of the other forms of union security, checkoff authorizations that purport to be irrevocable for up to a year have been challenged in the arbitration forum on the basis of their apparent inconsistency with state right-to-work laws. On this issue, however, labor arbitrators have consistently held that state right-to-work laws are inapplicable.[44] This is consistent with the Supreme Court's *SeaPAK* decision which held that state regulation of checkoff arrangements is preempted by federal law.[45]

---

[42] 52 LAB. ARB. 1057 (1969) (Grohsmeyer, Arb.).

[43] *Id.* at 1060 (emphasis added).

[44] *See* Holeproof Hosiery Co., 24 LAB. ARB. 347 (1955) (Williams, Arb.); Textile Workers Union, 17 LAB. ARB. 53 (1951) (Barrett, Arb.); Allied Maintenance Corp., 66 LAB. ARB. 875 (1976) (Richman, Arb.).

[45] SeaPAK v. Industrial Employees, National Maritime Union, 300 F. Supp. 1197 (S.D. Ga. 1969), *affirmed per curiam*, 423 F.2d 1229 (5th Cir. 1970), *affirmed per curiam*, 400 U.S. 985 (1971).

Union Use of Checkoff Monies—The Employer's Obligation

Under collective bargaining agreements, what an employer is obligated to deduct is frequently limited to the "periodic membership dues" of the employees. This type of checkoff arrangement has given rise to a recurring issue—distinguishing "membership dues" from "special assessments." There is fairly wide agreement over the controlling principle. As stated in *Saco-Lowell Shops*,[46] it is as follows:

[T]he critical distinctions between assessments and dues are that assessments are for special purposes and are limited to a specific period in time. When *both* elements are present in the facts the increase involves an assessment rather than an increase in dues. . . . But where the increase involves both special purpose and [a] specific period in time the proper ruling is that the increase is in reality an assessment. . . .[47]

In this case, one local had voted to provide strike relief funds to a sister local for the duration of that local's strike; the funds were to be raised through an increase in the membership dues. The arbitrator, however, found this to be an assessment and thus not collectable through the checkoff. On the other hand, where an international union levies a tax on its locals for the purpose of replenishing a strike fund, and the locals meet this obligation by increasing dues, most arbitrators will treat this as a bona fide dues obligation rather than as an assessment.[48] The fact that the money is not earmarked for a specific strike and the fact that duration of the increase is "indefinite" (*i.e.*, to last until the fund reaches a certain level) are the matters usually relied on by arbitrators in reaching this conclusion.

Revocation of Checkoff Authorizations

Most of the problems that have confronted arbitrators in the matter of checkoffs have centered on the timing and circumstances under which the employer's obligation to honor checkoff authori-

---

[46] 25 LAB. ARB. 18 (1955) (Hogan, Arb.).

[47] *Id.* at 21-22.

[48] Tokheim Corp., 57 LAB. ARB. 22 (1971) (Kates, Arb.) (increase in dues that was to last until the International Union strike fund reached a certain level was held to be "indefinite" in time); Globe-Democrat Publishing Co., 41 LAB. ARB. 65 (1963) (Smith, Arb.); John Deere Waterloo Tractor Works, 14 LAB. ARB. 910 (1950) (Updegraff, Arb.) (the International Union levy was specifically identified as an "assessment"); *but see* Bemis Bros. Bag Co., 14 LAB. ARB. 685 (1950) (Lindquist, Arb.).

zation ceases. In this regard, arbitrators have been called upon to construe not only the collective bargaining agreement, but also the checkoff authorization form itself and the federal statutes that touch on this matter.

Statutory Limits on Irrevocability. Under Section 302 of the Taft-Hartley Act, a checkoff authorization "shall not be irrevocable for a period of more than one year, or beyond the termination date of the applicable collective agreement, whichever occurs sooner. . . ."[49] The law has been construed, however, as allowing the authorization to be automatically renewable, provided the employee is given a reasonable period within which to exercise this statutory right of revocation.[50] These provisions, directly or indirectly incorporated into collective bargaining agreements, have been the subject of a considerable amount of arbitral construction.

One recurring issue has been the revocability of checkoff authorization during so-called contract hiatus periods. In *Washington Post Co.*,[51] the contract provided that an employee could revoke his checkoff authorization only during a period of from thirty to fifteen days prior to the anniversary date of the authorization or the expiration of the collective bargaining agreement, whichever occurred sooner. If an employee did not revoke, the authorization was automatically renewed. In this case, the contract expired, and it was several weeks before a new contract came into force. During this hiatus period, a number of employees revoked their checkoff authorizations, and these revocations were honored by the employer. The employer contended that once a collective bargaining agreement expires, checkoff authorizations become revocable at will, and that an employer's refusal to honor such revocations would violate federal law.

The arbitrator, however, held that since the employees in question did not revoke during the contractually designated thirty to fifteen day period, their authorizations were automatically renewed for one year as of the date the contract expired. Thus, during the hiatus period when no collective bargaining agreement was in force, federal law in effect provides that the maximum period of irrevocability be determined only by reference to the

[49] 29 U.S.C. § 186(c) (1974).

[50] Monroe Lodge 770, IAM v. Litton Business Systems, 334 F. Supp. 310 (W.D. Va. 1971), *aff'd*, 80 L.R.R.M. 2379 (4th Cir. 1972), *cert. denied*, 409 U.S. 879 (1972).

[51] 66 LAB. ARB. 553 (1976) (Gamser, Arb.).

renewal date of the authorization itself. This being so, federal
law did not require the employer to honor checkoff revocations
submitted during the hiatus period.[52]
Other arbitrators, however, have reached a contrary conclusion
on this issue. For example, in *Samsonite Corp.*,[53] the checkoff was
irrevocable for one year, or the expiration of the collective bargaining agreement, whichever was shorter. But unless the authorization was revoked during the ten days immediately following the period of irrevocability, then it was deemed automatically
renewed for another year. During a contract hiatus period, a
number of employees revoked their checkoff authorization, and the
arbitrator held that the employer was entitled to honor them.
He said:

> The Company is on sound ground in stating that employees were
> at liberty to revoke check-off authorizations during the period in
> which no contract was in force between the parties.[54]

Other decisions have similarly noted that during a hiatus period,
checkoff authorizations can be revoked at will.[55] To a large extent,
however, peculiar facts are deemed to be of controlling importance in these cases, and thus it is nearly impossible to state a
general principle for the revocability of checkoff authorizations
during contract hiatus periods.

Notifying the Union of a Checkoff Revocation. Collective bargaining agreements frequently require an employee to notify the
union of his desire to terminate a checkoff authorization. Indeed,
one arbitrator read such a requirement into the contract on the
grounds that this was an administrative necessity.[56] On the other
hand, where the contract contains no technical requirements for
the form and nature of the notice (such as that it be by registered mail or be individually submitted, etc.), such requirements

---

[52] The arbitrator relied heavily on a prior arbitration decision which had
reached the same result on similar facts. The award in that case was later
found by the NLRB to be "not clearly repugnant to the purposes and policies
of the Act," a conclusion the court of appeals concurred with. *See* The
Associated Press, 199 N.L.R.B. 1110 (1972), *order enf'd*, 492 F.2d 662 (D.C.
Cir. 1974).

[53] 58 LAB. ARB. 469 (1972) (Hon, Arb.).

[54] *Id.* at 473.

[55] *See, e.g.,* Sperry Rand Corp., 44 LAB. ARB. 965 (1965) (Stein, Arb.);
Murtha v. Pet Dairy Prod., 42 L.R.R.M. 2850 (Tenn. Ct. of App. 1957);
accord, Jewish Board of Guardians, 43 LAB. ARB. 665 (1964) (Rose, Arb.).

[56] Chromium Process Co., 45 LAB. ARB. 190 (1965) (Altieri, Arb.).

will generally not be read into the contract.[57] In one case, where notification by registered mail was required, the arbitrator held that this was merely intended "to affect proof of delivery in disputed cases and does not affect the validity of the notice itself" when receipt is otherwise conceded by the union.[58]

One recurring issue has been whether a resignation from the union is also effective as a revocation of a checkoff authorization. The general rule seems to be that resignation from union membership does not automatically have this effect. The arbitrator in *Bell Helicopter Co.*[59] noted, "The matter of Union membership has absolutely nothing to do with the *continuation* of dues deduction for the relevant annual or collective agreement period."[60]

The general rule, however, for resignation and revocation is not universally adhered to. For example, in *Chromium Process Co.*,[61] the arbitrator said that "to give them a different effect because of a possible admitted conceptual distinction between revocation of authorization and withdrawal from union membership would be a legalistic approach not in accord with the sound administration of industrial relations."[62] Likewise, in *Douglas & Lomason Co.*,[63] the arbitrator held that a resignation from union membership that was submitted prior to the negotiation of the collective bargaining agreement also served to revoke a prior checkoff authorization. In this case, the arbitrator read the collective agreement as requiring the employer to honor only the checkoff authorization of employees who had membership dues obligations at the time the contract became effective, or thereafter. Since an employee who has resigned his membership does not have such a dues obligation, the employer is not required to honor his checkoff authorization.

---

[57] Franklin Electric Co., 50 LAB. ARB. 41 (1967) (Kates, Arb.).

[58] *Id.* at 45.

[59] 36 LAB. ARB. 933 (1961) (Shister, Arb.).

[60] *Id.* at 937; *see also* Samsonite Corp., 58 LAB. ARB. 469 (1972) (Hon, Arb.); Telex Computer Prod., 58 LAB. ARB. 961 (1972) (Shearer, Arb.); Franklin Electric Co., Inc., 50 LAB. ARB. 41 (1967) (Kates, Arb.); Minneapolis-Honeywell Regulator Co., 36 LAB. ARB. 1138 (1961) (Ruckel, Arb.); Ranney Refrigerator Co., 13 LAB. ARB. 378 (1949) (Whiting, Arb.).

[61] 45 LAB. ARB. 190 (1965) (Altieri, Arb.).

[62] *Id.* at 195.

[63] 58 LAB. ARB. 334 (1972) (Brandschain, Arb.).

Termination of Employment. Obviously, when a person's employment is terminated and he is no longer receiving wages, the checkoff of union dues necessarily stops. There is a question, however, about whether this operates as a total revocation of the authorization or merely as a suspension. In *Link-Belt Co.*,[64] an employee who had authorized a checkoff was terminated; when he was subsequently rehired, the employer declined to honor the prior authorization. The arbitrator upheld this on the ground that the termination operated as a revocation of the authority. A similar result was reached in *Armstrong Cork Co.*[65] An employee was transferred out of his unit, and the checkoff was discontinued. Subsequently, the employee was transferred back into the unit. The arbitrator, however, held that the company was not required to renew the checkoff since the transfer-out had operated as a revocation.

Deauthorization of the Union Security Agreement. Consistent with NLRB law on this issue,[66] labor arbitrators generally hold that when the union security agreement that underlies a checkoff arrangement has been voided by the employees through a Board-conducted deauthorization election, checkoff authorizations either became immediately revocable or are simply void by operation of law.[67]

CONCLUSION

Like the statutes that authorize them, union security agreements are often ambiguously worded and, many times, merely copy the exact words of the statute itself. As have the courts, labor arbitrators have thus been confronted with many difficult problems of interpretation. They must not only determine what

---

[64] 16 LAB. ARB. 242 (1951) (Baab, Arb.).

[65] Armstrong Cork Co., 65 LAB. ARB. 907 (1975) (McKelvey, Arb.) ; *compare* Minnesota Mining & Mfg. Co., 62 LAB. ARB. 1013 (1974) (Belkin, Arb.) (employer required to honor the checkoff authorizations of employees who were promoted out of the unit but who retained their unit seniority for one year).

[66] *See* Penn Cork & Closures, Inc., 156 N.L.R.B. 411 (1965), *enforced*, 376 F.2d 52 (2d Cir. 1967), *cert. denied*, 389 U.S. 843 (1967).

[67] *See, e.g.,* North Hills Electronics, 46 LAB. ARB. 789 (1965) (Christensen, Arb.) (after a union security deauthorization election, checkoff authorizations can be revoked despite "irrevocability" clause) ; Ferris Sales & Service, Inc., 36 LAB. ARB. 848 (1960) (Benewitz, Arb.) (checkoff void after union is decertified by NLRB).

the law allows, but also, within that maximum, determine exactly how far the parties intended to go, and then apply the contract to factual situations that are often excruciatingly complex.

By and large, labor arbitrators have done an admirable job in this field. The decisions reflect a keen appreciation of the underlying interests of both the employer and the union. But more important is the apparent arbitral regard for the rights of the individual employee who stands to lose the most through an adverse decision.

CHAPTER X

Union Security and the Right to Work in the Public Sector

Twenty years ago collective bargaining by public sector employees was virtually nonexistent; indeed, in most jurisdictions it was positively illegal.[1] In states without any express statutory authorization of public employee collective bargaining, this is still often the case,[2] although in several jurisdictions bargaining has been allowed even in the absence of express statutory authorization.[3] Since 1955, however, the picture has changed radically. At the present time, the federal government expressly affords most

[1] *See generally* Blair, *State Legislative Control over the Conditions of Public Employment: Defining the Scope of Collective Bargaining for State and Municipal Employees*, 26 VAND. L. REV. 1 (1973).

[2] ALABAMA—Operating Engineers Local 321 v. Birmingham Water Works, 163 S.2d 619 (Ala. 1964); COLORADO—Fellows v. Latronica, 151 Colo. 300, 377 P.2d 547 (1962); KENTUCKY (public school teachers)—Attorney General's Opinion No. 75-126, Feb. 12, 1975; MISSOURI (public school teachers)—Attorney General's Opinion No. 276, Dec. 12, 1968; SOUTH CAROLINA—Attorney General's Opinion No. 1778 (1964); TENNESSEE—Weakley County Municipal Electric System v. Vick, 309 S.W.2d 792 (Tenn. 1957); UTAH (State employees)—Attorney General's Opinion No. 60-003, Jan. 12, 1960.

[3] ARIZONA—Local 266, Electrical Workers v. Salt River Project, 78 Ariz. 30, 275 P.2d 393 (1954); ARKANSAS—Attorney General's Opinion, Sept. 19, 1972; City of Fort Smith v. Arkansas State Council No. 38, 245 Ark. 409, 433 S.W.2d 153 (1968); IDAHO (municipal employees)—Attorney General's Opinion, March 18, 1959; ILLINOIS (local government employees)—Chicago Division of Illinois Educational Ass'n v. Board of Education, 76 Ill.App.2d 456, 222 N.E.2d 243 (1966); LOUISIANA—Attorney General's Opinion No. 74-413, April 4, 1974; New Orleans Firefighters Ass'n v. City of New Orleans, 204 S.2d 690 (La. Ct. of App. 1967); NEW MEXICO (local government employees)—Attorney General's Opinions Nos. 70-7 and 71-96; IBEW Local 611 v. Town of Farmington, 75 N.M. 393, 405 P.2d 233 (1965); NORTH DAKOTA (political subdivisions)—Attorney General's Opinion, Apr. 24, 1969; UTAH (teachers)—Attorney General's Opinion, Oct. 1, 1945; VIRGINIA (local government employees and teachers)—Attorney General's Opinions, July 30, 1962, and Feb. 16, 1970; WEST VIRGINIA—Attorney General's Opinions, June 29, 1962, Feb. 23, 1966, and June 26, 1974.

of its employees the right to bargain collectively; [4] and forty-one of the states likewise have statutes that authorize collective bargaining by one or more categories of public employees.[5] Legisla-

---

[4] Executive Order Number 11,491, 3 C.F.R. 861 (1966-1970 Compilation), reprinted in 5 U.S.C. § 7301 (1970), *as amended*, 3 C.F.R. 254 (1974) (employees in the executive branch); Postal Reorganization Act of 1970, 39 U.S.C. §§ 1201-09 (1970).

[5] ALABAMA—ALABAMA SCHOOL CODE, L. 1973, Act Nos. 1022 and 1023, and Act No. 385 (1963), *as amended* (school teachers).

ALASKA—ALASKA STAT. §§ 14.20.550 to 14.20.610 (1972) (school teachers); ALASKA STAT. §§ 23.40.070 to 23.40.260 (1972) (public employees).

CALIFORNIA—CAL. GOV'T CODE §§ 3500 to 3510 (Supp. 1976) (municipal employees, except teachers); CAL. GOV'T CODE §§ 3525 to 3536 (Supp. 1976) (state employees); CAL. GOV'T CODE §§ 3540 to 3549 (1976) (public school employees); CAL. PUB. UTIL. CODE §§ 70120 to 70127 (1973) (transit workers).

CONNECTICUT—CONN. GEN. STAT. ANN., Public Act No. 75-566 (Appendix Pam. 1976) (state employees); CONN. GEN. STAT. ANN. §§ 7-467 to 7-477 (1972) (municipal employees); CONN. GEN. STAT. ANN. §§ 10-153a to 10-153g (1977) (teachers); CONN. GEN. STAT. ANN. § 7-273j (1972) (transit employees).

DELAWARE—DEL. CODE ANN. tit. 19, §§ 1301 to 1312 (1975) (public employees); DEL. CODE ANN. tit. 14, §§ 4001 to 4013 (1975) (teachers); DEL. CODE ANN. tit. 2, §§ 1613 to 1614 (1975) (transit employees).

FLORIDA—FLA. STAT. ANN. §§ 447.201 to 447.605 (Supp. 1976) (public employees generally); LAWS OF FLORIDA, ch. 59-1424 L. 1960 (teachers in counties with from 390,000 to 450,000 population); Laws of Florida, ch. 71-686 L. 1971 (teachers in Hillsborough County); Laws of Florida, ch. 71-875 L. 1971 (teachers in Pinellas County).

GEORGIA—GA. CODE ANN. §§ 54-1301 to 54-1315 (1974) (firefighters).

HAWAII—HAWAII REV. STAT. §§ 89-1 to 89-20 (Supp. 1975) (all public employees).

IDAHO—IDAHO CODE §§ 33-1271 to 33-1276 (Cum. Supp. 1975) (teachers); IDAHO CODE §§ 44-1801 to 44-1811 (Cum. Supp. 1975) (firefighters).

ILLINOIS—EXECUTIVE ORDER No. 6, §§ 1.0 to 22.0 (Sept. 4, 1973) (state employees); SMITH-HURD ILL. ANN. STAT. ch. 111 2/3 § 328a (1966) (transit workers).

INDIANA—BURNS IND. STAT. ANN. §§ 20-7.5-1-1 to 20-7.5-1-14 (1975) (teachers); BURNS IND. STAT. ANN. §§ 22-6-4-1 to 22-6-4-13 (Cum. Supp. 1975) (public employees).

IOWA—IOWA CODE ANN. §§ 20.1 to 20.27 (Supp. 1976) (public employees).

KANSAS—KANSAS STAT. ANN. §§ 72-5413 to 72-5425 (1972) (teachers); KANSAS STAT. ANN. §§ 75-4321 to 75-4337 (Cum. Supp. 1975) (public employees).

KENTUCKY—KY. REV. STAT. §§ 345.010 to 345.130 (Cum. Supp. 1976) (firefighters); KY. REV. STAT. §§ 78.400, 78.480 (Cum. Supp. 1976) (police).

LOUISIANA—LA. STAT. ANN. § 23.890 (Supp. 1976) (transit employees).

[Footnote continued]

⁵ [Continued]

MAINE—ME. REV. STAT. ANN. tit. 26, §§ 961 to 972 (1974) (municipal employees); ME. REV. STAT. ANN. tit. 26, §§ 979 to 979-N (1974) (state employees); ME. REV. STAT. ANN. tit. 26, §§ 1021 to 1034 (Cum. Supp. 1976) (university employees).

MARYLAND—MD. ANN. CODE art. 64B, § 37(b) (1972) (transit employees); MD. ANN. CODE art. 77, § 160 (Supp. 1973) (public school teachers); MD. ANN. CODE OF PUBLIC LOCAL LAWS art. 1, § 64B (1974) (Allegany County public employees).

MASSACHUSETTS—MASS. GEN. LAWS ANN. ch. 150E §§ 1 to 15 (Supp. 1976) (all public employees); MASS. GEN. LAWS ANN. ch. 161A, § 19 (Supp. 1976) (transit employees).

MICHIGAN—MICH. STAT. ANN. §§ 423.201 to 423.216 (1967) (public employees).

MINNESOTA—MINN. STAT. ANN. §§ 179.61 to 179.76 (Cum. Supp. 1976) (public employees).

MISSOURI—VERNON'S ANN. MO. STAT. §§ 105.500 to 105.540 (1969) (all public employees except police and teachers).

MONTANA—MONT. REV. CODES ANN. §§ 41-2201 to 41-2209 (Cum. Supp. 1976) (nurses); MONT. REV. CODES ANN. §§ 59-1601 to 59-1617 (Cum. Supp. 1976) (other public employees).

NEBRASKA—NEB. REV. STAT. §§ 79-1287 to 79-1295 (1976) (teachers); NEB. REV. STAT. §§ 48-801 to 48-838 (1976) (other public employees).

NEVADA—NEV. REV. STAT. §§ 288.010 to 288.280 (1975) (local government employees).

NEW HAMPSHIRE—N.H. REV. STAT. ANN. §§ 273-A:1 to 273-A:16 (Supp. 1975) (public employees).

NEW JERSEY—N.J. STAT. ANN. §§ 34:13A-1 to 34:13A-11 (Supp. 1977) (all public employees); N.J. STAT. ANN. §§ 34:13B-1 to 34:13B-29 (Supp. 1977) (public utilities).

NEW YORK—N.Y. CIVIL SERV. LAW §§ 200 to 214 (McKinney 1973) (public employees); N.Y. CITY COLLECTIVE BARGAINING LAW, §§ 1173-1.0 to 1173-13.0, LABOR LAW REPORTER (CCH) ¶ 47,450 (1972) (New York City employees).

NORTH DAKOTA—N.D. CENT. CODE §§ 15-38.1-01 to 15-38.1-15 (1971) (teachers).

OHIO—PAGE'S OHIO REV. CODE ANN. § 306.12 (Supp. 1975) (transit workers).

OKLAHOMA—OKLA. STAT. ANN. tit. 11, §§ 548.1 to 548.14 (Supp. 1975) (firemen, police, and municipal employees); OKLA. STAT. ANN. tit. 70, §§ 509.1 to 509.10 (1972) (public school teachers).

OREGON—ORE. REV. STAT. §§ 243.650 to 243.782 (1975) (all public employees).

PENNSYLVANIA—PA. STAT. ANN. tit. 43, §§ 1101.101 to 1101.2301 (Supp. 1976) (public employees generally); PA. STAT. ANN. tit. 43, §§ 217.1 to 217.10 (Supp. 1976) (firemen and police); PA. STAT. ANN. tit. 43, §§ 721 to 726 (transit employees).

RHODE ISLAND—R.I. GEN. LAWS ANN. §§ 36-11-1 to 36-11-11 (Supp. 1976) (state employees); R.I. GEN. LAWS ANN. §§ 28-9.4-1 to 28-9.4-19 (Supp. 1976) (municipal employees except teachers, policemen, and firemen); R.I. GEN. LAWS ANN. §§ 28-9.3-1 to 28-9.3-16 (Supp. 1976) (teachers); R.I. GEN. LAWS

tion to extend even further the collective bargaining rights of public employees is pending both in Congress and in several of the state legislatures. Coincident with the phenomenal growth of public sector collective bargaining has been the growth of public sector labor unions.[6] These unions, like their private sector counterparts, have manifested the normal institutional imperative of attempting to obtain for themselves the benefit of union security agreements. The federal and state governments, however, have tended to resist this demand. In most jurisdictions, in deference to considerations of public policy and constitutional law, public employees have been guaranteed the right to work for the state free from any requirement that they join or pay money to the union that negotiates the terms and conditions of employment under which they work.

ANN. §§ 28-9.1-2 to 28-9.1-15 (Supp. 1976) (firemen); R.I. GEN. LAWS ANN. §§ 28-9.2-1 to 28-9.2-15 (Supp. 1976) (policemen); R.I. GEN. LAWS ANN. §§ 28-9.5-1 to 28-9.5-13 (Supp. 1976) (certified administrators in City of Providence).

SOUTH DAKOTA—S.D. COMPILED LAWS ANN. §§ 3-18-1 to 3-18-17 (1974) (all public employees).

TENNESSEE—TENN. CODE ANN. § 6-3802 (Cum. Supp. 1975) (transit employees).

TEXAS—TEX. REV. CIV. STAT. art. 5154C-1, §§ 1 to 20 (Supp. 1974) (police and firemen); TEX. REV. CIV. STAT. art. 5154c, §§ 1 to 7 (1971) (all other public employees).

UTAH—UTAH CODE ANN. §§ 34-20a-1 to 34-20a-9 (Supp. 1975) (firefighters).

VERMONT—VT. STAT. ANN. tit. 3, §§ 901 to 1007 (1972) (state employees); VT. STAT. ANN. tit. 22, §§ 1721 to 1734 (Cum. Supp. 1975) (municipal employees); VT. STAT. ANN. tit. 16, §§ 1981 to 2010 (Supp. 1975) (school teachers).

WASHINGTON—WASH. REV. CODE ANN. §§ 41.59.010 to 41.59.950 (Supp. 1976) (teachers); WASH. REV. CODE ANN. §§ 28B.52.010 to 28B.52.200 (Supp. 1976) (academic employees of community colleges); WASH. REV. CODE ANN. § 28B.16.100 (Supp. 1976) (higher education employees); WASH. REV. CODE ANN. §§ 41.56.010 to 41.56.950 (1972) (most employees of political subdivisions); WASH REV. CODE ANN. §§ 53.18.010 to 53.18.060 (Supp. 1976) (port district employees); WASH. REV. CODE ANN. § 47.64.030 (1972) (toll bridge employees); WASH. REV. CODE ANN. §§ 54.04.170, 54.04.180 (Supp. 1976) (public utility employees).

WISCONSIN—WIS. STAT. ANN. §§ 111.80 to 111.97 (1974) (state employees); WIS. STAT. ANN. §§ 111.70 to 111.71 (1974) (municipal employees); WIS. STAT. ANN. § 66.94(29) (1965) (transit employees).

WYOMING—WYO. STAT. ANN. §§ 27-265 to 27-273 (1967) (firemen).

[6] The 1972 Bureau of Labor Statistics HANDBOOK OF LABOR STATISTICS shows an increase in union membership among state and local government employees of 556,000 in 1964 to 948,000 in 1970, an increase of approximately 70 percent in a relatively short period.

In this chapter, we will examine the scope of that guarantee and the exceptions that have been made to it. The underlying considerations of public policy and constitutional law will be dealt with in subsequent chapters.

FEDERAL EMPLOYEES

In 1962, President Kennedy granted employees within the executive branch of the federal government the right to bargain collectively; but at the same time he prohibited compulsory unionism among federal employees. Section 1(a) of Executive Order 10988 provided:

> Employees of the Federal Government shall have, and shall be protected in the exercise of, the right, freely and without fear of penalty or reprisal, to form, join and assist any employee organization *or to refrain from any such activity.*[7]

When, in 1969, President Nixon revised the rules governing labor relations in the federal service, he retained the substance of Section 1(a) quoted above, but went even further in making it clear that no form of union security would be allowed in collective bargaining agreements negotiated by federal agencies. Section 12(c) of Executive Order 11491 provides:

> [N]othing in the agreement shall require an employee to become or to remain a member of a labor organization, or to pay money to the organization except pursuant to a voluntary, written authorization by a member for the payment of dues through payroll deductions.[8]

Up until 1970, postal workers were classified as federal employees and, thus, subject to the Executive Orders quoted above. That status was technically changed by Congress in the Postal Reorganization Act of 1970, but the right not to become a member of a postal union was preserved. The Act contains a provision, known as the "Right to Work Amendment," which is substantially similar to Section 1(a) quoted above.[9] On the other

---

[7] Executive Order Number 10,988, § 1(a) 3 C.F.R. 521 (1959-63 Compilation), reprinted in 5 U.S.C. 631 (1964), issued on January 17, 1962 (emphasis added).

[8] Executive Order Number 11,491, § 12(c) 3 C.F.R. 861 at 870 (1966-70 Compilation), reprinted in 5 U.S.C. § 7301 (1970), as amended, 3 C.F.R. 254 (1974).

[9] Postal Reorganization Act of 1970, 39 U.S.C. § 1209 (1970).

hand, the Postal Act also contains a provision which allows the checkoff of union dues, provided that the employee signs an authorization which shall be "irrevocable for not more than one year." [10] This, of course, is an indirect form of maintenance of membership; once an employee authorizes a payroll deduction in favor of the union, he must remain a dues payor for up to a year.

Subject only to that limited exception, it would appear that among executive branch and Postal Service employees, the right to work is fully preserved. Although the federal government has chosen to give the majority of its employees within various units the right to choose an exclusive bargaining representative for all the employees in that unit, it has given dissenting minority employees the coextensive right not to be forced to join or pay money to the labor union that serves in that capacity.

There are, however, proposals pending in Congress that would change the stance of the federal government with respect to the right to work of its employees. For example, H.R. 2881 [11] would repeal the right-to-work guarantee of the Postal Reorganization Act of 1970, thus opening the way for the same kind of union security agreements that are allowed in the private sector by the Taft-Hartley Act. [12] Another proposal, applicable to federal employees, would automatically impose upon all employees represented by a majority union the duty to pay to the union an amount equal to the dues, fees, and assessments that are customarily charged members. [13] Comprehensive federal employee collective bargaining laws have also been proposed by Congressmen Hanley of New York [14] and Forsythe of New Jersey. [15] Both bills provide that

> upon request by an exclusive representative an agency shall agree to require as a condition of employment membership in the exclusive representative labor organization or the payment of a repre-

---

[10] Postal Reorganization Act of 1970, 39 U.S.C. § 1205 (1970).

[11] H.R. 2881, 94th Cong., 1st Sess. (1975).

[12] The Postal Reorganization Act provides that "employee-management relations shall, to the extent not inconsistent with provisions of this title, be subject to the provisions of sub-chapter II of Chapter 7 of Title 29 [the Taft-Hartley Act]," which thus includes the authorization of certain kinds of union security agreements. 39 U.S.C. § 1209(a) (1970).

[13] H.R. 9784, 93rd Cong., 1st Sess. (1973).

[14] H.R. 6912, 94th Cong., 1st Sess. (1975).

[15] H.R. 79, 94th Cong., 1st Sess. (1975).

sentation fee equal to the amount of periodic dues uniformly required, on or after the thirtieth day following the beginning of
such employment or on the effective date of such agreement, whichever is later. . . .[16]

By speaking disjunctively of "membership . . . or . . . payment,"
this provision appears to sanction either the union shop or the
agency shop. This ambiguity, however, is arguably resolved by a
subsequent proviso which prohibits a government agency from
discriminating against an employee for nonmembership in a union
if the agency "has reasonable grounds for believing that membership was denied or terminated for reasons other than the
failure of the employee to tender the periodic dues and the
initiation fees uniformly required as a condition of acquiring
or retaining membership." An identical proviso in the Taft-
Hartley Act has been construed by the Supreme Court as requiring nothing more than the equivalent of the agency shop,[17] and
it is probable that the proposed legislation is intended to be construed in the same fashion.

Another comprehensive federal employee collective bargaining
proposal, introduced by Representative Henderson of North Carolina, takes the opposite tack with respect to union security:

> Nothing in any agreement negotiated under this subchapter shall
> require an employee to become or to remain a member of a labor
> organization, or to pay money to the organization, except pursuant
> to a voluntary, written authorization by a member for the payment
> of dues through payroll deductions.[18]

That proposal also provides, however, any written assignment of
union dues "shall be irrevocable for a period of 1 year," which
again amounts to the authorization of a form of maintenance-of-
membership arrangement.

Finally, several members of Congress have introduced bills
which, while not a part of any comprehensive collective bargaining statute, guarantee the right to work of all federal employees.
Representative Ashbrook's proposal states:

> Notwithstanding any provision of law or presidential executive
> order, no employee of the Federal Government shall be required

---

[16] Section 701(a)(2), H.R. 79, 94th Cong., 1st Sess. (1975).

[17] *See, e.g.*, NLRB v. General Motors Corp., 373 U.S. 734 (1963).

[18] Section 7108(c), H.R. 4800, 94th Cong., 1st Sess. (1975).

without his consent to join or become a member of any union of Government employees or to pay dues to such organization.[19]

It remains to be seen exactly what direction federal law will take regarding collective bargaining among federal employees and regarding the right to work in particular.

STATE AND LOCAL EMPLOYEES

The legal status of union security agreements covering non-federal public employees varies widely from state to state and varies even among different classes of employees within the same state. At one extreme are statutes which simply impose union security by operation of law—obviating the necessity of any contractual agreement on the matter. At the other pole are the express guarantees of a right to work in the traditional sense, which outlaw agency shop or service fee arrangements and all of the more compulsory forms of union security agreement. Between the two are the statutes which expressly authorize the negotiation of some kind of union security, ranging from the true union shop to an irrevocable (for no longer than one year) checkoff authorization. Finally, there are also large numbers of public employees who are not covered by any statute at all or who are covered by a statute that is either silent on the question of union security or that speaks by implication only. These state laws, moreover, are subject to constant change, and any survey is quickly apt to become dated. Nevertheless, a broad overview of the laws of the various states will be attempted here.

Express Statutory Authorization

Authorized Union Security. At the present time, eighteen states expressly authorize some kind of union security agreement among one or more classes of public employees.[20] None of the statutes

---

[19] Section 7103, H.R. 1581, 94th Cong., 1st Sess. (1975).

[20] ALASKA (all public employees except teachers); CALIFORNIA (public school employees); CONNECTICUT (state employees); HAWAII (all public employees); KENTUCKY (firefighters); MAINE (university employees); MARYLAND (noncertified public school employees, Baltimore City employees); MASSACHUSETTS (all public employees); MICHIGAN (all public employees); MINNESOTA (all public employees); MONTANA (university/college teachers, all public employees except nurses); NEW JERSEY (transit employees); OREGON (all public employees); PENNSYLVANIA (all public employees except firemen and police); RHODE ISLAND (state employees, teachers); VERMONT (municipal employees); WASHINGTON (port district employees, most local government

directly authorize a closed shop, although a New Jersey statute
dealing with state-owned public utilities is susceptible of being so
construed. The statute provides that "it shall not be unlawful to
require as a condition of employment, membership in any labor
organization. . . ." [21] Assuming that "membership" here means
formal membership, the absence of any provision about becoming
such a member within thirty days, as is found in nearly all
statutes authorizing the union shop, could suggest that union
membership can also be a condition of initial employment as
under a closed shop arrangement.

On the other hand, the forms of union security that are expressly authorized are the union shop, the agency shop, service
fee arrangements, and maintenance-of-membership agreements.

The union shop, which requires actual union membership as a
condition of public employment, is allowed in only a few states.
The most direct authorization of this particular kind of union
security is to be found in a Maine statute which provides that
"Nothing in this chapter shall be interpreted to prohibit the
negotiation of union security, excepting closed shop." [22] A Washington statute is similarly worded.[23] The intent of the legislatures
here was to authorize every kind of union security except the
closed shop, thus authorizing the union shop.

Other statutes that could be construed as authorizing the union
shop are those that talk of requiring union membership as a condition of continued employment. For example, one provision of
the Kentucky firefighters statute prohibits discrimination that
either encourages or discourages union membership, but then
states that this shall not be construed to "preclude a public employer from making an agreement with a labor organization to
require as a condition of employment *membership* therein. . . ." [24]
As far as it goes, this provision is identical to Section 8(a)(3) of
the Taft-Hartley Act. But the Kentucky statute does not contain
the second proviso of Section 8(a)(3) which provides that non-

---

employees, teachers, higher education employees, state employees) ; WISCONSIN
(state employees, municipal employees). For citations to the relevant statutes,
see n. 5, *supra*, and nn. 21-67, *infra*.

[21] N.J. STAT. ANN. § 34:13B-2 (1965).

[22] ME. REV. STAT. ANN. tit. 26, § 1027.3 (Cum. Supp. 1976).

[23] WASH. REV. CODE ANN. § 41.56.122 (Supp. 1977) states that "a collective bargaining agreement may . . . contain union security provisions:
Provided, that nothing in this section shall authorize a closed shop provision."

[24] KY. REV. STAT. § 345.050 (Cum. Supp. 1976) (emphasis added).

membership in the union will not be grounds for discharge unless it was because of a failure to tender periodic dues and fees. It was the wording of this second proviso which, in part, led the Supreme Court in *General Motors* to construe the word *membership* as meaning nothing more than the payment of money—as under the agency shop.[25] The absence of this second proviso in the Kentucky statute thus gives rise to the implication that, as used there, the term "membership" means actual membership—the kind required by the true union shop.

More confusing yet is one of the Washington public employee statutes. It allows "as a condition of employment membership in the certified exclusive bargaining representative on or after the thirtieth day following the beginning of employment. . . ."[26] On its face, that seems to suggest that the statute contemplates actual union membership, as under a true union shop arrangement. But then the statute goes on to say that "for purposes of this clause membership in the certified exclusive bargaining representative shall be satisfied by the payment of monthly or other periodic dues and shall not require payment of initiation, reinstatement or any other fees or fines and shall include full and complete membership rights." While it may seem unfair to entitle an employee to the rights of full membership without at the same time forcing him to assume the obligations thereof (enforced through union disciplinary procedures), this provision seems to suggest that the payment of periodic dues is all that can be required of an employee, as under the agency shop. But the statute goes on to provide that religious objectors can designate a union program to which they do not object and pay toward it "an amount of money equivalent to regular union dues minus any included monthly premiums for union-sponsored insurance program"—a benefit that is usually available only to formal union members. Further, the statute provides that "such employee[s] [religious objectors] shall not be a member of the union but shall be entitled to all representation rights of a union member." The last two clauses intimate that actual or formal membership is contemplated for everyone *except* religious objectors.[27]

---

[25] *See* pp. 42-45, *supra.*

[26] WASH. REV. CODE ANN. § 28B.16.100 (Supp. 1976).

[27] The WASHINGTON STATE PERSONNEL BOARD MERIT SYSTEM RULES, § 356-42-043, also seem to contemplate formal membership for everyone except religious objectors, who in lieu of "membership" can elect to pay an amount equivalent to dues less the cost of insurance premiums.

Statutory provisions that are phrased disjunctively, authorizing either one kind of union security or another, pose their own problems of construction—not only regarding the kinds of union security that are authorized, but also regarding who enjoys the option of choosing the one to be adopted. One of the Alaska public employee collective bargaining statutes, for example, provides:

> Nothing in this chapter prohibits a public employer from making an agreement with an organization to require as a condition of employment
> (1) membership in the organization which represents the unit on or after the 30th day following the beginning of employment or on the effective date of the agreement, whichever is later; or
> (2) payment by the employee to the exclusive bargaining agent of a service fee to reimburse the exclusive bargaining agent for the expense of representing the members of the bargaining unit.[28]

Since part (2) provides for one of the two forms of union security requiring only the payment of money, it is reasonable to assume that part (1) contemplates something more than that— to wit, membership in the formal of actual sense.

A Vermont statute is similarly worded. It provides that nothing in the statute shall be construed as preventing a municipal employer and a union from agreeing

> to require an agency service fee to be paid as a condition of employment, or to require as a condition of employment membership in such employee organization on or after the 30th day following the beginning of such employment. . . .[29]

It would appear that this statute authorizes both the agency shop and the union shop. This statute, however, goes on to say that a municipal employer cannot discharge an employee because of that employee's nonmembership in the union if, *inter alia*, the employer

> has reasonable grounds for believing that membership was denied or terminated for reasons other than the failure of the employee to tender the periodic dues and the initiation fees uniformly required as a condition of acquiring or retaining membership.[30]

This proviso is identical to that contained in the Taft-Hartley Act, and in the *General Motors* case the Supreme Court construed it as providing a definition for the term *membership,* which—as

---

[28] ALASKA STAT. § 23.40.110(b) (1972).

[29] VT. STAT. ANN. tit. 21, § 1726(a)(8) (Cum. Supp. 1976).

[30] *Id.* 1726(a)(8)(B).

under one of the two options available under the Vermont act—can validly be required as a condition of employment. What this means, the Supreme Court held, is that an employee can only be required to pay agency shop fees.

If the *General Motors* construction is applied to the Vermont statute, then what appears to be an authorization of two kinds of union security agreement is in fact merely the authorization of one—the agency service fee arrangement. Alternatively, if the *General Motors* construction is rejected with respect to this state statute, then what it authorizes is either an agency shop or a union option version of the union shop. This latter form of union security, which accommodates both the requirement of membership and the limitations of the proviso, would require an employee to apply for formal membership (as under a union shop), would give the union the option of denying such membership, but would preclude the employer from discharging the employee, pursuant to an agreement calling for membership as a condition of employment, unless the union's reason for denying membership was that the employee refused to tender the required dues and fees.[31]

After all of the employment-relations confusion and expensive litigation that has been caused by the ambiguously worded language of the Taft-Hartley Act's authorization of union security, one would think that a state legislature intending to authorize some kind of union security among public employees would be more exact in the drafting of its statutes. This, however, has not been the case.

Another example of this can be found in one of the Oregon statutes. In one section it states that

> any agreements entered into involving union security including an all-union agreement or agency shop agreement must . . . [alternatively allow religious objectors to pay an equivalent of union dues to a selected charity].[32]

Since "all-union agreement" is commonly thought to refer to a union shop arrangement, this statute would appear to sanction two kinds of union security. On the other hand, the statute goes on to prohibit an unfair labor practice discrimination that encourages or discourages union membership and excepts from this

---

[31] The union option version of the union shop is discussed more fully at pp. 37ff, *supra.*

[32] ORE. REV. STAT. § 243.666 (1975).

prohibition only so-called fair-share agreements which are defined
as agreements requiring the payment of the equivalent of union
dues.[33] It would appear that the unfair labor practice provisions
of the statute outlaw what the statute elsewhere refers to as the
all-union agreement to the extent that that term connotes actual
membership in the union as a condition of employment.

Those, then, are some of the statutes that authorize, or appear
to authorize, union shops among public employees. Next in the
order of alleged compulsoriness is the agency shop, an arrangement whereby an employee is not required to join the union, but
is required to pay the equivalent of union dues and fees. A
Washington statute covering public teachers expressly states:

> A collective bargaining agreement may include union security pro-
> visions including an agency shop, but not a union or closed shop.[34]

Other statutes, such as the one covering Connecticut state employees, provide that employees may be required to pay the union
"an amount equal to the regular dues, fees and assessments that
a member is charged." [35] Finally, there are a number of statutes
which require employees to pay a "service fee" [36] or to bear a
"proportionate share of the cost of the collective bargaining
process," [37] but which also define the amount owed by reference
to the normal dues and fees of union members. These should be
classified as agency shop arrangements, rather than fair-share
payments to be discussed next.

A true *fair-share* union security agreement is one like that
authorized by the Massachusetts statute; the amount of money
owed by a nonunion member is determined, not by reference to
dues and fees a member pays, but rather by reference to "the
cost of collective bargaining and contract administration." [38] The
Hawaii statute defines a *service fee* as

> an assessment of all employees in an appropriate bargaining unit
> to defray the cost for services rendered by the exclusive representa-
> tive in negotiations and contract administration.[39]

---

[33] ORE. REV. STAT. § 243.672 (1975).

[34] WASH. REV. CODE ANN. tit. 41, § 59.100 (Supp. 1976).

[35] CONN. GEN. STAT. ANN. Public Act No. 75-566, § 11 (Conn. Legis. Serv.
Supp. 1975).

[36] CAL. GOV'T CODE § 3540.1(i)(2) (Supp. 1976).

[37] WIS. STAT. ANN. § 111.70(1)(h) (1974).

[38] MASS. GEN. LAWS ANN. ch. 150E, § 12 (Supp. 1976).

[39] HAWAII REV. STAT. § 89-2(16) (Supp. 1975).

Under the Railway Labor Act, where the most that can be required of an employee is that he pay the equivalent of a service fee to reimburse the union for the expenses of collective bargaining and contract administration, difficult issues have arisen over the computation of that figure.[40] Similar problems have arisen under some of the state public employee collective bargaining laws.

The Minnesota statute, for example, authorizes a fair-share fee

> in an amount equal to the regular membership dues of the exclusive representative, less the cost of benefits financed through the dues and available only to members of the exclusive representative, but in no event shall the fee exceed 85 percent of the regular membership dues.[41]

If the amount set by the union is challenged, the contesting employee must

> specify those portions of the assessment challenged and the reasons therefor but the burden of proof relating to the amount of the fair share fee shall be on the exclusive representative.[42]

In *Schleck* v. *Freeborn County Welfare Board*,[43] an employee brought a challenge under this statute against a fair-share deduction that was, except for one brief period, always exactly 10¢ less than whatever the union was charging its members as dues. The deductions were thus in excess of the eighty-five percent of the regular union dues—the maximum amount of a fair-share deduction allowed by the statute. The court, however, went beyond this and held that since the union had not met its burden of coming forward with records or other evidence to prove exactly how much of its expenditures went toward contract negotiation and administration, the deductions in their entirety were illegal.

Under the Hawaii public employee collective bargaining statute, the union is merely required to submit to the employer

> a written statement which specifies an amount of reasonable service fees necessary to defray the costs for its services rendered in negotiating and administering an agreement and computed on a pro rata basis among all employees within its appropriate bargaining unit. . . .[44]

---

40 *See* pp. 125-144, *supra*.

41 MINN. STAT. ANN. § 179.65 (Cum. Supp. 1976).

42 *Id.*

43 88 L.R.R.M. 3525 (Freeborn Cty. Conciliation Ct., Minn. 1975).

44 HAWAII REV. STAT. § 89-4 (Supp. 1975).

The reasonableness of this amount is subject to review by the Hawaii Public Employment Relations Board, but in one case this Board approved a service fee which was actually in excess of the amount the union usually charged as dues and which included as a legitimate expense a $190,000 fine that the union had paid for engaging in an illegal strike.[45]

One state statute, while not going the full "service fee only" route, does go nearly as far as the Supreme Court went in the *Street* and *Allen* cases. The Montana statute generally provides for an agency shop arrangement, but then also makes it an unfair labor practice for a union to

> use agency shop fees for contributions to political candidates or parties at state or local levels.[46]

The theory behind fair-share arrangements is that an employee should pay for the services he allegedly receives. Under most statutes, by virtue of the union's right of exclusive representation, the services are forced on the employee; the payment, therefore, is also forced. A Vermont statute, however, contains a variation on this theme that obligates the employee to pay only if he elects to avail himself of certain of the union's services. One section of the Vermont statute provides:

> An employee, who is eligible to join an employee organization and elects not to do so may not be compelled to contribute to the support of such employee organization directly or indirectly in any way including the payment of dues or of an amount equivalent thereto or of any other amount of money, except as provided in Sec. 941(k) of this title.[47]

Section 941(k) then says that an employee may represent himself in grievance proceedings, but that

> [e]mployees who are eligible for membership in a collective bargaining unit who exercise their right not to join such union may avail themselves of the services of the union representative(s) in grievance proceedings before the board [only] upon payment to the unit of a fee equal to one-year's membership dues.[48]

The maximum form of union security that some states allow is the so-called maintenance-of-membership agreement, where if

---

[45] *In re* Hawaii State Teachers Ass'n, No. 36, Decision of the Hawaii Public Employment Relations Board (Sept. 13, 1973).

[46] Mont. Rev. Codes Ann. § 59-1605(2)(c) (Cum. Supp. 1976).

[47] Vt. Stat. Ann. tit. 3, § 903(a) (1972).

[48] Vt. Stat. Ann. tit. 3, § 941(k) (1972).

an employee is or becomes a member of the union during the term of the contract, that employee must remain a member for the duration. In two such states, the kind of membership that must be maintained is, however, radically different. Under a California statute, one of the forms of union security that is authorized is defined as

> [a]n arrangement pursuant to which a public school employee may decide whether or not to join an employee organization, but which requires him, as a condition of continued employment, if he does join, to maintain his membership in good standing for the duration of the written agreement.[49]

Clearly, formal membership in the union is contemplated by that form of maintenance-of-membership agreement.

On the other hand, the Pennsylvania statute expressly authorizes maintenance-of-membership agreements, but expressly provides that "the payment of dues and assessments while members, may be the only requisite employment condition."[50] The employee can be required to do nothing more than continue to pay agency fee dues, not maintain actual membership.

The final kind of union security expressly authorized by several state statutes, usually in conjunction with one of the other kinds mentioned above, is the checkoff arrangement. From the individual employee's perspective, the least compulsory checkoff arrangement is one requiring the individual's written authorization which is revocable at will. Ohio has a statute calling for this kind of checkoff.[51] This is not really a form of union security at all. More common are statutes that require an employee to give thirty[52] or sixty[53] days notice before revoking a prior written checkoff authorization. A New Jersey statute allows revocation at any time, but provides that it will not become effective until the following January 1 or July 1, whichever is sooner.[54] Carrying the notice requirement one step further, both Washington and the Baltimore City Code provide that a checkoff authorization, once

---

[49] CAL. GOV'T CODE § 3540.1(i) (1) (Supp. 1976).

[50] PA. STAT. ANN. tit. 43, § 1101.705 (Supp. 1976).

[51] PAGE'S OHIO REV. CODE ANN. § 9.41 (Supp. 1975).

[52] FLA. STAT. ANN. § 447.303 (Supp. 1976); IOWA CODE ANN. § 20.9 (Supp. 1976).

[53] BURNS IND. STAT. ANN. § 22-6-4-4 (Cum. Supp. 1975); MASS. GEN. LAWS ANN. ch. 180, § 17A (1958).

[54] N.J. STAT. ANN. § 52:14-15.9e (Cum. Supp. 1977).

executed by an employee, "shall be irrevocable for the period of one year."[55] This is an indirect and somewhat limited form of maintenance of membership; once the employee becomes a union-fee payor, he is required to maintain that relationship for up to a year. Many statutes are, unfortunately, silent on the question of revocability.[56]

From the perspective of the interests of the public agency, two issues are of importance regarding the checkoff. The first relates to whether or not the law absolutely obligates an agency to enter into a checkoff arrangement with its employees and the union that represents them. Some statutes merely make the checkoff a subject of bargaining.[57] Presumably, if the employer agency bargains in good faith but ultimately declines to agree to a checkoff, the agency's legal obligations are discharged. On the other hand, some statutes make the checkoff, whether authorized by the individual or not, an integral part of whatever kind of union security the employer is allowed to agree to.[58] Finally, some public agencies are affirmatively required to deduct union dues either upon receipt of a written authorization from an employee[59] or at the request of the union that such individual authorizations be honored.[60] Whether a union has the right to have money deducted from the salaries of the employees it represents, regardless of whether the employer agrees to it or the individual employees have authorized it will be dealt with subsequently.

Also of concern to the public agency is the issue of who bears the administrative cost of checkoff arrangements. A few statutes place this cost on the unions,[61] while at least one other makes it

---

[55] BALTIMORE CITY CODE, art. I, § 120 (1974); WASH. REV. CODE ANN. tit. 41, § 59.060(2) (Supp. 1976) (checkoff "shall not be irrevocable for a period of more than one year").

[56] *See, e.g.,* ALASKA STAT. § 23.40.220 (1972); DEL. CODE ANN. tit. 19, § 1311 (1975).

[57] MASS. GEN. LAWS ANN. ch. 150E, § 12 (Supp. 1976); WASHINGTON STATE PERSONNEL BOARD MERIT SYSTEM RULES, § 356-42-043 (1973); WIS. STAT. ANN. § 111.70(1)(h) (1974).

[58] *E.g.,* MONT. REV. CODES ANN. § 59-1605 (Supp. 1975); WIS. STAT. ANN. § 111.81(6) (1974).

[59] ALASKA STAT. § 23.40.220 (1972); DEL. CODE ANN. tit. 19, § 1311 (1975); BURNS IND. STAT. ANN. § 20-7.5-1-8 (1975); KY. REV. STAT. § 345.110 (Cum. Supp. 1974); MONT. REV. CODES ANN. § 59-1612 (Cum. Supp. 1976).

[60] FLA. STAT. ANN. § 447.303 (Supp. 1976); N.Y. CIVIL SERV. LAW § 208 (McKinney 1973).

[61] N.M. STATE PERSONNEL BOARD REGULATIONS, § 13 (1976).

a matter for negotiation.[62] In the absence of some express statutory provision, the agency is presumably expected to bear the cost. *Union Security by Operation of Law.* For the most part, as in the private sector, union security in the public sector is a consequence of a contractual arrangement between various public employers and labor unions representing public employees. In a few states, however, the legislature has chosen to make union security an incident of exclusive representation, thus denying the various public agencies covered by the statute the option of refusing to agree to such an arrangement.

The Connecticut statute, for example, provides:

> If an exclusive representative has been designated for the employees in an appropriate collective bargaining unit, each employee in such unit who is not a member of the exclusive representative shall be required, as a condition of continued employment, to pay to such organization for the period that it is the exclusive representative, an amount equal to the regular dues, fees and assessments that a member is charged.[63]

The statute then goes on to authorize the parties to negotiate a checkoff as a means of enforcing this automatic obligation, if they choose to do so. In other states, however, the checkoff too is automatic. The Rhode Island statute, for example, provides that

> in areas where employees have selected an exclusive bargaining representative organization . . . all non-members of the exclusive bargaining representative organization shall pay to the exclusive employee organization a service charge as a contribution toward the negotiation and administration of any collective bargaining agreement in an amount equal to the regular bi-weekly membership dues of said organization with the state controller being hereby directed upon certification of the exclusive bargaining organization to deduct bi-weekly from said employee's salary said above amount and remit the same to the treasurer of the exclusive bargaining organization.[64]

Though worded differently, the Hawaii statute operates in essentially the same fashion.[65]

---

[62] FLA. STAT. ANN. § 447.303 (Supp. 1976).

[63] CONN. GEN. STAT. ANN., Public Act No. 75-566, § 11 (Conn. Legis. Serv. Supp. 1975).

[64] R.I. GEN. LAWS ANN. § 36-11-2 (Supp. 1976).

[65] HAWAII REV. STAT. § 89-4 (Supp. 1975).

Under the Minnesota statute, union security is not automatically imposed; but neither is it a product of contract negotiations. The union, rather, has the option of unilaterally imposing a service fee upon the employees it represents and of having this obligation discharged through a checkoff arrangement with the employer.[66] In Washington, on the other hand, union security is achieved other than as a result of contract negotiations provided only that a majority of the employees in the unit vote to impose such an obligation.[67]

Religious Objectors Exemption. Several states which authorize the negotiation of union security agreements also expressly provide an exemption for public employees whose religious beliefs would be offended by association with a labor organization. Montana, for example, provides that an employee who is a member of a "bona fide religious sect, . . . the established and traditional tenets or teachings of which" proscribe membership in or financial support of labor organizations, may elect instead to give to a nonreligious charity chosen by the union a sum of money equivalent to the normal union dues, initiation fees, and assessments.[68] Washington [69] and Oregon [70] statutes have similar provisions, except that under these statutes the charity must be one mutually agreeable both to the employee and the union. Whether any rational or legitimate purpose is served by requiring religious objectors to pay the equivalent of union dues to someone other than the union is a question that will be discussed subsequently.

Some exemptions for religious objectors are not as broad as those discussed above. One of the Washington statutes merely provides that a religious objector may designate a union program that is "in harmony with his individual conscience" and pay into that program the equivalent of regular union dues less the cost of premiums for union-sponsored insurance policies.[71] The rules of the Washington State Personnel Board Merit System, covering state employees, similarly provide that religious objectors, in

---

[66] MINN. STAT. ANN. § 179.65 (Cum. Supp. 1976) ; Attorney General Opinion No. 270-D (Sept. 28, 1973).

[67] WASHINGTON STATE PERSONNEL BOARD MERIT SYSTEM RULES, §§ 356-42-043, 356-42-045 (1973).

[68] MONT. REV. CODES ANN. § 59-1603(5) (Cum. Supp. 1976).

[69] WASH. REV. CODE ANN. § 41.56.122 (Supp. 1977).

[70] ORE. REV. STAT. § 243.666 (1975).

[71] WASH. REV. CODE ANN. § 28B.16.100 (Supp. 1976).

deference to their right of nonassociation, are exempt from the requirement of union membership, but that they must pay to the union an amount like that described above.[72] Since both of these provisions require the payment of money to the union, it is doubtful that they satisfy the religious objections of employees to whom any kind of association, financial or otherwise, with a labor union is prohibited. The constitutional aspects of this problem will be discussed later.

Enforcement of the Union Security Obligation. The obligation that a public employee has to become a member of or pay money to a labor union is enforced in two ways. When the obligation arises by virtue of a collective agreement between the public employer and the union, the obligation is normally enforced through discharge or the threat of discharge. The employee's obligation exists only in the sense that the employer has contractually agreed with the union to discharge any employee who fails to join or pay the required dues. In the private sector, this is the only way that a union security agreement can be enforced.

In the public sector, however, another method is available. This is through the operation of a checkoff arrangement. Under some state public employee collective bargaining statutes, the checkoff is imposed automatically or merely upon the request of the union. This method of enforcement is not available in the private sector nor under some of the state employee statutes which require individual authorization of checkoff assignments.

A third technique or method for enforcing union security obligations, which may have important tactical ramifications, is being attempted by a union in Michigan. Under the relevant state statute, a public employer and a union are permitted to negotiate agreements making the payment of a service fee a condition of continued employment.[73] Presumably, the statute contemplated that where such an agreement was reached, an employee who refused to comply would be faced with discharge or the threat of discharge—which is the traditional method of enforcing union security obligations. In the case of a contract between a union and Central Michigan University, the agreement provided that employees who do not pay the fee within the required time period "shall be liable to the Association in a civil action for money damages or for requitable enforcement of the bargaining unit

---

[72] WASHINGTON STATE PERSONNEL BOARD MERIT SYSTEM RULES, § 356-42-043 (1973).

[73] MICH. STAT. ANN. § 423.210 (1967).

member's obligation." When an employee in the unit refused to
pay the required service fee, the union brought suit pursuant to
this contract term and, in *Central Michigan University Faculty
Association* v. *Central Michigan University,* recovered the amount
sued for; the district court stated:

> In seeking recovery of the representation fee, . . . Plaintiff is doing
> far less than could otherwise have been done under settled law, i.e.
> requiring the employer to fire her from her teaching position for
> failure to pay the membership service fee. Obviously, then, the
> Agreement allowing the Plaintiff to recover its membership service
> fee by civil action is less stringent than the remedy normally af-
> forded, hence it would appear that it is a legal and proper condition
> in the Collective Bargaining Agreement.[74]

While the court's argument has superficial appeal, it totally
ignores the nature of a collective bargaining contract, which is
after all still a contract. Clearly, at common law, *A* could not
effectively contract with *B* and thereby obligate *C* to pay *A* some
money. As the statutory agent of the employees, a union may
contract with an employer and thereby, to some extent, obligate
the employees to the employer in a contractual sense. But it
seems rather strange to suggest that, via a contract with the
employer, the union could use its power of agency to make itself
the beneficiary of new obligations on the part of its principal,
the employees.

The decision was affirmed on appeal. The Michigan county circuit court noted that it was clearly the intent of the legislature
to authorize, within a public employee collective bargaining agreement, a requirement that all employees pay a service fee. Moreover, the court noted, the statute does not say that discharge is
the only way this requirement can be enforced. Rather, "since
PERA does permit the requirement in a Collective Bargaining
Agreement that a member pay, it is certainly permissible that
the commonly accepted methods of enforcing a contractual obligation be utilized." The court did not explain, however, how a suit
by an agent against its principal to enforce an obligation the
agent created in a contract with a third party could possibly be
considered a "commonly accepted method of enforcing a contractual obligation." Indeed, such a method is totally unheard of at
common law.

---

[74] 81 CCH Lab. Cas. ¶ 55,040 (Mich. Dist. Ct. 1976).

An appeal to the Michigan Court of Appeals is pending, and in the absence of any proof that the legislature consciously intended to authorize a law suit of this kind, it is probable that the two lower court decisions will be reversed.

Implied Statutory Authorization

Some of the state employee collective bargaining statutes neither expressly authorize nor expressly prohibit union security agreements. When faced with the question of the legality of such agreements, a few courts have held that the statutory authority of public employers to bargain over "wages, hours, and other terms and conditions of employment" implicitly includes the authority to bargain for a union security provision.[75] Similar language in the Taft-Hartley Act, which deals with collective bargaining in the private sector, has been construed to encompass bargaining over union security.[76] On the other hand, a contrary conclusion might be reached under statutes which define the scope of bargaining more narrowly. For example, an Indiana statute states:

> A school employer shall bargain collectively with the exclusive representative on the following: salary, wages, hours, and salary and wage related fringe benefits.[77]

Union security would probably not be encompassed by any of those terms.

STATUTORY GUARANTEES OF THE RIGHT TO WORK

In thirty-two states, one or more classes of public employees are covered by laws containing language which is at least susceptible of being construed as guaranteeing the right to work. The source and scope of this guarantee, the wording of the statutory language, and judicial constructions thereof vary appreciably from state to state.

---

[75] Warczak v. Board of Education, 73 L.R.R.M. 2237 (Mich. Cir. Ct. 1970); Nagy v. City of Detroit, 60 CCH Lab. Cas. ¶ 52,105 (Mich. Cir. Ct. 1969); *cf.* Tremblay v. Berlin Police Union, 108 N.H. 416, 237 A.2d 668 (1968).

[76] NLRB v. Andrew Jergens Co., 175 F.2d 130 (9th Cir. 1949).

[77] BURNS IND. STAT. ANN. § 20-7.5-1-4 (1975).

Applicability to Public Employees

Of the twenty state right-to-work laws, five of them expressly include public employees within their coverage.[78] Public employees are expressly excluded from the Georgia right-to-work statute; and, a North Carolina statute not only exempts public employees from the general right-to-work statute, it also prohibits such employees from even joining a union that has as one of its purposes collective bargaining with the state.

Of the right-to-work laws that are silent with respect to their applicability to public employees, four have been construed as applying to such employees, and one has been construed to the contrary. This latter conclusion was reached by the Tennessee Supreme Court in *Keeble* v. *City of Alcoa*.[79] The court there noted that as a matter of general statutory construction, "a state, or political subdivision thereof, is not subject to a statute unless specifically mentioned therein or unless application thereto is necessarily implied." [80] This same rule had previously been cited by the Arkansas Supreme Court in *Potts* v. *Hay* [81] and was even said to be generally applicable to constitutional interpretations, such as the Arkansas right-to-work provision.[82] The court's conclusion in that regard is questionable. Unlike statutes, which for the most part are intended to create private rights and duties, constitutions are primarily directed against the state itself. When a state constitution contains a right-to-work provision, the presumption should be that this flows against the state as well as anyone else specifically enumerated. This was the approach the Arkansas court actually took in the *Potts* case. The court stated that "we perceive no compelling reason to believe that the people intended to exclude public employment from the positive, unequivocal command of [the right-to-work provision]. . . ." [83] The other courts that have found state right-to-work laws (constitutional and statutory) to be applicable to public employees have followed a similar approach. In the absence of express exclusion

---

[78] Arizona, Kansas, Nevada, Utah, and Virginia. For the citations to these laws, *see* Chapter VIII, n. 1, *supra*.

[79] 204 Tenn. 286, 319 S.W.2d 249 (1958).

[80] *Id.* at 287, 319 S.W.2d at 250.

[81] 229 Ark. 830, 318 S.W.2d 826 (1958).

[82] *Id.* at 832, 318 S.W.2d at 827.

[83] *Id.*

of the state from the coverage of the law, the right-to-work guarantee will be construed without the distinction between public and private employees.[84] All of the state right-to-work laws have been construed as prohibiting not only the kinds of union security that require formal membership, but also those that merely require the payment of money. Thus, in states where the right-to-work law applies to public employees, all of the traditional forms of union security—from the service fee arrangement to the closed shop—are prohibited.

Right-to-Work Guarantees in State Employee Collective Bargaining Statutes

Although a majority of the state employee collective bargaining laws purport to disallow some kind of union security agreement, it is not clear exactly what kinds of union security are proscribed by each of the various forms of prohibition.

The most comprehensively worded prohibition, which includes all types of union security agreement, is one like that contained in an Oklahoma statute:

> No person shall be discharged from or denied employment . . . by reason of membership or nonmembership in, or the payment or nonpayment of any dues, fees or other charges to, an organization of such members for collective bargaining purposes as herein contemplated.[85]

Only slightly less comprehensive are the statutes which give an employee not only the right to refuse to join a labor union, but also the right to refrain from "assisting" the union or "participating" in its affairs. Clearly, statutes of this kind are intended to prohibit agreements requiring actual membership in the union, and the courts have also construed language of this kind as proscribing the agency shop.[86]

In *City of Hayward* v. *United Public Employees Local 390*,[87] a California court explained:

---

[84] Dade County Classroom Teachers Ass'n v. Ryan, 225 S.2d 903 (Fla. 1969); Levasseur v. Wheeldon, 79 S.D. 442, 112 N.W.2d 894 (1962); American Fed'n of State, County and Municipal Employees v. Woodward, 406 F.2d 137 (8th Cir. 1969).

[85] OKLA. STAT. ANN. tit. 11, § 548.2 (Supp. 1975).

[86] *See, e.g.,* CAL. GOV'T CODE § 3502 (Supp. 1976); N.J. STAT. ANN. § 34:13A-5.3 (Supp. 1977).

[87] 91 L.R.R.M. 2898 (Cal. Ct. of App. 1976).

The forced payment of dues or their equivalent is, at the very least, "participation" in an employee organization. Practically, it would have the effect of inducing union membership on the part of unwilling employees. While increased participation and membership is a legitimate goal of labor organizations, coercion toward that end is forbidden by statute.[88]

Similarly, in *New Jersey Turnpike Employees' Union* v. *New Jersey Turnpike Authority*,[89] the court held that the agency shop violated the public employees' statutory right to refrain from assisting labor organizations. The court, however, also intimated that the compulsory payment of a service fee representing the individual's proportionate share of the union's collective bargaining expenses would not be illegal.[90] Apparently, what the court had in mind was this: While an employee cannot be required to take a "forced journey" with the union insofar as the union's nonstatutory activities are concerned, at the same time the employee cannot be permitted to be a "free rider" when the union acts as the exclusive representative of the unit employees. This reading of the statute is clearly based on a presumed legislative intent to pursue what this judge clearly thought was a wise policy, rather than on anything in the statute or the actual legislative history.[91]

There are a few state statutes which merely say that public employees "shall have the right to join or refuse to join any [labor] organization,"[92] or that "membership in any . . . [labor organization] shall not be required as a condition of employment."[93] These right-to-work guarantees prohibit the closed or union shop, but do they also prohibit an agency shop or service fee arrangement?

On the one hand, it could be argued that in labor legislation the word *membership* (or its infinitive equivalent, *to join*) is a term

---

[88] *Id.* at 2901; *accord,* Farrigan v. Helsby, 346 N.Y.S.2d 39 (3d Dep't 1973).

[89] 303 A.2d 599 (Super. Ct. of N.J. 1973), *aff'd,* 64 N.J. 579, 319 A.2d 224 (1974).

[90] 303 A.2d at 604. Although the collective bargaining agreement purported to relate the agency fee to the costs of the collective bargaining and contract negotiation, the court apparently considered this to be a fiction since the fee was also the exact equivalent of normal initiation fees and membership dues.

[91] *See also* Town of North Kingstown v. North Kingstown Teachers Ass'n, 110 R.I. 698, 297 A.2d 342 (1972). This case, in which the policy preference is openly relied on, was cited approvingly by the New Jersey court.

[92] CONN. GEN. STAT. REV. § 10-153a (1977).

[93] DEL. CODE ANN. tit. 14, § 4003 (1975).

which includes the mere payment of sums of money. Both the federal act and state right-to-work provisions containing the term *membership* have been consistently construed in this fashion. On the other hand, in the only case on this point to be decided under a state employee collective bargaining law, a contrary conclusion was reached. In *Town of North Kingstown* v. *North Kingstown Teachers Association*,[94] the court noted the general validity of the above argument. But it also acknowledged the contrary argument that if the legislature had intended to prohibit agency shops, it could and would have used express language effective to that end as some other states have done. Having thus found the purely legal arguments, pro and con, to be in a state of contraposition, and the true legislative intent unascertainable, the court then felt justified in resolving the case by reference to its own notions of "justice and social utility." In this regard, the court asserted that "it would be manifestly inequitable to permit those who see fit not to join the union to benefit from its services without at the same time requiring them to bear a fair and just share of the financial burdens." [95] The court thus concluded that the compulsory payment of a service fee did not violate the employee's statutory right to "decline to join" a labor organization.[96]

In a few states, the only statutory guarantee of a right to work is expressed in terms of a prohibition against discrimination. An Indiana statute is typical in this regard. It makes it an unfair labor practice for a public employer to

> discriminate in regard to hiring or condition of employment to encourage or discourage membership in any employees' organization. . . .[97]

Requiring formal membership in a union as a condition of employment is obviously a proscribed form of discrimination under such a statute; the question is whether it also proscribes the agency shop or service fee arrangements. In *Smigel* v. *Southgate Community School District*,[98] the Michigan Supreme Court held

---

[94] 110 R.I. 698, 297 A.2d 342 (1972).

[95] *Id.* at 706, 297 A.2d at 346.

[96] The statute was later amended to allow a "service charge . . . in an amount equal to the regular dues of said labor organization." R.I. GEN. LAWS ANN. § 28-9.3-7 (Supp. 1976) ; *see also* Des Jarlais v. Taft, 95 L.R.R.M. 2169 (R.I. Super. Ct. 1977).

[97] BURNS IND. STAT. ANN. § 22-6-4-5 (Cum. Supp. 1975).

[98] 388 Mich. 531, 202 N.W.2d 305 (1972).

that since the agency shop was, as a matter of established labor-relations law, the practical equivalent of the union shop, which the antidiscrimination provision clearly proscribes, the agency shop is also proscribed.[99] Three members of the court, however, also suggested that a true service fee arrangement, which obligates an employee to pay only his share of the union's collective bargaining expenses, would not be tantamount to membership, and that discrimination against a person who refused to pay such a fee would not be an unfair labor practice.

On the other hand, in *Board of School Directors of Milwaukee* v. *Wisconsin Employment Relations Commission*,[100] the Wisconsin Supreme Court held that even an exclusive checkoff arrangement was illegal, since it was merely another form of union security which the antidiscrimination provision of the statute was designed to prohibit.

PUBLIC EMPLOYEES NOT COVERED BY A COLLECTIVE BARGAINING STATUTE—THE PERMISSIBILITY OF UNION SECURITY AGREEMENTS

With respect to public employees who are not covered by a collective bargaining statute, an initial question arises as to whether the employer even has the authority to enter into a collective contract with a union purporting to represent these employees. On this issue, the authority is divided.[101] But assuming that collective bargaining is generally allowed even in the absence of any specific statutory authority, a subsidiary issue is whether a public employer can enter into a union security agreement.

In states with a right-to-work statute that is applicable to public employees, the negotiation of union security agreements is obviously proscribed. Other possible sources are the state civil service and tenure laws. Under these laws, a public employee can usually be discharged only for "just cause," "incompetency," "misconduct," or the like. Although some courts have held that these laws do not control where the legislature has also authorized

---

[99] *Accord,* Farrigan v. Helsby, 346 N.Y.S.2d 39 (3d Dep't 1973).

[100] 42 Wis.2d 637, 168 N.W.2d 92 (1969).

[101] *Compare* Operating Engineers, Local 321 v. Birmingham Water Works, 163 S.2d 619 (Ala. 1964) *with* Local 266, Electrical Workers v. Salt River Project, 78 Ariz. 30, 275 P.2d 393 (1954).

the imposition of union security,[102] in the absence of such authorization it would appear that it would be impermissible under these laws to discharge an employee because of his refusal to join or pay money to a labor organization. This is the conclusion that the Ohio courts have consistently reached. In *Hagerman* v. *City of Dayton*,[103] the Ohio Supreme Court held that an ordinance calling for a mandatory checkoff was both beyond the power of the municipality (because it served no "public purpose") and in violation of the state civil service laws which made public employment a matter of "merit" and "fitness" —criteria which are not violated by an employee's refusal to authorize the checkoff of union dues.

MEMBERS-ONLY COLLECTIVE BARGAINING

In an abstract sense, the doctrine of exclusive representation is the fundamental and undoubtedly most important form of union security. Conversely, a thoroughgoing sustainment of the right to work would include a prohibition against the imposition on an employee of an unwanted collective bargaining representative. Although in the private sector, right-to-work laws have not been allowed to extend that far, a surprising number of public employee collective bargaining statutes do give employees the right to opt out of the collective bargain and to serve as their own individual negotiator.

The Oklahoma statute, for example, provides for the election of a bargaining representative by majority vote, but further provides that "Any person who desires not to be represented by any organization, as provided for herein, may so state in writing to his board of education." [104]

Similarly, the Florida statute which gives public employees the right to be represented in collective bargaining by a labor organization also provides that "public employees shall have the right

---

[102] City of Warren v. Local 1383, Firefighters, 68 L.R.R.M. 2977 (Mich. Cir. Ct. 1968) ; Clampitt v. Board of Education, 68 L.R.R.M. 2997 (Mich. Cir. Ct. 1968) ; Smigel v. Southgate Community School District, 70 L.R.R.M. 2042 (Mich. Cir. Ct. 1968), *rev'd on other grounds*, 24 Mich. App. 179, 180 N.W.2d 215 (1970), *rev'd on other grounds*, 388 Mich. 531, 202 N.W.2d 305 (1972) ; *contra*, Oregon Attorney General Opinion No. 6449 (1968).

[103] 147 Ohio 313, 71 N.E.2d 246 (1947) ; *accord*, Foltz v. City of Dayton, 272 N.E.2d 169 (Ohio Ct. of App. 1970) ; State v. Ensign, 76 L.R.R.M. 3031 (Ohio Ct. of Common Pleas 1971).

[104] OKLA. STAT. ANN. tit. 70, § 509.2 (1972).

to refrain from exercising the right to be represented."[105] The Florida Supreme Court has also held that the state right-to-work law, to the extent that it applies to public employees, also prohibits any compulsory exclusive-representative scheme.[106] In California, only teachers are subject to exclusive representation. The statutes provide for most of the other public employees that they "shall have the right to represent themselves individually in their employment relations with the state."[107] The Nebraska statute is similarly worded.[108]

PROPOSED FEDERAL LEGISLATION

Presently pending in Congress are several proposals which would subject state and local employee labor relations to a uniform federal law. Representative Thompson of New Jersey has introduced a bill which would simply extend the coverage of the Taft-Hartley Act to include state and local governments.[109] Insofar as union security is concerned, this would authorize the negotiation of agency shops or service fee arrangements. A similar result would be reached under a comprehensive public employee collective bargaining statute introduced by Representative Roybal of California.[110]

On the other hand, a bill introduced by Representative Clay would impose as a matter of law an obligation on employees to pay an agency shop fee to the exclusive bargaining representative.[111]

It seems doubtful, however, that any of these proposals could withstand constitutional scrutiny.[112]

---

[105] FLA. STAT. ANN. § 447.301 (Supp. 1976).

[106] Dade County Classroom Teachers Ass'n v. Ryan, 225 S.2d 903 (Fla. 1969).

[107] CAL. GOV'T CODE §§ 3502, 3527 (Supp. 1976).

[108] NEB. REV. STAT. § 79-1288 (1976).

[109] H.R. 77, 94th Cong., 1st Sess. (1975).

[110] H.R. 1488, 94th Cong., 1st Sess. (1975).

[111] H.R. 8677, 93d Cong., 1st Sess. (1973).

[112] *See* Chapter VIII, *supra*.

CHAPTER XI

Union Security and the Right to Work — The Constitutional Issues

It has been said that all matters of grave public concern and controversy ultimately cast themselves into the form of a constitutional issue and wind their way to the Supreme Court where they are resolved by reference to the highest law of the land. For generations, the union security and right-to-work issue has embroiled the hearts and minds of much of the citizenry. It is no surprise, therefore, that recourse to the Constitution has been frequently made by the protagonists of the respective sides of the debate. While many specific issues have now been resolved by the courts—subject, as always, to erosion by the tides and eddies of a constantly evolving corpus of constitutional law—other issues, some of them quite fundamental in nature, have yet to receive adequate judicial attention. The purpose of this chapter is to map out only the broader contours of this extremely complex and often baffling constitutional controversy.

THE PRIVATE SECTOR

Reaching the Constitutional Issue

When evaluating the constitutionality of union security agreements in the private sector, one immediately confronts a threshold difficult: How can a constitutional issue even be said to exist? There would appear to be only two possible approaches to the matter: a direct attack upon the union security agreement itself, or an attack upon the federal legislation that authorizes such agreements. Neither line of approach, however, is free from major analytical obstacles.

Ostensibly, a union security agreement is a contract between two private parties—labor and management. It is axiomatic that constitutional limitations apply only to governmental acts and not to the acts of private individuals operating in a purely private capacity. Thus a direct constitutional attack on union security agreements seems out of the question.

Moreover, although the Taft-Hartley Act and the Railway Labor Act are undoubtedly subject to constitutional scrutiny, neither statute actually commands the negotiation of union security agreements. Indeed, the statutes only provide that such agreements are not to be considered illegal under federal law. There is, therefore, no constitutional question over governmental compulsion.

Since these arguments, if valid, would preclude the necessity of any substantive constitutional evaluation of union security agreements, an analysis of them is in order at this point.

Statutory Authorization of Union Security Agreements—The Problem of Being "Merely Permissive." Mr. Justice Frankfurter was a leading proponent of the view that because of its permissive nature, the statutory allowance of union security agreements could not be said to invade any constitutionally protected substantive rights. In *International Association of Machinists* v. *Street,*[1] he stated:

> Were we to assume, *arguendo*, that the plaintiffs have alleged a valid constitutional objection if Congress had specifically ordered the result, we must consider the difference between such compulsion and the absence of compulsion when Congress acts as platonically as it did, in a wholly noncoercive way. Congress has not commanded that the railroads shall employ only those workers who are members of authorized unions. Congress has only given leave to a bargaining representative, democratically elected by a majority of workers, to enter into a particular contractual provision arrived at under the give-and-take of duly safeguarded bargaining procedures. . . . And this Court in *Hanson* noted that "The union shop provision of the Railway Labor Act is only permissive. Congress has not . . . required carriers and employees to enter into union shop agreements." . . . When we speak of the Government "acting" in permitting the union shop, the scope and force of what Congress has done must be heeded. There is not a trace of compulsion involved—no exercise of restriction by Congress on the freedom of the carriers and the unions.[2]

The other members of the Court, however, did not agree with Mr. Justice Frankfurter. In *Railway Employees' Department* v.

---

[1] 367 U.S. 740 (1961).

[2] *Id.* at 806-07; *see also* Otten v. Baltimore & Ohio Railroad Co., 205 F.2d 58 (2d Cir. 1953).

Hanson,[3] after conceding that "the union shop provision of the Railway Labor Act is only permissive" in that "Congress has not compelled nor required carriers and employees to enter into union shop agreements," the Court nevertheless proceeded to a somewhat limited examination of the constitutionality of Section 2, Eleventh. The Court explained its rationale for reaching the constitutional question in the following terms:

> If private rights are being invaded, it is by force of an agreement made pursuant to federal law which expressly declares that state law is superseded. . . . In other words, the federal statute is the source of the power and authority by which any private rights are lost or sacrificed. . . . The enactment of the federal statute authorizing union shop agreements is the governmental action on which the Constitution operates, though it takes a private agreement to invoke the federal sanction.[4]

A legal enactment cast in permissive form can raise an issue of constitutionality if the "permission" or "authorization" has the effect of providing a preemptive legality to private conduct which would otherwise constitute an invasion of a right protected under some subordinate state law. Thus, in *Hanson* the Court suggested that when Congress affirmatively and preemptively sanctioned or authorized an invasion of a right previously protected by the Nebraska right-to-work law, this action by the federal government was susceptible to constitutional scrutiny.

In *Hanson,* the preemption theory was used to justify the Court's scrutiny of the union security authorizations of the Railway Labor Act. The next question is, can the same theory be used in the context of a Taft-Hartley Act suit? The answer would appear to be no.

Unlike the Railway Labor Act, Taft-Hartley specifically provides that the exemption of certain union security agreements from the Act's antidiscrimination provisions shall not operate to preempt state laws that make such agreements illegal. Thus, since there is no preemption, the *Hanson* theory would appear to be inapplicable. We are left again with the assertion that Taft-Hartley is permissive insofar as union security agreements are concerned, raising no constitutional issues in this regard.[5]

---

[3] 351 U.S. 225 (1956).

[4] *Id.* at 232.

[5] For judicial expressions of this view, *see* Reid v. McDonnell Douglas Corp., 443 F.2d 408, 410 (10th Cir. 1971); Linscott v. Millers Falls Co., 440 F.2d 14, 19-20 (1st Cir. 1971) (Coffin, concurring), *cert. denied,* 404 U.S. 872 (1971).

On the other hand, the language of the *Hanson* decision quoted above is susceptible of a broader interpretation, one which does not depend upon the element of preemption. In *Linscott* v. *Millers Falls Co.*,[6] the First Circuit Court of Appeals took such an approach and read *Hanson* as saying that when federal law creates federally enforceable rights, then such a law is subject to constitutional scrutiny. Since both the Railway Labor Act and the Taft-Hartley Act give unions the right to negotiate union security agreements and then to enforce them in a federal forum,[7] the union security provisions of both statutes are equally subject to constitutional review. From this perspective, it was irrelevant that Congress preempted state law in one statute, while in the other statute it declined to do so.

There is language in the *Linscott* opinion, however, that suggests another rebuttal to the "merely permissive, and thus not reviewable" argument. The *Linscott* court said at one point that "the LMRA's recognition of the union shop . . . constitutes governmental *endorsement* in an area in which Congress makes the rules."[8] Elsewhere, the court spoke of the Railway Labor Act, as construed by *Hanson*, as providing "federal *support*" for the union shop.[9] The court's emphasis was that both the Railway Labor Act and the Taft-Hartley Act do more than merely permit union security agreements; that these acts actively encourage such agreements.

Mr. Justice Black implicitly followed the "active encouragement" argument of the *Hanson* rationale for reaching the constitutional issue. In *International Association of Machinists* v. *Street,* he noted in summary of the *Hanson* holding that "[e]ven though Section 2, Eleventh is permissive in form, Congress was fully aware when enacting it that the almost certain result would be the establishment of union shops throughout the railroad industry,"[10] thus giving rise to a constitutional issue.

---

[6] 440 F.2d 14 (1st Cir. 1971), *cert. denied,* 404 U.S. 872 (1971).

[7] In Abood v. Detroit Board of Education, 45 U.S.L.W. 4473 at 4476 n. 12 (1977), the Supreme Court seemed to read *Hanson* in this fashion when it reiterated the fact that "once courts enforce the agreement the sanction of government is, of course, put behind them."

[8] 440 F.2d at 16 n. 2 (emphasis added).

[9] *Id.* at 16 (emphasis added).

[10] 367 U.S. at 789 n. 13 (Black, dissenting).

The author of the *Hanson* decision, Mr. Justice Douglas, recently explained the justification for reaching the constitutional issue by the perception of federal "encouragement" of union security agreements. In *Buckley* v. *American Federation of Television & Radio Artists*, he noted that in the Taft-Hartley Act:

> The fact that § 8(a)(3) is phrased in permissive rather than mandatory terms would not, in and of itself, prevent a finding of governmental action. The Federal Government has undertaken extensive regulation of the field of labor-management relations, and by its approval and enforcement of union-shop agreements, may be said to "encourage" and foster such agreements.[11]

The encouragement theory reading of *Hanson* by no means posits something novel. Such a theory has been used several times by the Supreme Court in reviewing the constitutionality of laws that are cast in the permissive mode.[12] Moreover, although Section 8(a)(3) is itself merely permissive of union security agreements, it is beyond dispute that, taken as a whole, the Taft-Hartley Act, whether by deliberate congressional design or otherwise, does facilitate and encourage the negotiation of this kind of agreement by imposing a duty on unions to represent everyone in the unit (thereby giving them a strong incentive also to seek financial support from everyone in the unit), by making union security a subject of mandatory bargaining, by enhancing union bargaining power, and by making such agreements legally enforceable.

Despite the "merely permissive" nature of the union security provisions of the Taft-Hartley Act, the courts have articulated a number of theories for subjecting both it and the Railway Labor Act to constitutional scrutiny.

Challenging the Constitutionality of Union Security Agreements Themselves—The Problem of Finding "State Action." Occasionally, the constitutional attack upon union security is directed, not at the underlying federal statutes, but at the union security agreement itself in a suit against the employer and union who negotiated the agreement. Before a court can reach the substantive constitutional law issue in such a case, however,

---

[11] 496 F.2d 305 (2d Cir. 1974), *cert. denied*, Lewis v. American Federation of Television and Radio Artists, 419 U.S. 1093, 1094-95 (1974) (Douglas, dissenting).

[12] *See* Reitman v. Mulkey, 387 U.S. 369 (1967); Robinson v. Florida, 378 U.S. 153 (1964); Moose Lodge 107 v. Irvis, 407 U.S. 163 (1972).

it must first determine that the constitution is in fact directly applicable to these parties, for constitutional limitations apply only to governmental acts. Thus, a suit of this kind can be successful only if the court finds that the employer and/or the union, in negotiating the union security agreement, were engaged in what has come to be called "state action."

The imposition of constitutional restraints upon private parties under the aegis of the "state action" doctrine is one of the most controversial developments of American constitutional law.[13] The Supreme Court cases allegedly finding state action in the guise of private conduct are not, however, known for their doctrinal clarity, and the theoretical underpinnings of state action have always been somewhat obscure. Indeed, the Supreme Court's various specific holdings, the Court's later interpretations of these prior holdings, the quotable language of the decisions, be it dicta or otherwise, and the concurring and dissenting opinions, all are like multicolored threads from which a variety of theoretical tapestries may legitimately be woven. As the Supreme Court recently conceded, "the question whether particular conduct is 'private,' on the one hand, or 'state action' on the other, frequently admits of no easy answer."[14]

Nevertheless, a number of theories have been advanced for subjecting unions, together with the collective bargaining agreements that they negotiate and administer, to constitutional scrutiny. It has been suggested, for example, that both unions and corporations should be subjected to constitutional limitation simply because of the social, economic, and political "power" which they allegedly possess.[15] Professor Wellington's rejection of this theory on the grounds that there are more effective instruments that one can use in regulating union power is cer-

---

[13] The literature on the "state action" doctrine is vast. For three of the most influential articles on the topic, *see* Williams, *The Twilight of State Action*, 41 Texas L. Rev. 347 (1963); Lewis, *The Meaning of State Action*, 60 Colum. L. Rev. 1083 (1960); Horowitz, *The Misleading Search for "State Action" under the Fourteenth Amendment*, 30 S. Cal. L. Rev. 208 (1957).

[14] Jackson v. Metropolitan Edison Co., 419 U.S. 345, 349-50 (1974).

[15] *See, e.g.*, Berle, *Constitutional Limitations on Corporate Activity—Protection of Personal Rights from Invasion Through Economic Power*, 100 U. Pa. L. Rev. 933 (1952); Miller, *Private Governments and the Constitution* (Occasional Paper for Center for the Study of Democratic Institutions, 1959); Malick, *Toward a New Constitutional Status for Labor Unions: A Proposal*, 21 Rocky Mt. L. Rev. 260 (1949); Rauh, *Civil Rights and Liberties and Labor Unions*, 8 Lab. L. J. 874 (1957).

tainly a valid, albeit secondary, grounds of demurral.[16] A more fundamental objection is this: Since obtaining and using private power is itself frequently a constitutionally protected right, it would be self-defeating and contradictory to apply indiscriminately the constitution to the exercise of such power simply because it exists. It is not the presence of power that is critical, but rather its quality and source.

It has also been suggested that unions should be subjected to constitutional restraints because they perform a "public function."[17] This theory of state action had its genesis in *Marsh* v. *Alabama*,[18] which involved the exclusion of a Jehovah's Witness from a privately owned "company town." Apart from the fact that recently the *Marsh* case itself has been narrowly construed by the Supreme Court,[19] the "public functions" theory—or "looks like government" theory, to borrow Professor Wellington's trenchant phrase [20]—suffers from the malaise of conceptual incompleteness. As Mr. Justice Douglas stated in *Evans* v. *Newton,* "The range of governmental activities is broad and varied, and the fact that government has engaged in a particular activity does not necessarily mean that an individual entrepreneur or manager of the same kind of undertaking suffers the same constitutional inhibitions."[21] Assuming thus that the regulation of the terms of the employment relationship is a public function—*i.e.,* because Congress and the states have enacted legislation which regulates it—does not convert a private contractual regulation into state action.

The Supreme Court, however, has recently refined and narrowed the "public functions" theory in such a way as to accommodate the Douglas *caveat*. In *Jackson* v. *Metropolitan Edison Co.,*[22] the Supreme Court, in reviewing the various state action theories that it apparently still considered legitimate, noted:

---

[16] Wellington, *The Constitution, The Labor Union, and "Governmental Action,"* 70 YALE L.J. 345, 348-50 (1961).

[17] *See* Symposium, *Individual Rights in Industrial Self-Government—A "State Action" Analysis,* 63 N. W. U. L. REV. 4, 19-30 (1968).

[18] 326 U.S. 501 (1946).

[19] Lloyd Corp. v. Tanner, 407 U.S. 551 (1972).

[20] Wellington, *supra* n. 16 at 348.

[21] 382 U.S. 296, 300 (1966).

[22] 419 U.S. 345 (1974).

We have, of course, found state action present in the exercise by a private entity of powers traditionally exclusively reserved to the State. . . . If we were dealing with the exercise by Metropolitan of some power delegated to it by the State which is traditionally associated with sovereignty, such as eminent domain, our case would be quite a different one.[23]

In short, what the Supreme Court was saying was that when government delegates to a private person the authority to exercise some of the government's unique sovereign powers, then the constitutional limitations on that power necessarily follow the delegation.

This version of the state action theory is not only one of the oldest [24] and most intellectually respectable of the Court's various approaches, it is also one of the few that has actually been applied within the context of labor union activity.

In *Steele* v. *Louisville & Nashville Railroad*,[25] the Supreme Court held that the Railway Labor Act imposed upon unions a "duty of fair representation" toward all members of the bargaining unit. The Act contains no specific provision of this kind; the Supreme Court read such a duty into the Act. But it is the Court's reason for this extraordinary bit of statutory construction that is of importance. The union in that case had negotiated a contract which blatantly discriminated against Negro employees in the unit. The Supreme Court noted:

> If, as the state court has held, the Act confers this power on the bargaining representative of a craft or class of employees without any commensurate statutory duty toward its members, constitutional questions arise. For the *representative is clothed with power not unlike that of a legislature which is subject to constitutional limitations* on its power to deny, restrict, destroy or discriminate against the rights of those for whom it legislates and which is also under an affirmative constitutional duty equally to protect those rights. . . . Since petitioner and the other Negro members of the craft are not members of the Brotherhood or eligible for membership, *the authority to act for them is derived not from their action or consent but wholly from the command of the Act.* . . . Congress has seen fit to clothe the bargaining representative with powers

---

[23] *Id.* at 352-53.

[24] *See* Olcott v. County Board of Supervisors, 83 U.S. (16 Wall.) 678 (1872) ; Nixon v. Condon, 286 U.S. 73 (1932) ; Smith v. Allwright, 321 U.S. 649 (1944).

[25] 323 U.S. 192 (1944) ; *see also* Carter v. Carter Coal Co., 298 U.S. 238, 311 (1936).

comparable to those possessed by a legislative body both to create
and restrict the rights of those whom it represents. . . .[26]

Arguably, what the Supreme Court in *Steele* was saying was
that the statutory grant of the right of exclusive representation
(whereby a union is empowered to negotiate collective labor contracts on behalf of employees, some of whom do not consent to
such representation) necessarily involves the exercise of powers
normally reserved to the sovereign; that whenever, pursuant to
this delegation of authority, the union acts in its representative
capacity, this *is* "state action"; and that such action is therefore
subject to the limits of the constitution.

The current validity of this theory is subject to doubt. Mr. Justice Powell's concurring opinion in *Abood* v. *Detroit Board of
Education* notes:

> Some have argued that this analogy [between a collective bargain-
> ing agreement and a legislative code] requires each provision of
> a private collective-bargaining agreement to meet the same limi-
> tations that the Constitution imposes on congressional enactments.
> But this Court has wisely refrained from adopting this view and
> generally has measured the rights and duties embodied in a collec-
> tive-bargaining agreement only against the limitations imposed by
> Congress.[27]

Although Mr. Justice Powell is undoubtedly correct in saying
that the *Steele* doctrine has not been extended as far as it might,
it nevertheless remains the leading theoretical justification for
raising constitutional issues within the context of ostensibly private collective bargaining agreements.

The Substantive Constitutional Law Issues

When governmental power is used to compel employees to join
a labor union as a condition of continued employment with a private employer, a number of constitutionally important interests
are touched upon. Whether the compulsion rises to the level of a

---

[26] 323 U.S. at 198-202 (emphasis added). Professor Clyde Summers has
aptly described it in these terms:

> Unions, in bargaining, are not private organizations but are govern-
> mental agencies garbed with the cloak of legal authority to represent
> all employees in the unit and armed with the legal right to participate
> in all decisions affecting terms and conditions of employment.

Summers, *Union Powers and Workers' Rights*, 49 MICH. L. REV. 805, 811
(1951).

[27] 45 U.S.L.W. 4473, 4484 (1977).

violation of a constitutional right remains to be seen. But at issue are the following: the constitutional liberty of work; freedom of association; freedom of speech; and freedom of religion. These will be taken up in turn.

The Fifth and Fourteenth Amendments. In *Railway Employees' Department* v. *Hanson* [28]—which, despite the inconclusivity of the Court's holding, is still said to be one of the leading cases on the constitutionality of union security agreements—the plaintiffs challenged a union security agreement that had been negotiated under the Railway Labor Act. They maintained that, *inter alia,* the agreement violated their constitutional right to work. The Supreme Court, speaking through Mr. Justice Douglas, apparently conceded that such a right did exist:

> It is said that the right to work, which the Court has frequently included in the concept of "liberty" within the meaning of the Due Process Clauses . . . may not be denied by the Congress.[29]

The Court's problem, however, was to define the proper scope of that right. In an earlier era, the Supreme Court had defined the constitutional right to work as a virtually unfettered freedom of contract. It was frequently held that an employee and an employer had the constitutional liberty to contract for such terms and conditions of employment as were mutually agreeable to both.[30] Under this approach, if neither an employer nor an employee desired to make union membership a condition of employment, then the imposition of such a requirement by government fiat (directly or indirectly through the exercise of governmental powers by a labor union) would be unconstitutional.[31]

---

[28] 351 U.S. 225 (1956).

[29] *Id.* at 234.

[30] In Adkins v. Children's Hospital, 261 U.S. 525 (1923), the Court stated the constitutional principle as follows:

> That the right to contract about one's affairs is a part of the liberty of the individual protected by [the 5th Amendment, due process] clause, is settled by the decisions of this Court and is no longer open to question. . . . Within this liberty are contracts of employment of labor. In making such contracts, generally speaking, the parties have an equal right to obtain from each other the best terms they can as a result of private bargaining.

Id. at 545. *See also* Lochner v. New York, 198 U.S. 45 (1905).

[31] *Cf.* Coppage v. Kansas, 236 U.S. 1 (1915); Adair v. United States, 208 U.S. 161 (1908).

By 1955, however, the Court had long since repudiated its liberty-of-contract philosophy. The prevailing doctrine was that individual employment contracts were subject to the states' police power or to its federal counterpart, the power of Congress under the Commerce Clause. Moreover, it was said that the police power could always be exercised in the public interest, and that the legislatures and not the courts had the primary responsibility of determining where the public interest lay. Thus, unless a regulation of contract was clearly arbitrary or contravened a specifically enumerated constitutional right, the courts would sustain its constitutionality.[32]

This was the approach the Court in *Hanson* took toward the so-called constitutional right to work. After paying deference to the right to work in the abstract, the Court continued:

> The question remains, however, whether the long-range interests of workers would be better served by one type of union agreement or another. That question is germane to the exercise of power under the Commerce Clause—a power that often has the quality of police regulations. . . . One would have to be blind to history to assert that trade unionism did not enhance and strengthen the right to work. . . . To require, rather than to induce, the beneficiaries of trade unionism to contribute to its cost may not be the wisest course. But Congress might well believe that it would help insure the right to work in and along the arteries of interstate commerce. No more has been attempted here.[33]

While a right to work is merely implicit in the liberty protected by the Fifth and Fourteenth Amendments and is subject to constitutional protection only to the extent of being insured against arbitrary interference, other constitutional "interests" affected by union security have received a greater measure of constitutional protection in other contexts.

The First Amendment. Although the United States Constitution does not specifically enumerate either a right of association or a right of nonassociation, the freedom of the individual to organize or join voluntary associations or to decline to do so is now well established as a constitutional right.[34] This was recognized by the Court in *Hanson*:

---

[32] *See* Lincoln Federal Labor Union v. Northwestern Iron & Metal Co., 335 U.S. 525, 536-37 (1949).

[33] 351 U.S. at 234-35.

[34] *See, e.g.,* NAACP v. Alabama, 357 U.S. 449 (1958); Bates v. City of Little Rock, 361 U.S. 516 (1960); Shelton v. Tucker, 364 U.S. 479 (1960);

It is argued that the union shop agreement forces men into ideological and political associations which violate their right to freedom of conscience, freedom of association, and freedom of thought
protected by the Bill of Rights.[35]

The Court, however, held that the record in the *Hanson* case did
not show any constitutional violation in the First Amendment
sense; that is, there was no evidence "that compulsory membership [was being] used to impair freedom of expression" or that
"the exaction of dues, initiation fees, or assessments [was being]
used as a cover for forcing ideological conformity or other action
in contravention of the First Amendment. . . ." [36] The Court thus
declined to pass on the issue.

Indirectly the Court did make a First Amendment judgment.
The Court stated that its holding was a narrow one in that

> [w]e only hold that the requirement for financial support of the
> collective-bargaining agency by all who receive the benefits of its
> work is within the power of Congress under the Commerce Clause
> and does not violate either the First or the Fifth Amendments.[37]

Implicit in the Court's First Amendment holding is the assertion that the mere payment of money to a labor union to defray
its collective bargaining expenses is either not a form of association at all (in the constitutional sense), or that there is some
countervailing constitutional justification for requiring this kind
of association. Although the *Hanson* Court did not indicate which
of these two possibilities formed the basis of its decision, the
Supreme Court has recently rejected the first one altogether.

In *Abood* v. *Detroit Board of Education*,[38] which involved the
constitutionality of an agency shop agreement in the public sector, the Court stated without equivocation that the payment of an
agency shop fee did involve a form of constitutionally recognized
"association." [39] The Court in *Abood* then construed *Hanson* as

---

Louisiana v. NAACP, 366 U.S. 293 (1961); Scales v. United States, 367
U.S. 203 (1961); NAACP v. Button, 371 U.S. 415 (1963); Emerson, *Freedom
of Association and Freedom of Expression*, 74 YALE L. J. 1 (1964).

[35] 351 U.S. at 236.

[36] *Id.* at 238.

[37] *Id.*

[38] 45 U.S.L.W. 4473 (1977).

[39] *Id.* at 4476-77. *See also* Shelton v. Tucker, 364 U.S. 479, 487-88 (1960);
Bond v. County of Delaware, 368 F. Supp. 618, 625-27 (E.D. Pa. 1973);
Pollard v. Roberts, 283 F. Supp. 248, 257-58 (E.D. Ark. 1968), *aff'd mem.*,
393 U.S. 14 (1968).

standing for the proposition that although the compulsory payment of dues does have a detrimental impact on the employees' constitutional right of nonassociation, such interference is nevertheless constitutionally justified. This understanding of *Hanson* is in line with the second interpretation mentioned above. What, however, is the nature of the justification? Normally, when a legislative enactment encroaches directly upon a First Amendment right, the Supreme Court will require that this be justified by reference to some "clear and present danger" to the Republic itself or, at the very least, to some "compelling governmental interest." [40] On the other hand, regarding economic or industrial legislation that is alleged to infringe on Fourteenth or Fifth Amendment "liberties," the Court has generally deferred to whatever policy the legislatures have chosen to follow, provided only that it is not patently arbitrary or unreasonable.[41]

In *Hanson*, the Court was confronted with a legislative enactment which, while dealing with a matter of industrial concern, infringed on a recognized First Amendment right. The Court was faced with a choice of which test to apply.

Apparently, the *Hanson* Court was of the view that because the compulsory dues were used only to finance collective bargaining activities, the enabling legislation was primarily economic, and the lesser standard of judicial review could be resorted to. The Court noted that there were arguments both pro and con over the issue of union security:

> But the question is one of policy with which the judiciary has no concern. . . . Congress, acting within its constitutional powers, has the final say on policy issues. If it acts unwisely, the electorate can make a change. The task of the judiciary ends once it appears that the legislative measure adopted is relevant or appropriate to the constitutional power which Congress exercises.[42]

Several years after the *Hanson* decision, the Supreme Court was again confronted with a case involving union security agreements under the Railway Labor Act. In this case, *International Association of Machinists* v. *Street*,[43] the plaintiffs hoped that the

---

[40] *See, e.g.,* Schenck v. United States, 249 U.S. 47 (1919); Schneider v. Irvington, 308 U.S. 147 (1939); Wisconsin v. Yoder, 406 U.S. 205 (1972).

[41] *See, e.g.,* Lincoln Federal Labor Union v. Northwestern Iron & Metal Co., 335 U.S. 525 (1949); Day-Brite Lighting, Inc. v. Missouri, 342 U.S. 421 (1952); Ferguson v. Skrupa, 372 U.S. 726 (1963).

[42] 351 U.S. at 234.

[43] 367 U.S. 740 (1961).

Court would decide the constitutional issue that it failed to decide in *Hanson*—whether it was constitutional for unions to use agency fee dues for political purposes. In *Street,* although the Court technically avoided the constitutional issue by holding that the Act simply did not authorize unions to use coercively obtained membership fees for such purposes, it is reasonably apparent that the Court was construing the Act in that way so that it would not have to declare it unconstitutional.

The controlling constitutional principle which the *Street* Court simply read into the statute was most eloquently stated by Mr. Justice Black, who dissented on the grounds that the cases should have been decided directly on a constitutional basis. Speaking in reference to the First Amendment, he said:

> Probably no one would suggest that Congress could, without violating this Amendment, pass a law taxing workers, or any persons for that matter (even lawyers), to create a fund to be used in helping certain political parties or groups favored by the Government to elect their candidates or promote their controversial causes. Compelling a man by law to pay his money to elect candidates or advocate laws or doctrines he is against differs only in degree, if at all, from compelling him by law to speak for a candidate, a party, or a cause he is against. The very reason for the First Amendment is to make the people of this country free to think, speak, write and worship as they wish, not as the Government commands.[44]

These sentiments were recently reaffirmed by the Supreme Court in the *Abood* case.

Hanson and *Street* dealt only with the constitutionality of the agency shop, which is the maximum form of union security allowed by federal law, and thus neither case addressed itself to the question of whether formal membership could be made a condition of employment. To the extent that formal membership entails a more literal form of association and would necessarily entwine the employee in the political, ideological, and other non-collective bargaining activities of the union, it would appear that such a requirement would be unconstitutional. In *Abood,* the Court noted that the requirement of formal membership, as under a true union shop, would raise constitutional issues not touched upon by *Hanson*; but the Court, since it too was concerned only with an agency shop situation, declined to pass on the issue.[45]

---

[44] *Id.* at 788 (Black, dissenting).

[45] 45 U.S.L.W. at 4475 n. 10 (1977).

Freedom of Speech. To the extent that the *Hanson* and *Street* cases can be construed as saying that the use of agency shop fees for political causes violates the associational rights of dissenting employees, so also can those cases be construed as saying that such use violates the freedom of speech of these employees. The two rights are very closely related, but not necessarily identical. As there is a right to speak, so also is there a right to refrain from speaking—a right which is violated when the union uses compulsorily obtained monies to finance political and ideological speech.

In recent years, it has been claimed that among certain kinds of employees, union security agreements also violate the First Amendment in that they serve as prior restraint upon the exercise of speech by the employees. This claim was made in the case of *Buckley* v. *American Federation of Television & Radio Artists.*[46] In this case, political commentators William F. Buckley, Jr., and M. Stanton Evans alleged that being required to join the union, AFTRA, as a condition of appearing on CBS operated as a prior restraint and had a chilling effect upon their speech. In particular, they alleged that the required membership subjected them to union discipline for violations of union rules, which among other things proscribed all conduct "prejudicial to the welfare of the Association." The Federal District Court for the Southern District of New York sustained their claim:

> Prior restraints on freedom of speech by federal, state or local government, or by those acting pursuant to Congressional authority, as is defendant, cannot be sustained in the absence of a competing and compelling necessity which, if not satisfied, will "surely result in direct, immediate and irreparable damage to our Nation or its people." [47]

The court then held that for persons like the plaintiffs—*i.e.*, commentators expressing their own views about political issues and national affairs—the state had no compelling reason for making them join the union as a condition precedent to the expression of their views.

The Federal Court of Appeals for the Second Circuit reversed. This court viewed the plaintiffs' claim as having two aspects: that the mere payment of dues constitutes a prior restraint; and

---

[46] 354 F. Supp. 823 (S.D. N.Y. 1973), *rev'd*, 496 F.2d 305 (2d Cir. 1974), *cert. denied*, Lewis v. American Federation of Television & Radio Artists, 419 U.S. 1093 (1974).

[47] 354 F. Supp. at 845.

that the threat of union discipline unconstitutionally "chilled" the plaintiffs' exercise of their right of speech. Regarding this second aspect, the Second Circuit held that the district court lacked jurisdiction even to decide the issue. It is highly doubtful, the court indicated, that the Taft-Hartley Act authorizes union security agreements requiring formal (discipline-subjecting) membership as a condition of employment. That being the case, AFTRA's attempts to force Buckley and Evans into the union was arguably an unfair labor practice and, thus, subject to the primary jurisdiction of the National Labor Relations Board.

On the other hand, with respect to the payment-of-dues aspect of the case, the court held that assuming *arguendo* the existence of state action, such a requirement was not unconstitutional as applied to these plaintiffs. The approach taken by the court was that the union dues requirement was analogous to an otherwise valid, nondiscriminatory tax, serving "substantial public interests." [48] The court noted that despite the incidental burden such taxes may have upon speech, they are not unconstitutional.

The United States Supreme Court denied *certiorari* in the *Buckley/Evans* case, over a strong dissent by Mr. Justice Douglas (joined by Chief Justice Burger). Douglas did not reach the substantive issue, but he did indicate that

> [t]here is a substantial question whether the union-dues requirement imposed upon these petitioners should be characterized as a prior restraint or inhibition upon their free-speech rights. In some respects, the requirement to pay dues under compulsion can be viewed as the functional equivalent of a "license" to speak.[49]

He also noted that in the *Street* case the Court had worked out an accommodation between the political rights of employees and their obligation to bear a share of the collective bargaining expenses. He then said, "Whether a similar accommodation could be worked out in the present case, I do not know." [50] He did, however, think that the issue should have been heard by the Court.

Freedom of Religion. The other constitutional liberty that has frequently been asserted against union security agreements is the First Amendment freedom of religion. Members of certain religious sects believe that membership in or financial support of

---

[48] 496 F.2d at 311.

[49] 419 U.S. at 1095.

[50] *Id.* at 1096.

labor unions is morally wrong.[51] Although the *bona fides* of these beliefs has never been disputed, the courts have consistently denied the pleas of these persons to be exempt from the requirements imposed by union security agreements under both the Railway Labor Act and Taft-Hartley.

Some of the earlier cases were dismissed on the grounds that because the statute was "merely permissive" and because the contract was between private parties, no constitutional issue could be raised.[52] Insofar as the Railway Labor Act was concerned, *Hanson* clearly overruled those holdings. In some of the religious cases to come later, the *Hanson* state action theory was applied to the Taft-Hartley Act as well.[53]

With respect to the substantive issue, the earlier decisions had occasionally relied in part on the notion that religious "action" is entitled to less constitutional protection than religious "belief," [54] and that the constitution provides no religious exception to otherwise valid, nondiscriminatory (against religion) statutory requirements.[55] Whatever validity these notions ever had, however, was undermined to some extent by the Supreme Court's recent decision in *Wisconsin* v. *Yoder*,[56] which dealt with the constitutionality of a state's compulsory education laws. The Court there rejected the state's argument "that 'actions', even though religiously grounded, are outside the protection of the First Amendment," [57] and further noted that "Nor can this case be disposed of on the grounds that Wisconsin's requirement for school attendance to age 16 applies uniformly to all citizens of the State and does not, on its face, discriminate against religions or a par-

---

[51] According to Representative Green of Oregon, there are at least seven religious groups in the country that do not allow their members to join or pay dues to labor organizations. 120 CONG. REC. 16915, 93d Cong., 2d Sess. (1974).

[52] Otten v. Baltimore & Ohio Railroad, 205 F.2d 58 (2d Cir. 1953); Wicks v. Southern Pacific Co., 231 F.2d 130 (9th Cir. 1956).

[53] Linscott v. Millers Falls Co., 316 F. Supp. 1369 (D. Mass. 1970), *aff'd*, 440 F.2d 14 (1st Cir. 1971), *cert. denied*, 404 U.S. 872 (1971).

[54] Otten v. Baltimore & Ohio Railroad, 132 F. Supp. 836 (E.D. N.Y. 1952), *aff'd*, 205 F.2d 58 (2d Cir. 1953).

[55] Gray v. Gulf, Mobile & Ohio Railroad, 429 F.2d 1064 (5th Cir. 1970).

[56] 406 U.S. 205 (1972).

[57] *Id.* at 219.

ticular religion, or that it is motivated by legitimate secular concerns." [58]

On the other hand, having had the constitutional issue thrust upon them by the *Hanson* state action holding, some courts concluded that *Hanson* also controlled on the merits of the freedom-of-religion claim. The Fifth Circuit clearly took such a position in *Gray* v. *Gulf, Mobile & Ohio Railroad*,[59] when it noted that

> Congress has clearly authorized such union shop agreements, and the Supreme Court [in *Hanson* and *Street*] has instructed us that such an arrangement does not violate the First Amendment. This being true, we cannot grant plaintiff's request that he be freed from the compulsions of the union shop agreement.[60]

The most thorough exposition of the freedom of religion issue, however, is to be found in the opinions of the district court and the court of appeals in *Linscott* v. *Millers Falls Co.*[61] Both courts concluded that the Supreme Court case of *Sherbert* v. *Verner* provided the controlling principles of law. Judge Wyzanski of the district court stated it as follows:

> In effect, the Sherbert case treats every officially authorized interference with religious freedom as a *prima facie* infringement of the free exercise of religion and hence as a presumptive violation of the First Amendment, but permits the alleged infringer to justify the supposed infringement by some compelling governmental interest.[62]

As the even more recent Supreme Court decision in *Wisconsin* v. *Yoder* demonstrates, this is an accurate statement of the controlling principle. In *Linscott*, however, both the district and the appellate court then went on to hold that such a "compelling governmental interest" did exist with respect to the imposition of union security obligations upon religious objectors.

Judge Wyzanski explained:

> Congress was concerned with the effect of labor disputes in disturbing the orderly flow of commerce. It sought to establish a new

---

[58] *Id.* at 220.

[59] 429 F.2d 1064 (5th Cir. 1970).

[60] *Id.* at 1072; *see also* Hammond v. United Papermakers, 462 F.2d 174 (6th Cir. 1972), *cert. denied*, 409 U.S. 1028 (1972).

[61] 316 F. Supp. 1369 (D. Mass. 1970), *aff'd*, 440 F.2d 14 (1st Cir. 1971), *cert. denied*, 404 U.S. 872 (1971).

[62] 316 F. Supp. at 1371 referring to Sherbert v. Verner, 374 U.S. 398 (1963).

order of labor relations. An important aspect of that new order was the right of a union, chosen by a majority of employees in an appropriate unit as the representative of all in the unit, and the employer of those employees to agree that every employee in the unit should contribute to the costs incurred by the representative. . . . Congress recognized that in some situations it would be a source of continual and serious interruptions of interstate commerce if there were free-riders. It was aware that to permit even a most sincere religious objector to escape the financial obligations of a union shop agreement might be an interference with the freedom of association, or rather of non-association, of those dues-paying employees who did not want the burden of carrying the costs of free-riders.[63]

It would appear that although the court in *Linscott* espoused a "compelling governmental interest" type of analysis, the interest or justification that it actually relied on is merely of the lesser kind normally used to sustain any economic or industry-regulating legislation. This judicial deference to what is little more than a congressional policy decision, while questionable, is, however, at least consistent with the approach the *Hanson* Court took in an analogous context.

The Constitutionality of Right-to-Work Legislation

Thus far, insofar as private sector law is concerned, the primary focus has been upon challenges to the constitutionality of either union security agreements themselves or the federal legislation that authorizes them. But the other side of this controversial coin has not escaped constitutional scrutiny either. For right-to-work laws, however, the issue seems fairly well settled.

In *Lincoln Federal Labor Union* v. *Northwestern Iron & Metal Co.*,[64] state right-to-work laws were alleged to be unconstitutional in four respects. First, it was argued that these laws violated the First Amendment rights of union members. The Supreme Court had some difficulty even grasping the union's First Amendment argument. It apparently consisted of the assertion that since workers had a constitutional right to organize and bargain collectively, since a closed or union shop is indispensable to the achievement of that end, and since right-to-work laws prohibit the closed or union shop, such laws should be declared unconstitu-

---

[63] *Id.* at 1372.

[64] 335 U.S. 525 (1949) ; *see also* American Federation of Labor v. American Sash & Door Co., 335 U.S. 538 (1949).

tional.[65] But this, the Supreme Court said, represented a misconstruction of the scope of the "right" originally relied on. The Court noted thus:

> The constitutional right of workers to assemble to discuss and formulate plans for furthering their own self interest in jobs cannot be construed as a *constitutional guarantee* that none shall get and hold jobs except those who will join in the assembly or will agree to abide by the assembly's plans.[66]

In summation, the right to attempt to achieve a goal is not the same as the right to have that goal assured.

Second, it was argued that the right-to-work laws violate the "obligations of contracts" clause of the constitution. The Court dismissed that claim without discussion,[67] consistent with the Court's other decisions in this area.

Third, the unions asserted that the right-to-work legislation in question denied unions and union members the equal protection of the law, in violation of the Fourteenth Amendment. This was allegedly so in two respects. First, it was asserted that "these laws weaken the bargaining power of unions and correspondingly strengthen the power of employers." [68] But the Court pointed out that the same legislation also protected independent unions (such as the plaintiff union) against the destructive influence of compulsory membership in company unions and thus could not be considered unfairly pro-employer. Second, it was also asserted that under these laws the protection for union members was not the same as the protection for nonunion members. The Court refuted this allegation on its facts, stating that

> in identical language these state laws forbid employers to discriminate against union and non-union members. Nebraska and North Carolina thus command *equal* employment opportunities for both groups of workers.[69]

Finally, it was argued that "due process of law is denied employees and union men by that part of these state laws that forbids them to make contracts with the employer obligating him to

---

[65] 335 U.S. at 530-31.

[66] *Id.* at 531 (emphasis added).

[67] *Id.*

[68] *Id.* at 532.

[69] *Id.* (emphasis added).

refuse to hire or retain non-union workers." [70] In support of this argument the union relied on a string of earlier Supreme Court decisions that had ensconced liberty-of-contract within the protections of the Fourteenth Amendment. In *Lincoln Federal Union,* however, the Supreme Court noted:

> This Court beginning at least as early as 1934 . . . has steadily rejected the due process philosophy enunciated in the [line of cases the union relied on]. . . . In doing so it has consciously returned closer and closer to the earlier constitutional principle that states have power to legislate against what are found to be injurious practices in their internal commercial and business affairs, so long as their laws do not run afoul of some specific federal constitutional prohibition, or of some valid federal law. . . . Under this constitutional doctrine the due process clause is no longer to be so broadly construed that the Congress and state legislatures are put in a strait jacket when they attempt to suppress business and industrial conditions which they regard as offensive to the public welfare.[71]

The Court here justified the states' interference with the unions' right to contract by reference to the same narrow standard of constitutional review that the Court was to later use in *Hanson* to justify the federal government's interference with the employees' right to work and the right not to associate.

THE PUBLIC SECTOR

Unlike the situation that prevails in the private sector, there are no major analytical difficulties to be encountered in the public sector in reaching the issue of the constitutionality of union security agreements. Both the statutory authorization of such agreements and the agreements themselves are literally and inexorably state action to which constitutional limitations obviously apply.

To say that the constitutional issue is easily raised is not, however, to say that it is easily resolved. There is, as a threshold matter, the problem of determining the proper constitutional standard for this kind of governmental conduct. Beyond that, there is the problem of applying the standard in a rational manner.

Finally, there is the question of who, within the federal system, has the constitutional power to legislate the terms and conditions of public employment. The issue is relevant to some of the pend-

---

[70] *Id.* at 533.

[71] *Id.* at 536.

ing federal legislation which would impose a uniform public employee collective bargaining statute on all the states and, thereby, authorize or simply impose security on a national scale. These matters will be discussed in turn.

The Proper Constitutional Standard

The constitutional rights of public employees has been a matter of much controversy and litigation over the years. Specifically at issue has been the nature and scope of the public employee's right to exercise various constitutional liberties without at the same time risking discharge from public employment. The resolution of this issue has been attended by considerable fluctuation in the language that the courts have used if not in the results.

At one extreme, there has been the view that public employment is a privilege to be withdrawn at any time or for any reason, subject only to contractual obligations. Mr. Justice Holmes succinctly stated this principle as follows:

> The petitioner may have a constitutional right to talk politics, but he has no constitutional right to be a policeman. There are few employments for hire in which the servant does not agree to suspend his constitutional rights of free speech as well as of idleness by the implied terms of his contract. The servant cannot complain, as he takes the employment on the terms which are offered him.[72]

At the other extreme, there is the view that if a particular activity is protected by the constitution against literal government sanction (fine or imprisonment, for example), then participation in that activity can also never be a cause for discharge from public employment. Under this view, it is immaterial whether the constitutional right is violated through the imposition of a sanction or through discharge from employment; in either case, the governmental activity is unconstitutional. The Supreme Court's language in *Perry* v. *Sindermann*,[73] is reflective of this view, although the decision itself does contain some limiting *caveats*. The Court noted that while an individual may have no right to a government job, the individual cannot be denied a job

> on a basis that infringes his constitutionally protected interests—especially, his interest in freedom of speech. For if the government

---

[72] McAuliffe v. Mayor of New Bedford, 29 N.E. 517, 517-18 (Mass. 1892); *see also* Adler v. Board of Education, 342 U.S. 485, 492-93 (1952).

[73] 408 U.S. 593 (1972).

could deny a benefit [public employment] to a person because of his constitutionally protected speech or associations, his exercise of those freedoms would in effect be penalized and inhibited. This would allow the government to "produce a result which [it] could not command directly." . . . Such interference with constitutional rights is impermissible.[74]

This version of the "unconstitutional conditions" theory would thus deny government the power ever to withhold (or terminate) a benefit, such as government employment, by reference to or because of the would-be recipient's exercise of a constitutional liberty.

Between these two extremes is an intermediate position which has been prevalent in Supreme Court decisions in recent years. This view recognizes that since the termination of an employment contract with the government is a radically different kind of detriment than being fined or sent to jail, not every exercise of a constitutional liberty that is privileged against criminal sanction is also privileged against a consequent denial or termination of government employment.[75] On the other hand, this view also recognizes that whenever government acts, whether by imposing bodily restraints or by withholding privileges and benefits, it has a constitutional obligation to act in a manner consistent with elementary notions of fairness and due process.[76]

Within the context of government employment, this then gives rise to a two-faceted test.[77] With respect to grounds for discharge that do not touch upon the exercise of any specific constitutional liberty, the discharge will be deemed unconstitutional only if it is arbitrary, discriminatory, or without any rational basis. On the other hand, if the reason for the discharge does relate to the exercise of a constitutional right, then the discharge will be deemed unconstitutional unless it can be justified by reference to some "compelling governmental interest." As the Supreme Court ruled in *Elrod* v. *Burns*:

[E]ncroachment "cannot be justified upon a mere showing of a legitimate state interest." . . . The interest advanced must be para-

---

[74] *Id.* at 597.

[75] *See, e.g.*, Civil Service Commission v. National Ass'n of Letter Carriers, 413 U.S. 548 (1973); Waters v. Peterson, 495 F.2d 91 (D.C. Cir. 1973).

[76] Board of Regents v. Roth, 408 U.S. 564 (1972).

[77] *Accord*, Huffmon v. Montana Supreme Court, 372 F. Supp. 1175 (D. Mont. 1974).

mount, one of vital importance, and the burden is on the Government to show the existence of such an interest.[78]

This standard of constitutional review is not as high as that which should be applied were the conduct in question a subject of direct criminal sanction rather than merely a grounds for discharge; but it does impose some rather rigorous limits on the government's power as an employer.

The standard that a court uses in a public employee case is important because this is often determinative of the result. This is well illustrated by the recent *Abood* v. *Detroit Board of Education*[79] case, where the Supreme Court considered the constitutionality of a requirement that public employees pay, as a condition of continued employment, an agency shop fee to the union that represents them in collective bargaining. Unfortunately, the standard adopted by the majority in that case does not fit neatly into any of the above categories.

The Court operated from the premise that the constitutionality of union security in the public sector should be judged by the same standard as in the private sector. This suggests that the Court was adopting the "if it cannot be compelled, it cannot be made a condition of employment" standard of review, which, when applied in other contexts, has amounted to an almost total ban on using the exercise of a constitutional liberty as a basis for discharge from government employment. But the adoption of that test in this context had an entirely different effect because the Court then also adhered to its *Hanson* standard for evaluating compulsory unionism in the private sector—namely, that it is a matter of legislative policy over which the judiciary has limited review.

The concurring opinion of Mr. Justice Powell, which on this point amounted to a virtual dissent, is also difficult to categorize. He too started with the proposition that the relevant "collective-bargaining agreement, like any other enactment of state law, is fully subject to the constraints that the Constitution imposes on coercive governmental regulation"[80] which again suggests a "if it cannot be compelled, it cannot be made a condition of employment" standard of review. But Powell, who was joined by Mr. Justice Blackmun and Chief Justice Burger, did not believe that

---

[78] 427 U.S. 347, 362 (1976).

[79] 45 U.S.L.W. 4473 (1977).

[80] *Id.* at 4484.

the *Hanson* decision reflected a constitutional evaluation of true compulsion. He contended that the abbreviated constitutional review that the Court undertook there could be explained by the fact that what was at issue was merely the legislative authorization of private union security agreements—which is a far cry from the direct imposition by the state of a duty to join or support a labor union.

Although Mr. Justice Powell rejected the limited *Hanson* standard of review, he did not at the same time adopt the view that the exercise of constitutional liberties by government employees entitles them to an absolute immunity to discharge on that basis—as might be suggested by his assumption that making something a condition of government employment is conceptually the same as coercing it. Mr. Justice Powell's position on that issue was neutralized, so to speak, by his view that First Amendment liberties against even coercive government action are far from absolute. Although he conceded that "a significant impairment of First Amendment rights must survive exacting scrutiny," [81] he then reiterated the "compelling governmental interest" standard of review as spelled out in *Elrod* v. *Burns*. In sum, Mr. Justice Powell's approach is the intermediate one described earlier. As was indicated, however, the majority proceeded on an entirely different basis.

Applying the Standard

Since the Court in *Abood* adopted the standard of review used by the Court in *Hanson*, it is not too surprising that the *Abood* Court also reached the same conclusion—that the compulsory payment of money to defray the costs of collective bargaining does not impermissibly infringe on the employees' constitutional right of nonassociation. In this regard, the Court simply noted that "the governmental interests advanced by the agency shop provision in the Michigan statute are much the same as those promoted by similar provisions in federal labor law." [82] On the other hand, the Court in *Abood* was required to go beyond this to some extent.

Relying on the *Street* doctrine to the effect that the use of compulsory dues for political purposes was constitutionally impermissible, the plaintiffs in *Abood* argued that since everything a

---

[81] *Id.* at 4486.

[82] *Id.* at 4477.

public employee union did was, by definition, political, the agency shop fee in the public sector was itself totally unconstitutional. The Court accepted the plaintiffs' premise but rejected its inference. The Court noted that "there can be no quarrel with the truism that because public employee unions attempt to influence governmental policy-making, their activities—and the views of members who disagree with them—may be properly termed political." [83] But the Court nevertheless concluded that public employees could be required to support the unions in these political activities. The Court's reasoning in this regard is obscure at best. It appears to be premised on the notion that since the so-called political activities in question are coincident with the wages, hours, and working conditions of the employees themselves, the public employee's objection to this kind of activity is really no different than the private employee's objection to similar activity by his union. What this ignores is that the public employee also occupies the role of a compulsory taxpayor, who must finance the union's demands, while the private employee occupies no analogous position *vis-à-vis* his employer's financing. This joint citizen-employee status had, in part, led the Court earlier in *City of Madison Joint School District* v. *Wisconsin Employment Relations Commission* [84] to hold that a public school teacher cannot constitutionally be prohibited from speaking out at a school board meeting on a matter relevant to collective bargaining—despite the union's rights as the exclusive *bargaining* representative. The Court in *Abood* concluded that the fact that what public employee unions do is intrinsically political "does not raise the ideas and beliefs of public employees onto a higher plane than the ideas and beliefs of private employees." [85]

Consistent with its approach to similar issues within the private sector, the Court in *Abood* also held that a public employee could not constitutionally be required as a condition of employment to finance such political activities as were unrelated to the union's duties as an exclusive bargaining representative. The Court recognized that it would be difficult to draw the line between the union's political activities as a collective bargaining agent and its other political activities, but left the resolution of this problem up to the lower courts.

---

[83] *Id.* at 4479.

[84] 97 S.Ct. 421 (1976).

[85] 45 U.S.L.W. at 4479.

With respect to an appropriate remedy, the Court tentatively suggested the *Allen* formula of a proportionate refund, subject to the possible requirement that the employee first exhaust his internal union remedies, in spite of the fact that this has proved virtually unworkable in the private sector. Mr. Justice Stevens concurred with the Court's opinion, but only on the understanding that the decision not be read as implying that such a remedy would necessarily be considered adequate under all circumstances.

The Court declined to pass on whether a state could require, as some apparently do, formal union membership as a condition of employment,[86] but since the courts have frequently held that public employees do have the constitutional right to join labor unions,[87] it would seem that they would also have the right to refuse to join in the formal sense.

FEDERAL REGULATION OF STATE AND LOCAL BARGAINING WITH PUBLIC EMPLOYEES

Earlier it was noted that several bills are presently pending in Congress which would impose a uniform public sector collective bargaining statute on all state and local governments. These bills would either authorize or directly impose union security obligations on all public employees represented by a majority union. In light of the Supreme Court's recent decision in *National League of Cities* v. *Usery*,[88] the constitutionality of such legislation is now in serious doubt.

---

[86] *Id.* at 4475 n. 10.

[87] *See* American Fed'n of State, County & Municipal Employees v. Woodward, 406 F.2d 137 (8th Cir. 1969) ; Hanover Township Teachers Local 1954 v. Hanover Community School Corp., 318 F. Supp. 757 (N.D. Ind. 1970), *aff'd*, 457 F.2d 456 (7th Cir. 1972) ; Lontine v. VanCleave, 483 F.2d 966 (10th Cir. 1973) ; McLaughlin v. Tilendis, 398 F.2d 287 (7th Cir. 1968) ; Orr v. Thorpe, 427 F.2d 1129 (5th Cir. 1970) ; Atkins v. City of Charlotte, 296 F. Supp. 1068 (W.D. N.C. 1969) ; Melton v. City of Atlanta, 324 F. Supp. 315 (N.D. Ga. 1971) ; National Ass'n of Letter Carriers v. Blount, 305 F. Supp. 546 (D.D.C. 1969), *appeal dismissed per stipulations*, 400 U.S. 801 (1970) ; Police Officers' Guild v. Washington, 369 F. Supp. 543 (D.D.C. 1973) ; Vorbeck v. McNeal, 407 F. Supp. 733 (E.D. Mo. 1976), *aff'd mem.*, 44 U.S.L.W. 3737 (1976) ; Bateman v. South Carolina State Ports Authority, 298 F. Supp. 999 (D. S.C. 1969) ; Elk Grove Firefighters Local 2340 v. Willis, 400 F. Supp. 1097 (N.D. Ill. 1975) ; Service Employees Int'l Union v. County of Butler, 306 F. Supp. 1080 (W.D. Pa. 1969) ; Teamsters Local 594 v. City of West Point, 338 F. Supp. 927 (D. Neb. 1972).

[88] 44 U.S.L.W. 4974 (1976).

In the *League of Cities* case, the Court held that the wage and overtime provision of the Fair Labor Standards Act could not constitutionally be applied to state and local governments. The Court indicated that although Congress generally had a plenary power to regulate under the Commerce Clause, the exercise of this power was necessarily limited by the Tenth Amendment, which provides that "the powers not delegated to the United States by the Constitution, nor prohibited by it to the States, are reserved to the States respectively, or to the people." What the Tenth Amendment means, the Court said, was that

> there are attributes of sovereignty attaching to every state government which may not be impaired by Congress. . . .[89]

The Court then went on to conclude:

> One undoubted attribute of state sovereignty is the States' power to determine the wages which shall be paid to those whom they employ in order to carry out their governmental functions, what hours those persons will work, and what compensation will be provided where these employees may be called upon to work overtime.[90]

The Court did not hold that every exercise of state sovereignty was immune from federal regulation. Rather, the Court emphasized that the Tenth Amendment merely provides that "Congress may not exercise power in a fashion that impairs the States' integrity or their ability to function effectively in a federal system." [91] Conversely, the question is whether the regulated state activity pertains to "functions essential to [the states'] separate and independent existence." [92]

The Court then proceeded to analyze in a rather detailed fashion the probable impact that the application of the FLSA would have upon the states' exercise of their sovereign powers. The Court noted, for example, that simply as a matter of cost, the application of FLSA would have "a significant impact on the functioning of the governing bodies involved." [93] Moreover, in some cases the Court noted that the result would be a "forced

---

[89] *Id.* at 4977.

[90] *Id.*

[91] Frye v. United States, 421 U.S. 542, 547 (1975), quoted *id.* at 4976.

[92] Lane County v. Oregon, 7 Wall. 71 (1869) quoted in Coyle v. Smith, 221 U.S. 559, 580 (1910) quoted *id.* at 4977.

[93] *Id.*

relinquishment of important governmental activities." [94] Finally, the Court observed that "quite apart from the substantial costs imposed upon the States and their political subdivisions, the Act displaces state policies regarding the manner in which they will structure delivery of those governmental services which their citizens require." [95] The Court then provided a bill of particulars of the various state policies that would be displaced and concluded that the extension of FLSA to state and local governments would "impermissibly interfere with the integral governmental functions of these bodies." [96]

The question that the *League of Cities* case raises is whether a similar conclusion would be reached with respect to a federal law imposing collective bargaining and union security upon state and local governments. Because of the fact-specific nature of the *League of Cities* analysis, the question is difficult to answer with assurance. The notion that a federal law on the subject would run afoul of the Tenth Amendment, however, is certainly suggested by the *Abood* Court's express recognition that public employee collective bargaining cuts deeply into the political processes of the states, affects the policies that they pursue, and has an obvious impact on their financial condition.

CONCLUSION

A review of the various decisions of the constitutional issues surrounding union security and the right to work reveals that the courts have been reluctant to apply constitutional law doctrines in any way that might offend the prevailing popular and legislative views on this subject. Moreover, the decisions in this area are marked by a lack of analytical and linguistic clarity which mars their value as precedent. Thus, it would appear that whatever the nation's policy is going to be on union security and/or the right to work, this policy is probably going to be achieved through processes other than constitutionally-based litigation.

---

[94] *Id.* at 4978.

[95] *Id.*

[96] *Id.* at 4979.

PART THREE

A Broader Perspective

The Continuing Debate Over Union Security and the Right to Work— A Jurisprudential Critique

The law on union security and the right to work is quite complex. The statutes, cases, and arbitration decisions that bear on this issue are legion; and any assertion of what the law is must necessarily be a qualified judgment over which people readily disagree. However difficult it may be to reach any consensus over what the law is, it is certainly no easier nor less controversial to assert what it ought to be.

Regardless of the state of the law at any time (and it has varied appreciably), from the early days of the Republic to the present, some segment of our society has always been of the view that the law ought to be changed and the debate over union security and the right to work has thus been as continuous as it has been heated.

In this chapter we will attempt to address the question of what the law "ought to be" by first summarizing and commenting on the policy arguments that are most often advanced in this debate; and second, by discussing the issue from a broader philosophical perspective.

THE STANDARD ARGUMENTS

The debate over union security and the right to work usually takes place in one of two closely related contexts. At the federal level, it is over the question of whether Congress should repeal Section 14(b) of the Taft-Hartley Act, which expressly authorizes the States to outlaw union security agreements. At the local level, it is over the question of whether a particular state should pass or repeal such a right-to-work law.

The arguments that are raised over Section 14(b) and specific state right-to-work laws are equally germane in yet another

271

context. That context concerns the possible repeal of those parts of the Taft-Hartley Act and the Railway Labor Act which provide the affirmative legal sanction to union security agreements. The repeal of those provisions would make union security agreements illegal under the general antidiscrimination provisions of both statutes, and this would provide the equivalent of a national right-to-work law.

Regardless of the context, the underlying arguments are essentially the same. There is an extensive body of literature on this subject,[1] and from these sources we have attempted to glean and restate the arguments that are both the most common and the most persuasive for each side—which is to say that the catalog is not a totally exhaustive one. Although in a broad way, the arguments on both sides either anticipate or respond to the arguments of the other side, no attempt has been made to include every possible point of rebuttal and counterrebuttal. At best, the following arguments represent the general parameters of the debate. Finally, the arguments here are intentionally being presented in an argumentative if not rhetorical form, since that is how they would appear in ordinary discourse—although, it is hoped that all purely emotional appeals have been eliminated.

For Union Security Agreements and Against Right-to-Work Legislation

Union Security Agreements Eliminate the "Free Rider." Under federal law, labor unions have the affirmative duty to represent everyone in the bargaining unit fairly and impartially. Thus, the union must negotiate wages and other benefits for everyone, not just union members. Indeed, many of the improve-

---

[1] *See, e.g.,* H. NORTHRUP & G. BLOOM, GOVERNMENT AND LABOR, Chapter VIII (1963); P. SULTAN, RIGHT-TO-WORK LAWS: A STUDY IN CONFLICT, Chapter 5 (1950); CONGRESS OF INDUSTRIAL ORGANIZATIONS, THE CASE AGAINST THE "RIGHT TO WORK" LAWS (1955), reviewed in Torff, *The Case for Voluntary Union Membership,* 40 IOWA L. REV. 621 (1955) and Loevinger, *The Case Against "Anti-Union Security" Legislation,* 40 IOWA L. REV. 627 (1955); W. HARRISON, THE TRUTH ABOUT RIGHT-TO-WORK LAWS (1959); E. KELLER, THE CASE FOR RIGHT-TO-WORK LAWS (1956); E. CHAMBERLIN, P. BRADLEY, G. REILLY & R. POUND, LABOR UNIONS AND PUBLIC POLICY, Chapter II (1958); Toner, *Right-to-Work Laws: Public Frauds,* 8 LABOR L. J. 193 (1957); Niebank, *In Defense of Right-to-Work Laws,* 8 LABOR L. J. 459 (1957); Toner, *There Is No Defense of Right-to-Work Laws,* 9 LABOR L. J. 566 (1958); Warshal, *"Right-to-Work," Pro and Con,* 17 LABOR L. J. 131 (1966); Spielmans, *Bargaining Fee Versus Union Shop,* 10 IND. & LABOR REL. REV. 609 (1956-57); Morris, *Compulsory Union Membership and Public Policy,* 18 SO. ECON. J. 72 (1951).

ments in working conditions that labor unions obtain through collective bargaining necessarily benefit everyone; if the union obtains better lighting in the plant, this benefits the union and nonunion employee alike, since such a benefit is not individually divisible. Moreover, if the employer violates the contract rights of a particular employee, whether this employee is a voluntary dues-paying member of the union or not, then the union must, under the statutory duty of fair representation, represent that employee in the processing of his grievance against the employer and by taking the matter to arbitration if necessary.

Obtaining these benefits and enforcing the contract in this manner is, however, an expensive matter. Even the most rudimentary notions of justice and fairness suggest that those who intentionally choose to share in a benefit should likewise be required to share in the cost of obtaining it. A union security agreement simply provides a way of enforcing that moral obligation.

In this regard, however, it is significant to note that labor unions are not analogous to other voluntary associations, like churches or the Red Cross, whose activities indirectly benefit a wide range of people—beneficiaries, however, from whom no demand for contribution could justly be made. Rather, when a labor union is acting in its statutory capacity as a collective bargaining representative, it is acting in a sovereign capacity. It is functioning as an agent of the government, discharging a public function. It stands to reason, therefore, that such a union should also enjoy the power of taxation, so to speak. Other semigovernmental bodies, like state bar associations, have been given the authority to finance their activities through the imposition of mandatory dues and fees. There is no reason why labor unions should not enjoy a similar privilege.

Similarly, an employee in a union shop is in no way analogous to the unwitting beneficiary of the public service activities of private voluntary associations. Unlike the citizen-at-large and his relation to the activities of these associations, the employee has actually had a say in whether or not the activities will be undertaken on his behalf (in the vote on whether to elect the union as a collective bargaining representative). Having lost on that issue, the employee is still at liberty to find work elsewhere and to avoid both the benefits of unionization and the cost of obtaining them.

Union Security Agreements Are Merely an Application of the Democratic Principle. Our society is governed by the principle of majority rather than minority rule. Union security agreements reflect the application of that principle to an industrial context. The Taft-Hartley Act expressly guarantees that no union security agreement can remain in force if a majority of employees vote to remove the union's authority to negotiate such a provision— a guarantee that is given for no other kind of contract term. Experience has shown, however, that the overwhelming majority of employees do favor union security agreements, and their will should prevail.

Right-to-work legislation, on the other hand, has just the opposite effect. Regardless of the fact that a majority of a particular employer's employees favor having a union security provision, the right-to-work laws cater to the will of the minority by outlawing such provisions altogether.

Union Security Agreements Insure that the Union's Status as the Bargaining Representative is not Undermined Through Employer Discrimination Against Union Members. Once a union obtains the support of a majority of the employees and becomes the duly recognized bargaining representative, the union should be entitled to discharge its functions free from invidious attempts by the employer to undermine its majority status. Historically, employers did this by firing union supporters and replacing them with nonunion employees or by using economic pressure to induce existing employees to resign from the union. Union security agreements, by making union membership a condition of employment of everyone, prevent an employer from resorting to such tactics. Moreover, when an employee who happens to be active in the union also engages in conduct that is cause for discharge, the employer can replace him without worrying about a charge of discrimination from the union. In short, the union shop gives everyone a sense of security, removes a possible source of conflict and suspicion between labor and management, and allows both parties to get on with the all-important business of negotiating and administering the collective bargaining agreement.

Union Security Agreements Promote Industrial Stability and Labor Peace. The linchpin of federal labor policy is the promotion of industrial peace and the establishment of stable bargaining relationships between labor and management. Union security agreements, especially of the closed or union shop variety, can be very instrumental in serving that end. Under the closed or union shop, an employee is required to be an *actual* member of the union, and as such is subject to the union's rules and disciplinary power. An employee who engages in wildcat strikes or otherwise violates plant rules is subject to sanction, not only by the employer, but also by the labor union through the imposition of fines. This is the way it should be. As the exclusive representative of all the employees, the union has struck a bargain with the employer; union security agreements merely give the union the power to insure that its own members adhere to the bargain it struck in their behalf. It is for this reason that many employers find union security agreements to be affirmatively desirable.

Indirectly, agency shop agreements have some of the same effects. An employee who is required to pay the equivalent of union dues will frequently elect also to join the union in a formal capacity, simply to insure that he has an effective voice in determining how his money is to be spent. Having done this, he will then be subject to the union's rules.

Similarly, union security agreements discourage factionalism, internal dissension, and "raiding" by rival unions; this in turn tends to eliminate a major source of labor unrest, namely strikes and other forms of "economic warfare" that are solely for the purpose of influencing the selection of a collective bargaining representative. Thus, union security agreements serve to promote industrial peace and stability.

Union Security Agreements Promote Responsible Union Leadership. In the absence of a union security agreement, the employees who join and become active in the union will tend to be the more militant, aggressive, and perhaps even irresponsible employees who will select leaders to represent their views, even though a majority of the workforce is much more moderate in its outlook. Moreover, even if that does not happen, a union without a union security agreement will nevertheless feel that in order to maintain the united support of its membership, it must constantly demonstrate its ability to extract concessions from the employer. This will then lead to a cycle of increasingly unreasonable demands, the unnecessary creation of conflict situations, and a preoccupation with immediate gains at the expense of long-term objectives—all to the ultimate detriment of the employees themselves.

On the other hand, a union security agreement frees the union from the immediate demands of the moment. It allows the union officials to exercise responsible leadership without the fear that the momentary displeasure of the membership will cost the union its representative status, and it allows the union to work with management on a cooperative rather than a purely adversary basis.

Union Security Agreements Enhance the Strength of Unions to the Benefit of the Employees and the Community as a Whole. It goes without saying that a labor organization which has as its dues-paying members every employee in the unit is a much stronger and more powerful organization. This then creates a more effective counterbalance to the inherently superior economic power of an employer, particularly of the corporate variety. This equalization of economic power between labor and management is a desirable social goal. The end result of an effective labor movement is, as experience has shown, an enhanced standard of living for millions of working class employees whose prosperity is shared by the community at large. This was one of the primary purposes of the original Wagner Act, and to the extent that union security agreements promote this end, they are clearly desirable.

Right-to-work legislation, on the other hand, is designed, intentionally or otherwise, to retard if not destroy the growth of labor unions and to insure that management retains the upper hand in unilaterally setting the terms and conditions of an individual's employment. Naturally, if they are left to management, wages are going to be as low as possible—a situation which benefits no one in the community except perhaps the plant owner. Certainly, no social policy is advanced in this regard.

Union Security Arrangements are Merely an Exercise of the Freedom of Contract. Federal law itself does not make union membership a condition of any person's employment. To the contrary, federal law merely permits an employer and a union to enter into a voluntary contract whereby the employer agrees to require of his employees, as a condition of their continued employment with him, that they join the union. But an employer is certainly not compelled by the law to agree to such a provision, and, indeed, he will do so only if he considers it to his advantage. Establishing the terms and conditions of employment through the process of free collective bargaining is an important part of American labor policy. It is merely an extension of our historical commitment to the philosophy of freedom of contract. It has worked well in the establishment of wages and other terms and conditions of employment; and, where allowed by state law, it has worked equally well in resolving the issue of union security.

Right-to-work legislation, however, deprives employers and unions of their freedom to contract in this regard. Rather than allowing the parties to work out an arrangement satisfactory to themselves, right-to-work laws impose a solution by government fiat. Given the fact that union security agreements are a product of free contract, it is a gross distortion to say that employees are "forced" to join a union. A collective bargaining agreement, of which a union security provision is but a part, merely determines in advance what terms and conditions of their employment contracts an employer is going to offer to individual employees. If the proffered terms and conditions are not satisfactory to a particular employee, then he is always free to accept employment elsewhere. This is true regardless of whether the employee is dissatisfied with the wages being offered or because union membership is being made a condition of this employment. In neither case is the employee forced to accept them. Again, this is an application of the principle of freedom of contract.

Put differently, in a contractual sense the right to work for someone else merely means that a person has the privilege of offering to work on certain terms and conditions. But under the philosophy of freedom of contract, there is no right to work for someone else in the sense that an employer has a corollary duty to give a person employment on terms and conditions that are not mutually acceptable to both!

And yet, the so-called right-to-work laws do artificially create such a right—in derogation of the principle of freedom of contract. By prohibiting an employer from making union membership a condition of employment, the right-to-work laws give an otherwise qualified applicant the right to be employed by an unwilling employer.

The Controversy Over Union Security and the Right to Work Should be Resolved by Reference to a Uniform Federal Policy Rather Than on a State-by-State Basis. Long ago it was determined that in order to insure the free flow of commerce, labor legislation should be both uniform and national in scope. Labor problems are never purely local in their impact; rather, they affect everyone throughout the entire nation. As such, they are properly resolved at the federal rather than at the state level.

Section 14(b) and the state right-to-work laws represent a glaring if not inexplicable exception to this exercise in federalism. By allowing each state to determine for itself an important issue of national labor policy, we are in effect resurrecting an outmoded and unworkable system of government—namely, that represented by the old Articles of Confederation.

For Right-to-Work Legislation and Against Union Security Agreements

Union Security Agreements Burden an Individual in the Exercise of His Most Precious Liberty—That of Engaging in Work. Work—or the productive activities that men engage in to provide for their subsistence—is said to be the most precious liberty man possesses. Given the importance of work to both the survival of the individual himself and to the prosperity of the community in which he lives, it is easy to see how this is so.

In an industrial society, the work that most people perform occurs in the context of the employment relationship. While no individual has an absolute right to enter into a contract of employment with another individual, social policy dictates that the liberty to contract for work should not be burdened by conditions and requirements that do not themselves relate directly to the performance of that work. The use of irrelevant employment criteria impedes qualified people from filling productive jobs which in the long run causes not only individuals but also society as a whole to suffer.

It is for this reason that society has undertaken to prohibit various forms of employment discrimination. A person's race, for example, is irrelevant to how well he can operate a printing press, and society has thus concluded that an individual's fundamental liberty to be employed as a printer should not be burdened by the fact that he happens to be black. Similarly, that person's membership or nonmembership in a labor union has nothing to do with his productive capacities. To deny him a job on this basis is to burden his liberty in a way that, to say the very least, demands some affirmative justification.

Union Security Agreements Also Burden an Individual in the Exercise of Fundamental Liberties—Those of Association, Speech, and Religion. It is basic to the American tradition that the individual should have the liberty to associate or not with organizations of his own choosing, to support only the political causes that he personally believes in, and to exercise his religious beliefs in a manner not inconsistent with the rights of others. These liberties are important not only for the sake of the individual himself, but also because their free exercise is conducive to the existence of a happy and productive community—something that affects everyone. It is for this reason that society is justified in protecting these liberties, not only against direct violation, but also against conduct which makes their exercise burdensome or which requires that the liberty be waived as a condition for obtaining something else.

When an employee is either required to join formally a union or even just pay dues, this operates in clear derogation of his fundamental liberty to choose the organizations with which he wants to associate. This forced association is particularly pernicious in light of the fact that labor unions are deeply involved in matters of political and social concern for which they lobby and on which they take public positions. Just as freedom of speech includes the liberty of having one's say on a matter, so also it includes the liberty of not saying anything and, indeed, of declining to subsidize the propagation of beliefs contrary to one's own—a liberty which is clearly violated by the operation of a union security agreement.

Likewise, union security agreements require many employees as a condition of their continued employment to violate their own religious beliefs, in that the support of or association with labor unions is contrary to the teachings of several important religious denominations.

Because union security agreements operate to the injury of the individual and society alike in derogating the exercise of these fundamental liberties, those agreements should be proscribed by law. To say the very least, some affirmative justification for these violations is called for.

An Employee Who, Against His Will, is Being Represented by a Union Has No Moral (and Should Have No Legal) Obligation to Reimburse the Union for Obtaining Alleged Benefits on His Behalf. Prior arguments have shown that union security agreements, since they burden the exercise of fundamental liberties, require some affirmative justification. The justification that is most often advanced in this context—that union security agreements are necessary to eliminate the "free rider"—is fallacious in a number of respects.

In the first place, the entire "free rider" argument is predicated on the notion that the duty to represent everyone in the unit was something Congress foisted upon unions against their will. To the contrary, unions actively sought, indeed demanded, the right to be the exclusive representative of all the employees in a unit, once a majority had designated a union as such. In short, unions have insisted on representing certain employees who do not desire such representation. Against that background, it is anomalous indeed that unions should complain of free riders. If uncompensated representation is what the unions are concerned with, then they should petition Congress to repeal the doctrine of "exclusive representation." This would enable unions to negotiate wage increases only for those who desire and are willing to pay for such representation; the nonunion employee would then have to bear the expenses of his own wage negotiations. The problem of the free rider would then disappear.

Even with respect to benefits that are not individually divisible, such as certain improvements in working conditions, the free rider argument does not provide a justification for forced compensation. It may be true that when a union negotiates for improved lighting in the factory, this benefits union members (who paid for the negotiations) and nonunion members alike. But situations like that are common to any society of men. If, for his own pleasure, my neighbor expends much time and effort planting a beautiful flower garden in his yard, the fact that I too derive pleasure (or benefit) from this would by no means give rise to a moral or legal obligation on my part to share in his expenses. It is no different when a union, on behalf of its members, negotiates improvements that incidentally benefit other employees.

This is especially true since the actual cost of negotiating such benefits is usually the same regardless of the number of employees that the benefit affects. Thus, by sharing in the benefit, the nonunion employee is not taking anything away from or adding to the cost of the union employee who originally sought the benefit.

This, of course, is not necessarily true with respect to the administration and enforcement of the contract. If a nonunion employee insists that the union, pursuant to its statutory duty, process or arbitrate a grievance on his behalf, then there may be justification for requiring that such an employee pay for such requested services.

Even within this context, however, one can argue that the employee who is insisting upon such representation is not a free rider at all, but that he had paid his dues in an entirely different fashion. The notion of a free rider suggests someone who receives benefits but who gives up nothing in return. From a union's perspective, it suggests a "carrier" who receives no compensation from someone who benefits from the "ride" that is being given. But by virtue of the union's right of exclusive representation, a nonunion employee has in fact given up something of value—it is the liberty and opportunity to negotiate his own terms and conditions of employment! Moreover, what the employee loses in this regard, the union gains. By virtue of the coerced unanimity of the workforce, the union obtains a bargaining power that it would not have if it merely represented a segment of the workforce. Thus, in a very real sense, there has been a *quid pro quo* for the benefits that the nonunion employee receives from union representation.

Finally, the notion that a nonunion employee always receives a benefit from union representation may be seriously questioned on at least two grounds. First, the wage gains that a union obtains for one group of employees nearly always come at the expense of another group of employees rather than out of profits, as is often alleged. Ironically, some of the employees at whose expense the increase ultimately comes may, in fact, be employees whom the union claims to be representing. A union, for example, may obtain an across-the-board 5 percent wage increase. Unable to absorb this out of profits or pass it on to the consumer (other employees who buy the product), the employer may eventually find it necessary to reduce his labor costs by reducing his workforce. In most instances, employees with the least skill and experience will be ones laid off. In the meantime under a union security agreement, they will have been reimbursing the union for its expenses in bringing about this result!

The notion that a nonunion employee receives a benefit from union representation and is thus a free rider is fallacious in an even more fundamental respect. It presupposes that the economic value of certain benefits can be ascertained by reference to some fixed and objective standard. To the contrary, the economic value of any object is simply a function of how badly a given individual wants it; as different individuals have different desires in differing degrees, so also does the economic value of any object vary from one individual to another. Two employees similarly situated may view from radically different perspectives the advent of union representation and the negotiation of a contract containing, for example, an increase in wages but a loss of overtime opportunities. To one employee, the loss of his liberty to bargain individually and the loss of overtime opportunities may be more than compensated for by the wage increase. He values the latter more than the former and has obtained a personal benefit from union representation. But the other employee, whose individual value judgments are different, may view the resulting bargain as a detriment.

By virtue of what moral authority can a union impose its own set of values of this employee, insist that he has received a benefit whether he recognizes it or not, and then coerce him into bearing a part of the expenses of obtaining the benefit? The philosophical implications of this kind of moral authoritarianism—all of which are implicit in the free rider argument— are quite awesome!

Voluntary Union Membership Promotes Responsive Union Leadership. When a labor union, in order to maintain its status as the exclusive bargaining representative of a group of employees, is required to obtain the continued voluntary support of those it purports to represent, then such a union is necessarily going to strive to represent the interests of its members rather than its own institutional interest. Regardless of whether what the employees want is reasonable or not, they are entitled to be represented—not dictated to, not paternalized, and not ignored by their agent in collective bargaining.

On the other hand, where a union security agreement exists, the union is effectively insulated from the employees in the unit. It can, without undue jeopardy, compromise the needs of its constituency in favor of its own institutional security. Indeed, as the name suggests, that is exactly what a *union* security agreement is designed to do.

Union Security Agreements Give Labor Unions Too Much Economic Power. As the proponents of union security suggest, agreements of this kind enhance the power of the recipient union. This is not to say that such a result is necessarily in the public interest. To the contrary, even without union security, compulsory collective bargaining has already resulted in a variety of forms of economic dislocation, including misallocation of resources, unemployment, inflation, and a stifling of productivity and capital investment.

To the extent that union security agreements exaggerate the economic power of unions, the desirability of this power may be seriously questioned. Union monies (which are far in excess of what is required for the mere negotiation and administration of a collective bargaining agreement) are used to finance (a) prolonged strikes for unrealistically high wages, (b) organizational campaigns at plants whose employees have shown no interest in the union, and (c) political candidates and programs especially advantageous to the parochial interests of organized labor.

Although some counterbalance to the economic power of corporate employers may be called for, union security agreements swing the pendulum too far in the opposite direction to the detriment of society as a whole.

Certain Kinds of Union Security Agreements Give Unions Too Much Power Over Hiring Decisions. Under the closed shop, a person must be a member of the union in order even to obtain a job. This in effect gives the union a monopoly over the labor supply of that particular employer. The possession of such monopoly power is not only inconsistent with the American tradition of competition, but experience has shown that it is a power which labor unions tend to abuse by denying a person membership and thus a job for reasons totally unrelated to his qualifications as an employee. The union shop, which only requires that an employee eventually become a member, is subject to some of the same objections. If the union refuses to admit or expels an employee from membership, that person loses his job regardless of what kind of worker he is.

This delegation to the union of the employer's prerogatives over hiring and firing is objectionable because the union does not have the corollary responsibility for the efficiency of the workforce. This ultimately leads to a decrease in productivity to the detriment of the workers themselves, the stockholders, and eventually society as a whole.

Although for these very reasons both the closed and the union shop are presently prohibited by federal law, the proponents of union security would like to have these laws repealed.

Since Federal Law Prohibits an Employer From Discriminating on the Basis of Union Membership, Considerations of Parity Require That Discrimination on the Basis of Nonmembership Should Likewise Be Prohibited. It is clearly illegal for an employer to discriminate against an employee because of that employee's membership in a labor organization. No one is seriously arguing that the law on this point should be changed. The underlying policy here is that an employee's choice with respect to union membership is something that should be completely divorced from the question of his continued status as an employee. The argument, rather, is that this policy should be applied neutrally, so as to prohibit discrimination either for or against union

membership. Just as an employer cannot enter into a yellow dog
contract whereby an employee agrees not to become a member of
the union during his term of employment, so also should an employer be prohibited from entering into a union security agreement whereby such membership becomes a condition of employment.

*The Power of States to Enact Right-To-Work Law Represents
a Proper Allocation of Responsibilities Between the State and
Federal Governments.* As a general matter, it may be true that
labor legislation should be uniform, national in scope, and thus
made at the federal level. But right-to-work laws represent a legitimate exception to that rule. Whether a person should be required to join a labor union as a condition of having a job is a
question that provokes strong feelings. Unlike most matters of
labor policy, there is no national consensus over the right-to-
work issue. The mores, traditions, and economic conditions of
each state determine how the people of that state are going to respond to the question of compulsory unionism. Going against
those feelings, in whichever direction they may happen to fall,
can only produce social upheaval and employment unrest. It is
for this reason that Congress wisely chose to allow each state to
determine its own policy in this regard.

COMMENTS ON THE STANDARD ARGUMENTS

Despite years of debate on the subject, during which time all
of the above arguments have been advanced time and time again,
public opinion remains divided on the right-to-work/union security controversy. The supporters of right-to-work legislation
naturally think they have the better of the argument, while
the proponents of union security think otherwise. Since neither
side has been able to marshal a consistent majority for its position, the arguments pro and con must be regarded as inconclusive.
And, indeed, the debate does have a certain unsatisfactory quality
to it.

In the first place, many of the arguments about union security
and the right to work are predicated on assertions about the
impact these situations allegedly have on the union's ability to organize, its bargaining power, wages, the conduct of labor-
management relations, the attitude of the union leadership toward those it represents, labor unrest, and other related matters. But the substantiation of these assertions leaves something
to be desired. Economic data, impartial analysis of that data, and

other hard empirical evidence of the actual effects of union security agreements and/or right-to-work legislation is not found in much abundance in the available literature.[2] It is suggested that further studies in this field would improve the quality of the debate and perhaps even finally resolve the matter in more people's minds.

Secondly, it would appear that the debate over union security and the right to work is much too specific in its focus. These matters can be properly evaluated only within a broader legal and economic context. Union security agreements are integrally related to federal law regulating the organizational rights of unions, the manner in which collective bargaining representatives are chosen, the doctrine of exclusive representation, mandatory collective bargaining, the legal immunities of labor unions, and the fiduciary duties of unions in general. The desirability of the law on such matters and others has a direct bearing on the consequent desirability of union security agreements themselves; yet these matters rarely enter into the debate except tangentially.

Similarly, the question of the economic impact of union security agreements and/or right-to-work legislation is but a part of the larger question concerning the effect of union power on the nation's economy. An intelligent position on this debate between union security and the right to work would have to be based on more than what is covered by the standard arguments.

---

[2] *But see* G. BLOOM & H. NORTHRUP, ECONOMICS OF LABOR RELATIONS, 167-73 (7th ed. 1973); F. MEYERS, "RIGHT-TO-WORK" IN PRACTICE (1959); Cohen, *Operating Under Right-to-Work Laws*, 9 LABOR L. J. 574 (1958); Palomba & Palomba, *Right-to-Work Laws: A Suggested Economic Rationale*, 14 J. LAW & ECO. 475 (1971); Tollefson & Pichler, *A Comment on Right-to-Work Laws: A Suggested Economic Rationale*, 17 J. LAW & ECO. 193 (1974); Moore, Newman & Thomas, *Determinants of the Passage of Right-to-Work Laws: An Alternative Interpretation*, 17 J. LAW & ECO. 197 (1974); Soffer & Korenich, *"Right-to-Work Laws As a Location Factor,"* The Industrial Experience of Agricultural States, 3 J. REGIONAL SCI. 41 (1961); Gilbert, *A Statistical Analysis of the Right-to-Work Conflict*, 19 IND. & LABOR REL. REV. 533 (1966); Comment, *A Statistical Analysis of the Right-to-Work Conflict*, 20 IND. & LABOR REL. REV. 447 (1967); Kuhlman, *Right to Work Laws: The Virginia Experience*, 6 LABOR L. J. 453 (1955); Glasgow, *That Right to Work Controversy Again?*, 18 LABOR L. J. 112 (1967); Lumsden & Petersen, *The Effect of Right to Work Laws on Unionization in the United States*, 83 J. POL. ECON. 1237 (1975); Gallaway, *The Economics of the Right to Work Controversy*, 32 So. ECON. J. 310 (1966), commented on in 33 So. ECON. J. 409, 411 (1967), 35 So. ECON. J. 265 (1969), 37 So. ECON. J. 356 (1971); Dempsey, *Right-to-Work Controversy*, 16 LABOR L. J. 387 (1965); Meyers, *Effects of "Right-to-Work" Laws: A Study of the Texas Act*, 9 IND. & LABOR REL. REV. 77 (1955); Kuhn, *Right-to-Work Laws—Symbols or Substance?*, 14 IND. & LABOR REL. REV. 587 (1961).

Thirdly, and in a similar vein, the standard arguments seem to lack any broad philosophical coherence. Words like *right* and *liberty* carry a great deal of emotional luggage with them, but they are philosophically ambiguous, and the standard arguments do little to clarify their meaning. But beyond that, in the standard debate between union security and the right to work neither side addresses itself adequately to the fundamental philosophical premises of their various positions. One suspects that such premises may not even exist, or that the debators are at least not aware of them.

This is easy to understand. Americans are not a particularly ideological or doctrinaire nation of people; we tend to resolve things of what appears to be a practical basis, rather than by reference to any abstract theories. But one cannot escape having a philosophy. Its various premises may be both articulated and reconciled into a coherent whole, in which case each specific application will then follow a consistent and rational pattern; or its premises may consist of nothing more than a intellectual "grab bag" of isolated value judgments with no perceived relationship between any of them, in which case the applied consequences will be equally chaotic and lacking in direction. Since the conscious use of man's intellect is necessary to his survival, it is strongly suggested that as a people we should address ourselves more often than we have to the broader philosophical implications of the social and political issues that confront us. In the section that follows, we will thus make a modest attempt to take such an approach to the debate over union security and the right to work.

THE PHILOSOPHICAL IMPLICATIONS OF THE CONTROVERSY

The apparent inconclusivity of the standard arguments over the right-to-work issue has led one commentator to suggest that, at bottom, each side merely reflects a different "value judgment on the position of the labor union in our economic society." [3] Or, as another writer put it, "the debate on the 'right-to-work' laws should center, not around the 'rights' involved, but on whether or not a country would be better off if its unions were stronger or weaker." [4]

---

[3] Cohen, *Operating Under Right-to-Work Laws*, 9 LABOR L. J. 574 (1958).

[4] M. OLSON, THE LOGIC OF COLLECTIVE ACTION 89 (1971).

In the first instance, these comments represent an attempt to move the debate onto a broader legal and economic plane— probably a desirable step. On the other hand, implicit in them is a certain philosophical approach. Those who would evaluate the right-to-work controversy solely in terms of the desirability or "social utility" of strong labor unions are, perhaps unwittingly, proceeding along the lines of the traditional utilitarian philosophers, whose touchstone of analysis—to reduce the philosophy to its most abbreviated form, with due apologies to Jeremy Bentham —has been "the greatest good for the greatest number." In short, the premise is that if strong labor unions and union security agreements generally benefit society, then laws promoting such an end are themselves "good" in a philosophical or moral sense.

Beyond all doubt, utilitarianism—in one form or another—has been the predominant social philosophy of our times. Because it is not based on transcendental considerations, utilitarianism has, however, been somewhat suspect as a moral philosophy— especially in contrast to those based on the natural law. Most recently, the preeminent Harvard philosopher, John Rawls, has argued that the utilitarian norm, carried to its logical conclusion, is capable of producing results that are clearly inconsistent with other more deeply held notions of individual justice and fairness, thus raising a question about its validity per se as a method for evaluating any moral issue.[5]

The broader arguments over utilitarianism are beyond the scope of this study. Suffice it to say that the "value judgment" thesis, in common with other instances of applied utilitarianism, seems to ignore the philosophical distinction between the question of how much power it is generally desirable for a labor union to have, on the one hand, and the more specific question of how a union should be allowed to obtain and/or exercise that power, on the other. The two questions are arguably not the same. For example, one could believe that strong unions and an active membership are socially desirable goals, but at the same time not believe that it is proper to achieve these goals through the operation of union security agreements. The moral propriety of the means that are used to obtain a goal raises a question that is, at least in the first instance, separate and apart from the question of the moral propriety of the goal itself.

Insofar as union security agreements are concerned, the issue is thus twofold. Among the various means that exist, how should

---

[5] J. RAWLS, A THEORY OF JUSTICE (1971).

one characterize the operation of a union security agreement? And, what moral justification exists for the use of this particular means?

In response to the first question, one commentator has answered, "Actually, the whole moral argument boils down to the problem of *coercion.* No one can deny that the union shop coerces a worker to join this union. . . ." [6] Unfortunately, but as is often the case, this author did not define what he meant by "coercion." Other writers, however, have followed up on this theme and have attempted to show how the coercion of the union shop can be justified.

One view, which concedes that the proponents of compulsory unionism started out in a somewhat embarrassing moral position because of their apparent support of coercive restraints on individual freedom, nevertheless attempts to justify this coercion by reference to the economic theory of "collective" or "public" goods.[7] Goods of this nature are said to have two salient characteristics. First, the increased consumption of such goods by growing numbers of individuals does not decrease the availability of this good to other consumers. For example, one individual's enjoyment (consumption) of the benefits of a lighthouse does not affect, one way or the other, the availability of this resource to other users. Second, a collective or public good is one that is incapable of being supplied only to those who are willing to pay for it. Lighthouse services cannot be supplied on a "subscription only" basis, for whenever the lighthouse is operating, anyone who sees it will benefit therefrom.

Next, the theory hypothesizes that once a society of men reaches a certain minimum size, individuals within that society —acting on a purely rational and nonaltruistic basis—will have no incentive to contribute to the cost of collective or public goods, because each person will perceive that, standing alone, his individual support, or the lack thereof, will have no noticeable effect on the availability of these goods, and that he can therefore enjoy them without making any contribution. Thus, the argument goes on to conclude that once a society decides that a collective or public good should be provided, it is morally legitimate for that society to coerce each individual within the society to contribute to the cost of providing it.

---

[6] Warshal, *"Right-to-Work," Pro and Con,* 17 LABOR L. J. 131, 132 (1966).

[7] Pulsipher, *The Union Shop: A Legitimate Form of Coercion in a Free-Market Economy,* 19 IND. & LABOR REL. REV. 529 (1965-66) ; *see also* OLSON, THE LOGIC OF COLLECTIVE ACTION, Chapter III (1971).

Apparently, the "collective goods" theory considers itself to be merely an extension of the democratic principle into the economic realm—a principle which in Western political thought serves as one of the primary moral justifications for any use of the inherently coercive power that governments exercise through law. Except for the rank "majoritarians," however, most of the political theory referred to *also* recognizes that there are certain moral limits on what even a duly constituted majority can do in the way of providing for the common good, in an economic sense or otherwise. At one extreme, there is the view that government can coerce individuals to contribute to the cost of providing only such collective or public goods as are actually necessary for the continuation of the civil society itself—such as an armed force to defend against foreign aggression, a domestic police force to deal with civil violence, and a court system to resolve private disputes. At the other extreme is the view that a democratic government can do virtually anything it chooses, except to infringe upon certain specific individual rights (such as those enumerated in the Constitution).

In short, the issue is a question of achieving the proper balance between individual rights, on the one hand, and collective rights, on the other. Clearly, the collective goods theory views the balance as resting heavily in favor of collective or community rights. These in turn are inevitably determined by reference to the utilitarian norm—which, in response to the initial question about coercion, says that whenever (subject only to narrow exceptions) a goal can be justified under considerations of social utility, then it is also morally permissible for society to use coercion in reaching that goal. We have, in short, come full circle back to the basic utilitarian position.

Carrying this theory over into the area of union security, the theory's supporters then argue that within the miniature society of a bargaining unit, the benefits obtained in a collective bargaining agreement partake of the nature of collective or public goods.[8] To the extent that a union security agreement coerces each individual to share in the costs of obtaining these goods and benefits, such coercion is nevertheless morally permissible, sub-

---

[8] Only some of the benefits a union negotiates are intrinsically *collective*, as that term was defined above; the others are collective only in the sense that federal law affirmatively requires the union to negotiate these benefits for everyone in the unit, thus precluding the application of the exclusion principle.

ject only to the possible exception that the political and religious rights of workers not be violated thereby.

Under this view, the Taft-Hartley Act's policy of allowing, if not encouraging, union security agreements are morally permissible, while the prohibitions of state right-to-work laws serve as an unnecessary impediment to the achievement of legitimate goals of the subsociety of the collective bargaining unit and, ultimately, of society itself.

That, then, serves to identify the fundamental premises of the moral argument in favor of union security agreements; basically, the argument is simply an application of the philosophy of social utilitarianism. Whether that philosophy, as a general matter, has any merit or not will be left for debate in other forums.

Turning now to the primary moral argument against the coercion of compulsory unionism, we see that it found itself in the seventeenth and eighteenth centuries' classical liberalism and natural rights philosophies, amplified and brought up to date by contemporary libertarian writers such as Hayek, Nozick, and Machan.[9] Within this broad school there are, of course, many divergent strands of thought. The argument that follows merely attempts, on a somewhat selective basis, to weave some of these ideas together into a coherent theory capable of dealing specifically with the union security issue.

By this approach, the place to begin is a proper understanding (if not a redefinition) of the term *right*—a term that is used far too casually in most contemporary political debate, including that on the right-to-work controversy. But, as used herein, the term *right* pertains to an individual's freedom of action, and a right is violated (the freedom of action impermissibly interfered with) only when another person's restraints on that freedom of action are of such a kind as to justify a forcible response.

By the traditional approach of the natural law, rights are deduced from the nature of man himself—rather, from a set of abstract characterizations of his nature. Of particular importance in this regard is the assertion that men are by nature autonomous entities; that is, each man as an individual has been endowed by his Creator with certain inalienable rights, and these flow to him directly rather than to the social group of which he happens to

---

⁹ *See* F. Hayek, The Constitution of Liberty (1960); R. Nozick, Anarchy, State, and Utopia (1974); T. Machan, Human Rights and Human Liberties (1975); *see also* R. Taylor, Freedom, Anarchy, and the Law (1973).

be a part. Thus, there is no such thing as a social or collective right, except in a derivative sense.

In the first instance, rights are of a moral nature; they identify the circumstances under which it is morally permissible for an individual to respond with the use of force. But, to the extent that these moral rights are codified into positive law, they also become legal rights; legal rights identify the circumstances under which the government, as the agent of the individuals within a society, will, on behalf of those individuals, respond with the use of force.

Given the fact that each human being is both autonomous and equal in his possession of fundamental rights, it is next hypothesized that everyone has the moral right to do anything he chooses, *except* to infringe upon the equivalent rights of others. That formulation, of course, is not specific enough itself to be very helpful. But it is then further suggested that this equilibrium of rights can be achieved by reference to the germinal *right of self-ownership*, which is violated whenever a person is, against his will, denied the exclusive possession and control of himself or of the fruits of his labor. According to classical theory, this could be done in only the following ways: by the initiation of physical force against person or property, threats to initiate such force, theft, fraud, breach of contract, and engaging in activities which involve a "high risk" that the person or property of another will be interfered with in any of these ways. These are often referred to as "natural law wrongs" or subsumed under the label "acts of aggression" (which is how they will be referred to hereinafter).

In short, each individual has the moral right to do anything he chooses except engage in any of the above acts of aggression, and the corollary of this is that if a person has been wronged in any of these ways, *but only on that condition*, then such a person has a moral right to respond with the use of force—*i.e.*, to use coercion in defense of his person or property. But the use of force or coercion under any other circumstances is itself an act of aggression as defined above and is a moral wrong.

Moving into the political arena, the theory next focuses on the nature of government, especially as it speaks through the organs of law. In this regard, borrowing a leaf from the legal positivists, the moral argument against compulsory unionism would suggest that in its essence *law* is nothing more than a statement of the circumstances under which the sovereign is going to exercise force or coercion. Moreover, since a legitimate government is, under the Lockean view, merely the agent or delegate of the individual citizens, the circumstances under which the government is morally permitted to respond with force are no different from the circumstances under which the individual citizen himself would be morally justified in so responding. Thus, the only things that the government can make "against the law" are the things previously identified as being acts of aggression. For the government to use force or coercion under any other circumstances is itself morally wrong.

Before attempting to apply this political theory to the specific problem of union security agreements and right-to-work laws, we should, however, first identify two further corollaries. First, under this theory, freedom of contract remains virtually unfettered. Offering or refusing to offer and accepting or refusing to accept a contract with another person, whatever the terms and conditions, is not itself an act of aggression as previously defined. Second, therefore, no person has the right to work for another person except on terms and conditions acceptable to both.

By reference to these two corollaries, it would appear that union security agreements represent an exercise of the freedom of contract and that right-to-work laws interfere with that freedom and give nonunion employees a right to work for a particular employer in spite of that employer's desire to make union membership a condition of employment. For the most part, however, this represents a misapplication of the libertarian theory.

As the term is used in classical liberalism, *freedom of contract* contemplates a freedom to choose who one will bargain with, a freedom to choose what one will bargain about, a freedom to choose what terms one will accept, and a freedom to choose to exercise whatever economic power one has to influence the outcome of the bargain. The parties, in other words, have the moral right to exercise these freedoms—which is to say that their choices in this regard, whatever they may happen to be, cannot in moral contemplation be considered acts of aggression. A true contract is thus the product of a purely consensual process.

Under federal law, however, a union security agreement is not consensual in any of these respects. The law imposes an affirmative duty on an employer to bargain with a certain union whether the employer wants to or not. The law requires an employer to bargain specifically about union security agreements. Although the law theoretically does not require an employer to agree actually to any specific contract term, experience has shown that it is difficult for an employer to refuse to agree to a union security provision and at the same time avoid a charge that he bargained in "bad faith" in violation of his statutory duty. Finally, the employer's freedom to use his economic power to induce the union to accept his position on union security is severely limited by the broad constraints of the Act.

A union security agreement, in other words, is a product of coercion, not consent. Moreover, the coercion in question is directed against acts, or refusals to act, that cannot themselves be classified as *aggressive* as that term is defined in the libertarian lexicon. Consequently, such coercion, the laws through which it operates, and the union security agreements which are its product, all must be considered morally impermissible.

In the first instance, this impermissible coercion operates against the employer in violation of his rights of true liberty of contract. But the consequence of this coercion, the union security agreement itself, has a secondary coercive effect on nonunion employees who, but for their lack of affiliation with a labor union, would have continued employment with an otherwise willing employer. This secondary coercion partakes of the impermissibility of its primary source. In that sense, the right to work of these employees is also being violated by the union security agreement.

It is against this background that a classical liberal or libertarian would evaluate right-to-work laws. To the extent that such laws nullify or limit an impermissibly coercive aspect of federal law, they are clearly to be favored; the same could be said about the repeal of the operative provisos of Section 8(a)(3) of the Taft-Hartley Act and Section 2, Eleventh, of the Railway Labor Act (which would in effect guarantee a national "right to work" as that phrase is used in the colloquial sense).

On the other hand, right-to-work laws themselves have a certain antilibertarian residuum. They coerce the employer who, quite apart from the influence of federal law, would be willing to agree with the union that only union members should be hired or who, even in the absence of agreement, would want to make this condition of employment. Such voluntary conduct on the part of an employer is not aggressive, in the natural law sense, and thus it should not be made against the law as it is under the right-to-work laws.

As a practical matter, because of the scarcity of employers with such inclinations, this is not a major problem. Ideally, however, the libertarian defense of the rights of the employer, employee, and union alike would be realized through, first, a repeal of all the impermissibly coercive provisions of the Taft-Hartley Act which promote union security agreements and, second, a subsequent repeal of the right-to-work laws. This would then leave the parties free to negotiate union security agreements, but on a purely voluntary basis.[10] Until, however, the first goal is realized, right-to-work laws must be considered the lesser of two evils by this argument.

Such are the philosophical underpinnings of the primary moral arguments against union security agreements and in favor of right-to-work laws; basically, the argument is that of the classical liberal or libertarian. As with the philosophy of social utilitarianism, the broader issue of the merits and demerits of this school of thought will be left for others to debate. Our function here has simply been to define these philosophies in terms of their respective positions on the union security and right-to-work issue.

CONCLUSION

Whether it is being argued from the legal, the economic, the political, or the philosophical perspective, the debate over union security and the right to work must always take into account the broader implications of the respective positions. The direction in which the nation moves on this issue and its reasons for doing so may well be a portent of other changes in social policy; and it is critically important that we be aware of exactly what we are doing and why. It is to that end that this study was undertaken.

---

[10] This is not necessarily to say, however, that the courts would enforce these agreements, for there is a serious question about whether collective bargaining agreements are truly "contracts"—*i.e.*, the kind of promise the breach of which would be considered an "act of aggression" under the former analysis. At common law, which relied on this kind of analysis in formulating the rules of contract, the parties were required to have exchanged "something of value"—commonly called "consideration"—in order for an agreement to be legally binding. It was for want of any consideration on the union's part that many early common-law judges refused to enforce collective labor agreements. The same result might well be reached under the philosophical approach being discussed here.

Index of Cases

Racial Policies of American Industry Series

Order from: Kraus Reprint Co., Route 100, Millwood, New York 10546

STUDIES OF NEGRO EMPLOYMENT

Vol. I. *Negro Employment in Basic Industry: A Study of Racial Policies in Six Industries (Automobile, Aerospace, Steel, Rubber Tire, Petroleum, and Chemicals)*, by Herbert R. Northrup, Richard L. Rowan, et al. 1970. $15.00

Vol. II. *Negro Employment in Finance: A Study of Racial Policies in Banking and Insurance*, by Armand J. Thieblot, Jr., and Linda Pickthorne Fletcher. 1970. *

Vol. III. *Negro Employment in Public Utilities: A Study of Racial Policies in the Electric Power, Gas, and Telephone Industries*, by Bernard E. Anderson. 1970. *

Vol. IV. *Negro Employment in Southern Industry: A Study of Racial Policies in the Paper, Lumber, Tobacco, Coal Mining, and Textile Industries*, by Herbert R. Northrup, Richard L. Rowan, et al. 1971. $13.50

Vol. V. *Negro Employment in Land and Air Transport: A Study of Racial Policies in the Railroad, Air Transport, Trucking, and Urban Transit Industries*, by Herbert R. Northrup, Howard W. Risher, Jr., Richard D. Leone, and Philip W. Jeffress. 1971. $13.50

Vol. VI. *Negro Employment in Retail Trade: A Study of Racial Policies in the Department Store, Drugstore, and Supermarket Industries*, by Gordon F. Bloom, F. Marion Fletcher, and Charles R. Perry. 1972. $12.00

Vol. VII. *Negro Employment in the Maritime Industries: A Study of Racial Policies in the Shipbuilding, Longshore, and Offshore Maritime Industries*, by Lester Rubin, William A. Swift, and Herbert R. Northrup. 1974. *

Vol. VIII. *Black and Other Minority Participation in the All-Volunteer Navy and Marine Corps*, by Herbert R. Northrup, Steven M. Di Antonio, and Dale F. Daniel. Spring 1978. $18.50

Order from the Industrial Research Unit
The Wharton School, University of Pennsylvania
Philadelphia, Pennsylvania 19104

* Order these books from University Microfilms, Inc., Attn: Books Editorial Department, 300 North Zeeb Road, Ann Arbor, Michigan 48106.

Date Due

FEB 8 1982			
FEB 2 7 1984			
MAY 1 '89			
MAY 2 2 '89			